LAW IN THE AMERICAN WEST

BLUE CLARK

Lone Wolf
v.
Hitchcock

Treaty Rights and Indian Law
at the End of the Nineteenth Century

University of Nebraska Press Lincoln & London

Portions of chapters 8 and 10 were originally published in "*Lone Wolf v. Hitchcock:* Implicatons for Federal-Indian Law at the Start of the Twentieth Century," *Western Legal History*, 5:1 (Winter/Spring 1992), 1–12. Reprinted with permission of the Ninth Judicial Circuit Historical Society. © 1994 by the University of Nebraska Press
Manufactured in the United States of America

∞

First Bison Books printing: 1999
Most recent printing indicated by the last digit below:
10 9 8 7 6 5 4 3 2 1

Library of Congress Cataloging in Publication Data
Clark, Blue, 1946–
Lone Wolf v. Hitchcock: treaty rights and Indian law at the end of the nineteenth century / Blue Clark.
p. cm.—(Law in the American West; v. 5)
Includes bibliographical references and index.
ISBN 0-8032-1466-9 (cl.: alk. paper)
ISBN 0-8032-6401-1 (pbk.: alk. paper)
1. Lone Wolf—Trials, litigation, etc.
2. United States—Trials, litigation, etc.
3. Kiowa Indians—Land transfers—History. 4. Kiowa Indians—Land tenure—History. 5. Indians of North America—Oklahoma—Land transfers—History. 6. Indians of North America—Oklahoma—Land tenure—History.
7. Indians of North America—Treaties—History. I. Title. II. Title: Lone Wolf versus Hitchcock. III. Series.
KF228.L66C58 1994
346.7304'32'08997—dc20
[347.30643208997]   94-7735
                                           CIP

CONTENTS

ILLUSTRATIONS

Plates
Following page 78
Kiowa pictographic representation of
Medicine Lodge Treaty Council
Medicine Lodge Council
Jerome Commission members
E. A. Hitchcock, Binger Herman,
and Samuel Brosius
Delos K. Lone Wolf
Kiowa delegation to Washington, D.C., 1902
Anadarko Townsite Auction, 6 August 1901
William Springer, Hampton Carson,
and Willis Van Devanter
Herbert Welsh
Supreme Court Justices

To examine *Lone Wolf v. Hitchcock* is to gain insight into United States Indian policy at the end of the last century and the beginning of the present century. The suit left an enduring imprint on the Kiowas and other American Indians who lost their land base and their treaty rights as a result of the decision. In some ways federal tutelage tightened, while in other instances federal supervision slighted the Indians. More important psychologically, the opinion cast a whole people into despair when not only their guardian but their friends abandoned them. For the Kiowas, the case serves as a byword for the worst traits in Anglo-American society in its relationship with the American Indian. To be sure, the Indians adjusted to the opening of their lands and to the swirl of American society around them. Even so, the bitterness lingered. The Indian Claims Commission in 1955 awarded the Kiowas, Comanches, and Plains Apaches, who shared the same Oklahoma reservation, $2 million for lands taken from them illegally in the past. However, the Indians pointed out that money could not restore land and heritage lost, pledges violated, and trust despoiled. The opinion set the stage for many disappointments in the years ahead for the American Indian.

For whites eager for opportunity, for the possibilities of quick wealth, for "open" lands awaiting the plow or the speculator, the Lone Wolf decision merely confirmed assumptions about their own superiority. The federal court system upheld the Manifest Destiny of American expansion into the last of the continental frontier spaces. Justices underscored federal dominance over aboriginal peoples, and judges certified that the land lottery and the bustle of town site speculation would engulf the three tribes.

There are a few outstanding instances in the nineteenth century of Indian presence in American courtrooms. Among the more notable are Corn Tassel's capital defense in a Georgia court, the Cherokee cases arguing for their sovereignty, Standing Bear's eloquent plea for Ponca rights, Crow Dog in South Dakota defending his life, and Lone Wolf upholding treaty rights in Oklahoma Territory. The Cherokee cases opened the century and the nation's dealings with Indian peoples; *Lone Wolf* closed the same century. Each of these examples of Indian litigation is important for an understand-

ing of the constitutional place of the American Indian and the evolution of
federal–Indian law in the United States.

My interest in the turn-of-the-century period for Indians focused on *Lone
Wolf* because of its importance for reservation Indians' rights and land loss
during the most crucial modern period for native peoples undergoing the
trauma of allotment. *Lone Wolf* had ramifications far beyond the boundaries
of the reservation in Oklahoma. *Lone Wolf* enshrined one of the fundamental
rules in federal–Indian law, plenary power. The decision made it legal to destroy tribes' land base in violation of treaty promises. The American frontier
juggernaut found its legal justification. Frontier expansion and reform sentiment for assimilation threatened Indian treaty obligations and tribes. Courts
abandoned both under the "political question doctrine" to a Congress in
no mood any longer to tolerate landed separateness. The case illustrates the
complexity of federal–Indian law throughout the United States.

I started out to examine the court decision. I soon found that the case law
is also the story of the Indians and how they adjusted to the world around
them. Too often, scholars stop only at the case law and do not see beyond
the citations into the lives of the people affected. Kiowa leaders responded
in a tangled variety of ways to the pressures they encountered. Kiowa leaders
and followers moved in and out of complicated issues, changing sides and
alliances as their own interests demanded. In many of the same ways, eastern humanitarians shifted their support from one approach to another in
their quest for solutions to what they considered the always vexatious "Indian
problem."

ACKNOWLEDGMENTS

Many people assisted in the search for information on *Lone Wolf*. A McNickle Fellowship at the Newberry Library during 1985–1986 provided the opportunity to complete the bulk of the research. People in the McNickle Center led me to think in new ways about questions the case raised. Robert Kvasnicka at the National Archives and Kathleen Baxter in the National Anthropological Archives located materials. Mary Lee Boyle and Bill Welge gave help in the Indian Archives of the Oklahoma Historical Society. Kiowa people in classes and at the interview table led me to much information. Over the years they have brought me to a much more profound understanding of the impacts of the 1892 agreement on their lives. Numerous attorneys, tribal judges, graduate students, and other scholars added to my knowledge regarding the case. Special appreciation goes to Floyd A. O'Neil and Gregory C. Thompson of the University of Utah, and Kirke Kickingbird of the Native American Legal Resource Center of Oklahoma City University, for their assistance. Kathleen Foster provided technical assistance.

My thanks to California State University in Long Beach for support of the project. Deep gratitude is extended to my mother and to my wife for their encouragement.

CHRONOLOGY OF THE LONE WOLF COURT SUITS

	In Oklahoma	In Washington	At the Supreme Court
1901 June 6	The Act opening the tract Restraining order/injunction filed in Canadian County probate court, with a justice of the peace presiding, to halt the opening.		
		William Springer filed the same case in the Supreme Court of the District of Columbia.	
1901 June 12		E. A. Hitchcock (via Van Devanter) asked a special appeal, again in the Supreme Court of the District of Columbia. Springer requests a special appeal to the Court of Appeals of the District of Columbia.	
1901 June 17	Injunction amended to add other KCA members to the suit Rebecca Young et al. file their suits.		
		Springer's brief of June 12 is amended with the same additional KCA names.	
1901 June 20		D.C. Supreme Court Justice A. C. Bradley turns down Lone Wolf, with chance for reargument and final decree on June 26.	
1901 July 29	Oklahoma Territory Second Judicial District Judge Clinton Irwin overturns the injunction, turning down Lone Wolf.		
1901 August 17	Judge Irwin does so again, after rearguments. Meanwhile, federal authorities ignored these activities and proceeded with platting, surveying, and setting up procedures for the land rush of the opening.		
			Meanwhile, because of the treaty issue involved, Springer and Van Devanter filed a Lone Wolf suit with the United States Supreme Court for the October 1901 term.
1901 December 4		D.C. Court of Appeals Chief Justice R. H. Alvey turns down Lone Wolf's appeal.	

	In Oklahoma	In Washington	At the Supreme Court
1902 March 4		Justice Alvey issues final opinion.	
1902 March 6		Springer's motion for reargument filed.	
1902 March 14		Springer's motion turned down in final decree.	
1902 March 18			Transcript filed, along with the March 14 Court of Appeals transcript.
1902 October 23			Oral arguments made. Springer given one week (and a slight extension) to file his brief to counter Van Devanter's telling claim that Indians, including Lone Wolf, had already accepted payment for the KCA lands.
1903 January 5			Justice White reads the Court's opinion.

1

Introduction

Allotment comprised the most important policy change for American Indians in nineteenth-century America. It proved disastrous for tribal government and land areas: allotment undermined both. The federal government's allotment policy assigned farmsteads to individual Indians in an attempt to merge the new Indian yeomanry into national life. Partitioning tribal estates liquidated tribal reservation land areas, terminated communal Indian land ownership, detribalized the individual Indian, and opened the surplus lands to homesteading.

Massachusetts Senator Henry L. Dawes embraced an earlier idea to compel Indians to take individual farmsteads, forcing an end to any Indian connections to a communal tribal organization. Senator Dawes came to symbolize allotment of Indian lands. He represented the assumptions of his era regarding the conquered status of Indians and their governments, as well as the disposition of their lands. He believed that their condition could be altered according to the will of Congress without regard to Indians' wishes. His rigid views remained constant in spite of lingering doubts about the effectiveness of the policy of allotment that would be identified with his name.[1] The Dawes Severalty or General Allotment Act of 1887 inaugurated vigorous American Indian reservation land division, which dominated United States Indian policy for over half a century.

Its effects took a variety of forms depending on the reservation, circumstances, effectiveness of resistance, and swings in national assimilation policy. Ultimately, over two-thirds of Indian land passed out of aboriginal control as a consequence of the measure. What little land was left in Indian possession was often marginal and unproductive. Fractionated division of surviving Indian allotted land left it equally poor. Unrelenting pressure for allotment after 1887 led directly to Indian landholding decline. After removal from their homelands earlier in the century, allotment was the most traumatic federal policy affecting Indian people. Its ramifications reach into the present.

In the words of President Theodore Roosevelt, who witnessed its application on the northern plains, allotment "was a mighty pulverizing engine to break up the tribal mass."[2] It tore away the tribal land base. Allotment left tribal members destitute. It prevented Indians from obtaining mortgages and capital for economic improvements. Allotment perpetuated a way of life lived in poverty, disease, and other ills. The era of allotment has correctly been called "the most critical period in the whole history of Indian–white relations in the United States"[3] because of the lasting and detrimental effects of government policy on Indians.

At the close of the nineteenth century, a Kiowa band chief, Lone Wolf, like many of his fellow Indians, took an allotment under coercion. However, he went into court to halt the selection and assignment of his own allotment, as well as those of his and neighboring tribal supporters. He wanted to prevent the allotment of his Kiowa, Comanche, and Plains Apache Reservation in southwestern Oklahoma and to stave off the opening of the "surplus" to white homesteaders. He based his suit on treaty pledges made between Kiowa and United States negotiators just after the conclusion of the American Civil War. The Indian litigation could have involved a half dozen reservations in the era as a result of assimilation pressures, land hunger, and Indian resistance. Because of the subjects involved—congressional authority, treaty rights, and the Indian—the Kiowa case went to the United States Supreme Court for argument in 1902.

The historical circumstances leading up to the *Lone Wolf* judgment demonstrate the overwhelming influence of the federal government in Indians' lives. At every major turn, the federal government had a substantial hand in precipitating either the action or the reaction to policies designed to coerce the Indian. The court case involving the Kiowas trapped the Indians. On the one hand, the 1867 Treaty of Medicine Lodge had mandated the consent of three-fourths of the Indian males to any land cessions. On the other hand, a majority of the Kiowas in 1892 agreed through the blandishments of deception to alter the land area in return for monetary payment from the federal government. Either way, the Indians were inexorably tied to the cession of a major part of their reservation. United States courts made legal the theft of Kiowa land and denial of Indian rights. Courts refused to halt the allotment, permitted the opening of the surplus, and encouraged Indian land loss on the reservation. In the wake of the Spanish-American War, American policy makers then transferred overseas that nearly absolute power over native peoples to newly acquired United States possessions in the Pacific and the Caribbean seized in the quick war against Spain.

The major participants survived the Lone Wolf litigation and went about their lives without physical scars from the legal battle. No one was executed as a result of the outcome of the suit. However, the legal struggle and its aftermath deeply affected them. Anglo-American homesteaders and towns inundated the Indians with an alien way of life. Circumstances forced the Indians to make a rapid and oftentimes unsuccessful adjustment. The decision also affected other participants. The court conflict marred the reputation of the secretary of the interior. Before the appeal, he had been seen as a stern but effective champion of Indians. After the bruising court fight, his reputation among reformers suffered, and his relationship with the nation's leading Indian reform body notably cooled. The controversy over the implementation of the court order after 1903 so preoccupied the commissioner of Indian affairs that his health deteriorated to a point such that he became increasingly ineffective in his office.

The major test case for American Indian treaty rights, congressional authority over Indian tribes, and land division during the peak of the allotment policy, *Lone Wolf v. Hitchcock* has often been cited in federal–Indian law but has rarely been the subject of scholarly study. It is surely one of the most famous, or infamous, court decisions dealing with American Indian rights in United States history. The 1903 Supreme Court opinion clearly established the dependent status of the Indian under the control of the federal government. It became the hallmark of federal paternalism over the Indian. The ruling had momentous consequences for American Indians and eventually for native people occupying American overseas possessions after 1898.

The Court's announcement is one of the most frequently cited judicial rulings on the American Indian, especially in court documents dealing with issues the case directly touched. It is considered one of the major cases in federal–Indian law. At the turn of the century, *Lone Wolf* was one of the judicial system's major levers used against recalcitrant tribal governments and obstinate individual Indians. Curiously, the case has been ignored in anthologies and passed over in histories dealing with American Indian developments in the era. Except to note that the High Court made the decision, most scholars have either missed or slighted the major pronouncement on abrogation of Indian treaty rights, congressional authority, and assessment of the allotment policy process.[4]

Some historians have discussed the historical, regional, and national impacts of the decision within the contexts of United States Indian policy, reform sentiment, and overseas implications.[5] Legal scholars have discussed the judicial import of *Lone Wolf* in treaty, trust, and federal–Indian relations because of the Supreme Court's influence on national and tribal policy. Legal casebooks dealing with federal–Indian law include excerpts from the 1903 decree because the opinion summarized nineteenth-century American jurisprudence regarding the American Indian within American law.[6] However, national treatments gloss over many of the aspects of the Kiowas' suit and cannot devote sufficient space to an examination of the impact of national policies on the local level, as well as divergences from federal policies at that level. No one studied the Kiowas' case specifically for its effects on their lives, lands, and national policies.

National American Indian policy has been complex and its effects diverse. Scholars like Francis Paul Prucha, Frederick Hoxie, and William T. Hagan have studied the national aspects of federal–Indian policy and reformers' attempts to integrate the Indian into American life. A case study focused on Lone Wolf's suit brings into light the impact of national policies on the local level. Such an undertaking provides insight into the historical, American legal, and Indian law aspects of Indian–white relations.

A case study grants a focus on federal officials' actions at both national and local levels. It emphasizes the difficulties involved in federal administration of both Indian reserves and public lands open to settlement. The court suit caught not only the Indians but the United States government as well in a dilemma. Federal authorities were charged with the duty to assist the nation's wards as their guardian. At the same time, national representatives also had to satisfy insistent parochial demands for additional lands for homesteaders. The study examines the activities of the land agents and the special allotting agent who had to work under great pressure to meet a presidential deadline for opening the reserve to homesteaders.

A case study permits a closer examination of the reservation involved, showing conditions that affected government decrees emanating from the Capitol but implemented at the lowest level. It also reveals changing alliances among Indian bands and individuals through time. A study of the Kiowa court opinion also underscores the immediate impact the suit had on the leader who initiated the appeal. Indian opinion regarding litigation is virtually nonexistent, but an attempt has been made to round out the story with insight into the Indian side of the case.

The Kiowa court case summarized end-of-the-century legal assumptions toward native peoples. A case study helps clarify some of the issues involving American Indian tribal rights. A narrowly focused study also follows judges' use of the decision in subsequent court decrees. It reveals the fall and rise of Indian tribal sovereignty in federal court opinions. It also shows that remnants from the 1903 ruling continue in judicial thinking regarding Indian tribal rights of self-government and landownership. However, no attempt has been made to trace each thread in the convoluted legal patchwork that makes up federal–Indian law because others have assessed specific aspects of the relationship, as for example 5th Amendment protections against arbitrary takings of Indian land. The literature detailing Indian case law, whether dealing with Congress's plenary authority, the abrogation of treaties, or Indian land claims, is vast. Many of the judicial dicta overlap with prior court pronouncements, making research of a particular holding a challenge. Tracking each finger of the legal hand involving the suit would result in a work prohibitively long.

The examination of Lone Wolf's case is arranged chronologically. It begins with a look into the important role of the United States Supreme Court in both the nation's industrial development and in Indian affairs. The study continues with an examination of the Kiowa leadership crisis and a glimpse of Kiowa life under the control of the federal government after the mid-1070s. The dreaded specter of allotted land loss is the center of attention thereafter, with an examination of the Indians' negotiating skills and delaying tactics until the Act of 1900 precipitated the start of the lawsuit. The work next trails the snarled course of judicial appeals leading to the Supreme Court's important pronouncement in 1903. The remainder of the book follows the various impacts of the Court's decree.

2

The Supreme Court

The United States Supreme Court has played a pivotal role in American political life and society. The Constitution simply states that "the judicial power of the United States shall be vested in one supreme court."[1] Since Chief Justice John Marshall asserted its independence from the legislative and executive branches, the Court has had a primary formative influence on the development of American society and governmental institutions.

THE COURT AND INDUSTRIALIZATION

During the period of rapid industrialization following the end of the American Civil War, the Supreme Court enlarged its role as an institution favoring economic progress and business development. Court opinions aided the completion of continent-wide transportation links that would eventually tie Pacific Ocean countries to East Coast American markets, while conveying European immigrants who had crossed the Atlantic Ocean to West Coast dockside jobs and Midwestern farms. The High Tribunal smoothed the progress of American industrialism. The justices led the flowering of laissez-faire monopoly capitalism and the enshrinement of eighteenth-century individualism. They prevented foreign competition from dominating and often from entering the domestic American market, protecting fledgling enterprises from foreign competition.

American energy and dynamism seized a continent in the 1840s, quashed a rebellious South in the 1860s, and turned their attention to unbridled industrial expansion in the 1870s. America was a vibrant, growing nation. Entrepreneurial endeavor cemented the great fortunes of such notable business leaders as Andrew Carnegie, John D. Rockefeller, and Andrew Mellon, among many in the period whose wealth made them prominent.

"Yankee ingenuity" helped change the world. New inventions permitted improved communications, longer working hours that extended into the nighttime, and increased manufacturing output. The telephone of Alexander Graham Bell linked business and society in ways undreamed of only a few months before March of 1876, when Bell finally perfected the communications device in his laboratory. Thomas Alva Edison, who would soon become a folk hero because of his patents and business acumen, perfected Bell's original telephone transmitter in 1878. He went on to manufacture the first electric lamp and set up an electric power distribution system. His laboratory started the electric lighting industry. Innovations by Edison provided light for whole cities beginning in the early 1880s. An employee of the Edison Illuminating Company in Detroit, Henry Ford, invented a car that moved under its own power in 1896. Ford began producing his automobile and in 1908 sold the Model T, a vehicle which "put the nation on wheels" as a result of mass production techniques and a low price.

Along the breezy sand hills of Kitty Hawk, North Carolina, the brothers Wright used an internal combustion engine of their own design to stay aloft for the first powered flight of a true airplane in December 1903. As a result of the Hay-Buna-Varilla Treaty the same year, the United States began the excavation of an isthmian canal across Panama linking the Atlantic and Pacific oceans. It became one of the modern engineering marvels of the world.

Legal innovations improved the flow of commerce and financial transactions. Monopoly control of basic raw materials, commodities, and finished products received an enormous boost when courts recognized the corporation as an individual for legal purposes, adopting the suggestion of Roscoe Conkling.[2] In the mid-1880s he had argued that the word "person" in the 14th Amendment included corporations, which allowed business entities to get their cases into federal courts when alleging that state legislatures denied corporations "due process" or "equal protection" under the laws. Trusts arose to take over entire one-product enterprises such as steel wire and sugar.

The Supreme Court in the period after the American Civil War and extending into the 1930s served as the staunch defender of the earlier Whig conservative political and economic tradition in the nation. The Court upheld the doctrine of strict limits on government interference in national affairs. The sanctity of the contract, representing the entrepreneurial spirit at its best, and the unfettered use of private property were bulwarks which the Court strongly safeguarded. Justices allied with legislators to prevent reforms of chronic monopolistic economic abuses in the nation and provide an atmosphere favorable to rapid industrialization.

Conservatives seized on the social theorizing of the Englishman Herbert Spencer as justification for public policies. Spencer applied Charles Darwin's studies of natural selection of the strongest and most capable members of a species to the economic realm. Spencer took the study of organisms a giant step further and pointed out that the struggle of humans through their lives resulted also in the survival of the fittest. The purest form of that necessary struggle took place without government interference. Spencer added a scientific veneer to the free trade ideas of Adam Smith: progress demanded individual freedom of action in economics; out of economic and social combat would emerge the highest happiness. Spencer summarized his uncompromising views of economic and social conflict: "The poverty of the incapable, the distresses that come upon the imprudent, the starvation of the idle, and those shoulderings aside of the weak by the strong, which leave so many 'in shadows and miseries,' are the decrees of a large, far-seeing benevolence" that must be left free to act.[3] Within the economic realm, Spencerian doctrine came to be known under the umbrella phrase "laissez-faire." Laissez-faire stood for unbridled individualism, monopoly capitalism, and unregulated industrialism.

Justices did not permit public regulation to interfere with private property and personal acquisition in the era. Judges, alarmed over rising violence and anarchy in labor disputes from the 1870s onward, desired to preserve society's contemporary order without significant concessions or changes. Midwestern legislatures that enacted granger laws in direct response to shippers' outcries of unfair railway practices and rates, and their demands to regulate railroad freight rate abuses, found that federal courts nullified the measures or led to their repeal under vigorous corporate lobbying efforts. Supreme Court Justice Edward Douglas White, during an opinion on the eight-hour law and railroads, put the matter succinctly: "[The] right to prohibit could not be applied to pig iron, steel rails, or most of the vast body of commodities."[4] The courts enshrined laissez-faire economic policy and blocked states from exercising their police power to enact changes which public petitioners, independent political parties, and reform groups demanded. Laissez-faire played so prominent a part in judicial rulings of the era that Justice Oliver Wendell Holmes went out of his way to lament in 1905, without much effect, that "the Constitution does not enact Mr. Herbert Spencer's *Social Statics*" into national law.[5]

In the 1886 Wabash case,[6] the Supreme Court justices declared that states could not regulate, even within their own borders, any railroad traffic that involved interstate commerce. Limiting regulation to one state would have a "deleterious influence upon the freedom of commerce among the States and upon the transit of goods through those States," Justice Samuel F. Miller announced for the Court. "[R]egulation of [interstate] commerce . . . should be done [only] by the Congress of the United States under the commerce clause of the Constitution." The announcement left railroads virtually unregulated until Congress acted the following year with a law that established an industry-run regulatory commission.

The same justices narrowed the interpretation of the due process clause of the 14th Amendment to the Constitution to constrict the use of government police power for regulatory purposes. In the Slaughter-House Cases of 1873, the Supreme Court decreed that regulation be "left to the State governments . . . and not [be left] . . . under the special care of the Federal government."[7] In effect, the justices permitted state legislatures, which were often subject to the corrupting influence of corporate largess which they were supposed to be supervising, to regulate monopolies. Furthermore, the justices in their opinion denied that the Congress had extended federal power to encompass enforcement of basic civil rights.

Leaders on the highest court also narrowly confined Congress from taking national action in the case of the E. C. Knight Company[8] in 1895. The government attempted to break up the American Sugar Refining Company, which in the words of Chief Justice Melville Fuller had "acquired nearly complete control of the manufacture of refined sugar in the United States."[9] In the first Supreme Court interpretation of the 1890 Sherman Antitrust Act, Chief Justice Fuller's opinion halted the enforcement of the act and froze nearly all antitrust prosecutions for a decade. The court order severely limited the act's application and refused to apply it to a nearly complete monopoly. After admitting that the American Sugar Refining Company held a monopoly over the manufacture of sugar in the United States, the Chief Justice held that "commerce succeeds to manufacture, and is not a part of it," that sugar refining in Pennsylvania, where the case focused after the company purchased four Philadelphia refineries through shares of its own stock, "bore no direct relation to commerce between the states."[10] The Chief Justice made law in an instance where the Congress had refused to act. The Knight case has often been pointed to as a flagrant example of judicial legislation on the part of the Court.[11] Time and again, judicial decisions blocked popular desires for reform.

The High Tribunal neutralized the civil rights thrust of the 14th Amendment itself in the 1883 *Civil Rights Cases*,[12] which limited congressional enforcement and effectively recognized the impossibility of overturning segregated life in America. In spite of a stirring dissent from Justice John Marshall Harlan that years later would dominate the Court's thinking, the justices in 1883 pointed out that "redress is to be sought under the laws of the State" in question and not from the national Congress. The Supreme Court's determination that the 1875 Civil Rights Act—passed as a cornerstone of Radical Reconstruction and as a guarantee for black civil rights—was unconstitutional left that segment of American society virtually unprotected against state actions to limit their rights. Supreme Court justices upheld states' rights. Earlier in 1876, they permitted discriminatory voting restrictions such as poll taxes,[13] stating that the federal government's role was now narrowly limited to instances of race and color only. Again, in the 1896 *Plessy v. Ferguson* decision, justices recognized the segregated "separation of the races" in America,[14] and accepted segregated railroad cars for blacks in the state of Louisiana, and, in effect, elsewhere, as long as the public facilities for blacks were "equal." The order also did not oppose the idea of "separate schools."[15] "Separate but equal" education in American schools rapidly spread. The highest court in the nation consented to the racial status quo for Jim Crowism in the United States.

Just as for blacks and Asians through the nineteenth century in establishing racial policy, lower courts frequently declared what federal law ought to be and the Supreme Court often affirmed it, just as the justices would do for Lone Wolf. That was particularly the situation in the American judicial system up to the establishment of a separate circuit court apparatus in 1891 within the federal court structure. *Plessy* was one such famous case. *Lone*

Wolf v. Hitchcock is another example. Through the nineteenth century the Supreme Court affirmed district and circuit judges' declarations of what the law ought to be.[16]

Reformers and political leaders believed they had solved the issue of blacks' freedom through war, emancipation, and legislation. They next called for the removal of the Indian as "a stumbling block in the pathway of civilization" and for the Indian's absorption "into the common life of the people of the United States." Building on Civil War experience, the Commissioner of Indian Affairs called for full citizenship for the Indian, just as the black possessed.[17] Reformers would echo that refrain throughout the era of assimilation in regard to the American Indian,[18] pointing out that once full citizenship had been granted to the Indians, they would no longer block American progress and stand in the way of the public good.[19] The nomadic aboriginal way of life seemed part of another era to Americans in bustling cities and noisy factories during the period. Only a few years earlier, the nation was shocked to learn of the defeat of the elite Seventh Cavalry under the ill-fated command of George Armstrong Custer during the same year as the disputed Hayes–Tilden election and the young republic's centennial celebration.

  The historian Francis Paul Prucha has demonstrated[20] that humanitarians believed the American Indian faced only the dual choice of total assimilation into American life or extinction in the face of a superior civilization. With rare exceptions, they never imagined that Indian enclaves could survive within American society. To the reformers, the superiority of American civilization was so overwhelming that its more sordid aspects were never questioned, and they assumed that once introduced to that culture, even by force, people would willingly accept it, at home and then abroad. Commissioner of Indian Affairs John Smith saw only two avenues for the Indian: "The civilization or the utter destruction of the Indians is inevitable. The next 25 years are to determine the fate of a race."[21] One humanitarian group set up specifically to aid the Indian, the Indian Rights Association (see chap. 6), had the goal of bringing about the "complete civilization of the Indians and their admission to [full] citizenship."[22] They believed that persistent patience and persuasion would move aborigines toward their inevitable absorption into American society, when everyone would live under the same laws.

THE COURT AND THE INDIAN

The Supreme Court has also played a vitally important role for American Indian tribes. Court interpretations drastically altered Indian sovereignty over the years. Through judicial decisions, Indian tribes in less than a century traveled the pathway from nearly complete independence to restricted dependence under the paternalism of the federal government. The Court served as a powerful instrument for confining Indians and forcing drastic changes upon them.

American justices and federal negotiators with tribes in treaty councils upheld federal power to accomplish national goals without regard to Indian tribal governmental rights as specified in treaties. They looked on Indians as conquered subjects whether they were friend or foe. The ultimate goal was obtaining Indian lands. Chief Justice Marshall early in the Supreme Court's career established the Court's approach to Indian tribes. Native peoples were a part of the land mass and subject to United States authority by right of discovery. In one of his earliest statements on the subject, *Fletcher v. Peck*, Chief Justice Marshall remarked on the fact that Indian reserved land in the way of expanding white settlement was merely "a temporary arrangement." [23] He further pointed out that Indian sovereignty was "diminished" and that Indian tribes were only "occupying" land which the United States owned, in the subsequent ruling of *Johnson v. McIntosh* in 1823.[24] The justices called federal authority "plenary" when dealing with tribal governments. Marshall clarified the overwhelming plenary power vested in Congress the following year in *Gibbons v. Ogden,* when he stated that such power "acknowledges no limitations" within the prescribed boundaries of the Constitution.[25] When discussing American Indian nations, the chief justice in 1831 used the phrases "domestic dependent nation," "state of pupilage," and "relation . . . of a ward to a guardian" to underscore the superior–inferior relationship.[26] Later opinions focused on the guardian–ward relationship to the detriment of independent status for tribespeople. Even the favorable decision in *Worcester v. Georgia* contained language which qualified and hedged Indian independence, as seen in comments that Indian self-government was to be understood "to be temporary," that Indian governments for a short time had "a very limited independence," and that aboriginal tribes would "become amalgamated" into the American nation's "larger political communities." [27] The Cherokee

Nation cases established the notion of tribal sovereignty at the same time they anchored the plenary doctrine in American law dealing with tribes.

The grip of wardship tightened just before and just after the American Civil War. Chief Justice Roger Taney in *U.S. v. Rogers* completely misconstrued the Cherokee cases and asserted in 1846 that Congress could legislate for both white and Indian crimes in the Indian Territory in spite of the treaty recognition of the latter's independence.[28] As the nation moved into actual warfare, secession and fighting bred demands for the assertion of congressional plenary authority over Indian lands and the opening of reserved lands following that conflict. The Supreme Court justices gave legal voice to that agenda in the Cherokee Tobacco decision in late 1870, which established the Court's recognition of congressional power to modify an Indian treaty and to pass an act in violation of the treaty, "as if the treaty were not an element to be considered."[29] Congress announced that the Indian was outside 14th Amendment guarantees, but at the same time emphasized the inviolability of past treaty obligations.[30] That body ended treaty-making with tribes the following year. Congress readily granted large tracts of reserved land to railroads without Indian consent or knowledge as the industrial output of the nation demanded wider markets and transportation to them.

The Court's favorable release of the Sioux Indian Crow Dog in 1883 contained phraseology that foretold of restrictions to come from Congress when the justices wrote about Indians who "had always been . . . wards subject to a guardian" and invited Congress to enact legislation that would interfere with internal tribal matters.[31] The measure came two years later in the Major Crimes Act[32] and damaged tribal self-government and undermined Indian tribal self-sufficiency. In an 1882 pronouncement, the Court stated that Colorado acquired jurisdiction over the Ute Indians without their consent when that state became a member of the Union, which also diminished tribal self-government powers.[33] Two years later, in the Elk case the Court decided that an individual Indian could not become a citizen without a special congressional enactment.[34] In its Kagama ruling, the Court never mentioned a treaty, but emphasized that Indians were wholly dependent on the United States, stressing the necessity for the federal government to appropriate tribal government functions such as jurisdiction over homicide.[35] The same year, in a case involving the Choctaw Nation's claims under removal treaties and a Court of Claims award, the Court in *Choctaw Nation v. U.S.* emphasized anew that the relationship was one of a "superior to an inferior."[36] The three opinions expanded federal intervention in tribal governmental affairs and lessened self-governance for the Indians.

Congressional frustration increased over Indian intransigence in the face of demands for allotment. American elected leaders gave vent to their views that Congress could exercise unlimited power over its wards. Speaker Joe Cannon concluded during a discussion of Kiowa Indian lands in 1898 that "the United States had plenary power touching these lands; that the Indians were the wards of the Government, and the United States could . . . settle this question according to the dictates of the conscience of the United States" without regard to prior treaty obligations with the Indians.[37] The secretary of the interior could lease Indians' lands in spite of their objections, permitting exploitation of resources and granting pipeline and railroad rights of way through reservations.[38]

Even in cases usually thought to be favorable toward tribal independence, such as *Talton v. Mayes* and *U.S. v. Winans* during the period, justices in an ominous warning found aboriginal peoples to be "subject always to the paramount authority of the United States," even when flagrant mistakes robbed the Indians of rights.[39] As the new century approached, the High Court grew less tolerant of Indian self-government and found that federal "paramount authority" had "allowed" Indians to govern themselves perhaps for too long.[40] In 1899 justices maintained the misinterpretation of the Cherokee cases and noted that "Chief Justice Marshall's description, that 'they are in a state of pupilage' . . . has become more and more appropriate as they have grown less powerful and more dependent" on the United States.[41] The crescendo peaked in the 1903 Lone Wolf pronouncement when the Court made its strongest summation of the Indian as dependent ward unprotected by outmoded treaty guarantees.[42] For thirty years the doctrine of guardianship dominated Indian affairs and remains an often-quoted precedent down to the present time.

The United States Constitution mandates that the Constitution itself, and enactments made under it, as well as treaties, shall be the supreme law of the land.[43] Chief Justice Marshall in the 1830s Cherokee cases pointed out that treaties set Indian nations apart from states within the national domain and contributed to the Indians' unique separate status. Treaties with tribal representatives conducted the Republic's business with Indians until just after the Civil War. In many of the same decisions that set forth plenary authority over

Indian nations, Court pronouncements advanced the progressive abrogation of Indian treaty rights. The Supreme Court in 1870 upheld congressional power to pass a revenue act in clear violation of a treaty with the Cherokee Nation in the pivotal Cherokee Tobacco case.[44] The justices wrote that "the act of Congress must prevail as if the treaty were not an element to be considered." Again, the High Court found that legislation creating the state of Colorado in 1875 "repeals . . . any existing treaty" standing in its path.[45] In 1888 the same Court chose between a treaty and a legislative enactment in favor of "the one last in date,"[46] borrowing from the Court's own *Cherokee Tobacco* statement regarding the document enacted "last-in-time." The justices said the next year that the "last expression of the sovereign will must control" in questions of treaties within the United States, accepting whatever damage that such action might entail to treaties.[47]

During the post-war debate over national expansion into the Far West, many Americans echoed the sentiments of Ohio Representative William Lawrence in his 1871 commentary on the necessity for an end to treaty-making with Indian tribes when he stated with relief "that hereafter the land policy of Congress cannot be broken up and destroyed by Indian treaties."[48] They must not be an obstacle to American progress. Shortly thereafter, Congress abolished treaty negotiations with Indian tribes in a rider to an Indian appropriations act.[49]

In 1890 the justices turned the issue of tribal rights around and noted that Congress had all governmental powers over Indians not specifically given them in their treaties, when in the Stephens case they upheld eminent domain through Indian reserved lands.[50] Former commissioner of Indian affairs Thomas Jefferson Morgan told the annual meeting of Indian reformers assembled in upstate New York's Lake Mohonk Lodge that conditions under which the original treaties had been made over fifty years before had so "totally changed" that the terms of Indian treaties were no longer applicable or binding.[51] Connecticut's Senator Orville Platt explained that treaty stipulations for Indian governments were "no longer obligatory" on the United States; that it was high time the federal government forced allotments and citizenship on the nation's reluctant wards.[52]

The next year the Supreme Court decided that it was unfortunately "too late" for the President of the United States "to protect the Indians in their treaty rights,"[53] leaving them to the mercy of congressional will. Justices the same year twisted treaty language to mean that treaties "should not be made an instrument for violating the public faith" and jeopardizing the rights of Wyoming to regulate American Indian hunting.[54] In the Stephens case, already mentioned, the High Tribunal ruled that Cherokee treaty land was "public" and subject to United States administrative control and ultimate disposal.[55] The Court kept to itself rights to interpret Indian treaty provisions in *Jones v. Meehan* in 1899 but put American Indian nations in the same "state of dependency and pupilage, entitled to the care and protection of the Government"[56] as did plenary authority cases of the same era. Indians remained dependent wards, with the emphasis on dependent status.

3

Kiowas and Americans

The Kiowas played a dominating role in the nineteenth-century history of the southern plains. Both their allies and their enemies felt the weight of Kiowa presence well beyond the impact of the tribe's small numerical strength. Their fierce independence fed Kiowas' headstrong attitudes even after their forced confinement to a reservation.

According to linguists, the Kiowas speak a language related to the Tanoan-language Pueblos of Taos, Jemez, Isleta, and San Ildefonso in New Mexico. Elderly Kiowa speakers, however, consider their tribal tongue unique. In their far northern home country located in Montana, the Kiowas made the transition from elk and antelope subsistence hunting to use of the horse and to a buffalo culture. They also took on ritual identifying them with plains warrior cultures and they acquired their sacred thanksgiving ceremony, the medicine lodge Sun Dance.

From their homeland in south central Montana, the Kiowas skillfully used diplomacy and alliances during their movement toward the southern plains in the middle of the eighteenth century. They made close and lasting ties with the Sarcees of the Canadian Rockies, the Crows of Montana, and the Arikaras of the northern plains. While still in the north, the Plains Apaches (or Kiowa-Apaches) merged with the Kiowas proper. The Kiowas, along with their allies the Comanches after 1780, dominated the southern plains region of the United States well into the nineteenth century. As mounted warriors, the Kiowas and the Comanches had few equals. At successive stages in their history on the southern prairies, the tribes blocked Spanish desires for Indian hegemony, harassed French and then Mexican attempts to forge a plains presence, and dominated emigrant Indian tribes and later white settlers well into the early nineteenth century.[1]

Official Kiowa relations with the American government began when the 1834 Dragoon expedition ventured onto the southern plains and contacted the Indian nations. In that earliest encounter, the Cherokee interpreter's poor knowledge of Spanish made initial communications faulty. Poor communications hampered good relations and fostered misunderstandings that would haunt mutual relations thereafter. Already trappers and traders had carried on commerce with the plains tribes for a long time, and Anglo-American trade goods brought awareness of the Americans into Kiowa camps. Indian tales of whiskered and hat-wearing strangers told the Kiowas of the Americans long before any reached their camps.

The Kiowas were not present for the 1835 negotiations that led to a Comanche–United States treaty.[2] Two years later, however, the Kiowas entered into an identical treaty of friendship with the Americans.[3] Again, in 1853, after a successful parley two years before at Fort Laramie for northern tribes, federal negotiators met Kiowa leaders at Fort Atkinson, Kansas, a post located on the Santa Fe Trail. The Kiowas agreed to allow military forts and roads in their region and accepted federal annuities.[4] Although the Kiowas did not participate in Confederate negotiations at the start of the American Civil War, they did attend the Little Arkansas Council after that conflict and agreed to a reservation with wide boundaries.[5] There the Plains Apaches formally allied with the Cheyennes and Arapahos. Authorities quickly realized that Indian cessions were not adequate for the rapidly expanding pioneers, who needed more land from the Indians.

In 1866, Kiowa leaders discussed post-war affairs with federal authorities but made no lasting agreements. A series of incidents, such as Indian depredations and frontier conflict, contributed to demands from reform advocates for a peaceful course of action in Indian affairs. Continued settler intrusions onto reservations and incessant charges of an "Indian Ring" defrauding peaceful wards on western reservations helped initiate congressional inquiries into Indian affairs. All these events fed a desire to try something new to find a solution to Indian troubles and led to the congressional formation of a Peace Commission in 1867 to "remove the causes of war," secure the frontier, "and establish a system for civilizing the tribes."[6]

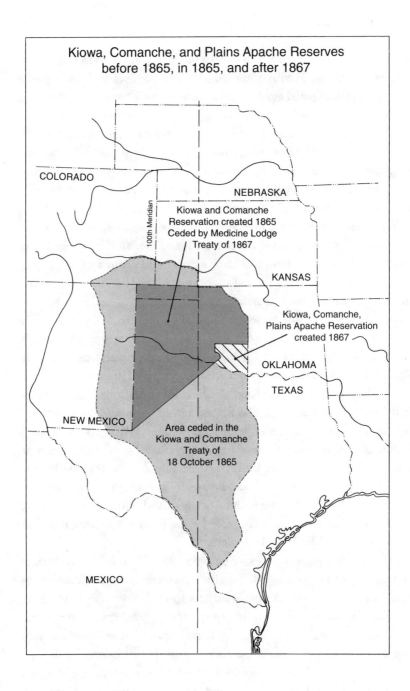

Map 1. Kiowa, Comanche, and Plains Apache reserves before 1865, in 1865, and after 1867.

It represented a dramatic shift away from the policy of using military force against the tribes, although the ultimate threat of force remained. The Peace Commission of 1867–1868 had come with the announced intention "to conquer by kindness" and included civilian and military officials who worked sincerely to reach accords with northern, central, and southern plains tribes. The commissioners sought to preserve natives as individuals, while at the same time changing Indian cultures through educational, agricultural, and missionary endeavors.

They also confined American Indians to reduced reservations so they could open the available lands to railroads cutting through the central plains. Commissioner of Indian Affairs Nathaniel G. Taylor in his report to the United States Senate called for the creation of a giant Indian Territory to be carved out of parts of Texas, New Mexico, and the existing Indian Territory.[7] Taylor assumed that the reserved area for the exclusive occupancy of the Indian would end Indian–white conflict because the root cause of outbreaks—Indian–white contact—would be blunted. Even though causes for warfare continued along with hostilities after their treaties had been concluded, both sides felt they had gained from the agreements. It marked the first time southern plains tribes had been required to give up rights to traditional hunting lands outside their large former reservations.

Because of the later importance of the 1867 treaties (see appendix 1) for the legal evolution of Kiowa land holdings, it is well to examine those deliberations closely. Comanche warrior Ten Bears was the first to suggest a meeting on Medicine Lodge Creek to Kiowa and Comanche Agent J. H. Leavenworth, who in turn convinced Superintendent Thomas Murphy, the man who selected the site.[8] Medicine Lodge directly affected the *Lone Wolf* case thirty-four years later. Kiowa participants and their descendants remembered the 1867 talks much differently than the federal negotiators sent in 1892 to close out Kiowa claims to their last remnant of the bison range.[9]

The Medicine Lodge Council witnessed history's largest assemblage of Indians on the southern plains. The impressive number of distinguished federal officials, notable Indian leaders, and even newspaper journalists in attendance attested to the importance of the proceedings for national Indian policy. About five thousand Indians met with some six hundred whites. Interspersed among the colorful Indian costumes and presents of bright cloth and top hats were many United States military uniforms. Negotiators for the United States included Commissioner of Indian Affairs Taylor, Chairman of the Senate Indian Affairs Committee and author of the peace commission bill John B. Henderson (Missouri), head of the Sand Creek massacre investigation Samuel F. Tappan, Little Arkansas Council negotiator John B. Sanborn, and leading soldiers like retired Major General William S. Harney, commander of the Department of the Dakotas Major General Alfred H. Terry, and commander of the Department of the Platte Major General Christopher C. Augur. The ranks were all brevet, a holdover from the recent Civil War. Augur replaced Lieutenant General William Tecumseh Sherman in the field. Sherman headed the Division of the Missouri, west of the Mississippi River, and his duties prevented him from being in Kansas. The Commission had earlier encountered Sioux obduracy on the northern plains, so the negotiators set their sights on their first agreement with southern tribes.

For the Indians, most of the notable leaders were present, with the exception of some of the more distant Comanche bands. Lone Wolf, a young and promising warrior, was an onlooker but did not directly participate in the talks. Satank, Stumbling Bear, and Satanta spoke for the Kiowas. Ten Bears and Little Horn led the Comanche presence, while Wolf's Sleeve and Brave Man represented the Plains Apaches. The Lipan Apaches did not attend, probably out of their enmity toward the Comanches. Although the Kwahadis were the most remote and aloof band of the Comanches, and most of them were nowhere to be seen, the young man Quanah Parker was present for the consultations but took no direct part in them.

The Kiowas called General Winfield Scott Hancock, the commander of the region in which the Kiowas resided, *Ganuan,* as they pronounced "General." Hancock was also referred to as *Pasot-kya'to,* "Old man of the thunderer," as a result of the thunderbird or eagle that he wore as an emblem on his shoulder.[10] For their part, United States representatives referred to the Indians as the "children" of the Great Father in the capital, and the Indians followed the example in referring to themselves. Kiowa deliberations with representatives of the Great Father centered on promises made but not kept, while United States representatives focused on the paternal aspects of the relationship. The Kiowas stressed the responsibility inherent in the social relationship among family members, while federal negotiators pressed for their contractual advantage in the document before them. One spoke of relationships; the other spoke of land transactions.

At the Medicine Lodge Council, tribes officially agreed to reside on drastically reduced Oklahoma reservations. The Kiowas and Comanches gave up claims to 90 million acres (some 50,000 square miles) in exchange for a 2.9 million acre reserve. They were to settle in what was called the Leased District on a tract taken from the Choctaws and the Chickasaws at the end of the Civil War in their reconstruction treaties.[11] The Kiowas, Comanches, and Plains Apaches were to be confined to a region that was to be one-tenth the size of the 1865 region. Indian signatories agreed to discontinuance of 1865 treaty annuities and substitution of 1867 annuity payments and gifts for a period of thirty years. Payments were to consist of one suit of woolen clothing for every male person, or flannel, cloth, and calico for every female, and $25,000 in goods for the tribes to be spent as the Indian Service deemed necessary. The Indians agreed to halt raids against railroad construction gangs, settlers, and military posts. Claims for Indian depredations would be paid from Indian annuities. The Indians could continue to hunt in the Texas panhandle.

For its part, the government only stated that whites would be barred from the new reservation but provided no means for removing trespassers, who were the persistent problem on Indian lands. The guarantee in Article 2 promised the Indians "absolute and undisturbed use and occupation" of reserved lands. The government pledged to construct ten buildings to house agency officials, schooling, blacksmithing, and other services. After a decade, the government had the option of channeling building funds up to $10,000 a year into education. Continuing maintenance of the agent was the sole exception. The government also assented to provide Indian employment preference in staffing agency positions in keeping with the policy of civilizing its wards and offering an outlet for the skills of students who would return from eastern educational institutions.

Federal officials targeted individual Indians who were heads of families with the offer of 320-acre farmsteads. Their aim was to turn the plains nomads into a sedentary yeoman citizenry. Indians who were adults but not heads of families could obtain 80 acres. The government would provide each head of an Indian family a total outlay of $175 over four years for agricultural implements and seeds for farming. The government held out $500 annual awards over three years to the leading Indian farmers as cash incentives for new converts to agriculture. The federal government also agreed to provide a carpenter, a blacksmith, a miller, an engineer, a teacher, and a physician to assist in the reformation of the Indians. The agreement also pledged that the national government would build a steam sawmill and gristmill on the reservation to enable the new farmers to market their products more easily.

Since they would be citizens on their farms, Anglo-American law would come into play. Indian reformers like the abolitionist Samuel Tappan pointed to the extension of civil law over the Indians as one of the most important aspects of the Peace Commission.[12] The first article of the treaty promised that the Indians would deliver "bad men among the Indians" to United States officials for punishment. The Indians accepted federal jurisdiction, and in Article 6 the United States agreed to establish Indian reservation governmental and police laws. Vital for the future was the requirement in Article 12 for the consent of at least three-fourths of male adult Indians for further cessions of their land. That provision underscored the government's approach to the Indian, treating each as an individual freeholder with a vote. The article would be the focus of renewed legal attention following the 1892 agreement for more land cessions.

The 1867 treaty also provided for missionary schooling for Indian children and at least one teacher for every thirty Indian children attending school. That obligation was to last for not less than twenty years. Indians agreed "to compel their children" to go to schools. In a separate treaty, the Plains Apaches officially rejoined the Kiowas and Comanches. The commissioners raised the annual annuity to $30,000 to the three tribes to make up for their additional numbers. The Medicine Lodge treaties set the government's course with the three tribes for the remainder of the century.[13]

The Kiowa warrior Satanta spoke for all the Indians when he reminded the commissioners on the first day of the grand council that the Indians did not want to be confined to a reservation. They preferred their life of freedom on the open prairie: "When we settle down, we grow pale and die." The Comanche spokesman Ten Bears eloquently made the same plea the following day, stating that "I was born upon the prairie, where the wind blew free and there was nothing to break the light of the sun. I was born where there were no enclosures and where everything drew a free breath. I want to die there and not within walls." Senator Henderson replied that to persist on the old pathway was to face extermination, and he quickly held out the prospect of government gifts, annuities, houses, and a new way of life as inducements for agreeing to the terms of the treaty.[14]

Many of the same problems that would later plague the 1892 Jerome Commission proceedings, which were to start Lone Wolf's court fight, arose at the Medicine Lodge Council. Communications proved to be a formidable hurdle. Mixed-blood Cherokee Jesse Chisholm served as one of the interpreters. Another was the Delaware Indian Black Beaver. White man Philip McCusker also served as an interpreter. He spoke only Comanche but was proficient in sign language. However, even when he spoke he often mumbled during the prolonged proceedings. Bao (Cat), also known as Having Horns, next translated from Comanche into Kiowa but lost much of the meaning in the process. Probably the Indians understood little of the entire affair, but because of the gifts, food, speeches, and pageantry, they "had a fine time," in the words of one who was there and recalled the events many years later.[15]

However, what little they did understand of council promises they took seriously. The Kiowa farmer Poor Buffalo later recalled that when touching the pen, "we raised our hands and told the Great Spirit that it was a sacred thing." Nearly a year before the conclusion of the sessions, Lieutenant General Sherman reported that the Kiowa "claim to the very letter the execution on our part of those treaties, the obligations of which they seem to comprehend perfectly."[16] One of the clauses the Indians later remembered most clearly and clung to stubbornly during the 1892 negotiations was their belief that the entire treaty ran for thirty years—the time period for the annuities and clothing outlays only, according to the American interpretation of the negotiations.

Even though the Indians did not understand the proceedings or what was said during the council regarding restrictions on their movement off their new reservation, their leaders signed the document. They were anxious to receive the presents the commissioners brought. Toshaway (Silver Brooch) of the far-ranging Penetethka Comanche eagerly anticipated his government-built house upon his consent to the document. United States authorities before had only loosely enforced treaty terms, and many of the war leaders probably believed that this one would be as easily evaded. After all, in the document Texas or that part of Texas that made up the panhandle remained a segment of their recognized hunting territory just as it had always been. More than one warrior taunted United States army officers and proclaimed the superiority of the mounted aboriginal soldier in the event of any contest over hegemony.

The commissioners played out a role that had taken place many times earlier in national Indian negotiations. The council was a counterfeit imitation of negotiation between equals. The commissioners spoke concepts that the Indians did not grasp and translators failed to convey. Federal representatives carried out a burlesque of a council. They submitted to Congress for ratification agreements they maintained were from all the plains Indians but which were not understood by the warriors who had gathered at Medicine Lodge Creek who moreover did not fairly represent all the Indians.

Commissioners did not gauge Indian opinion, much less unanimity, at the council. Some Indians were not even present, such as the Kwahadi Comanches. Still others had listened but refused to be bound by the agreements, such as Lone Wolf's Kiowa band and the Kotsoteka Comanches. The commissioners were not daunted. They had dictated terms they had brought from Washington to their listeners. The commissioners adhered to a familiar policy of quieting frontier conflict, confining Indians to smaller parcels of land, opening the remainder to settlers, and introducing Anglo-American civilization through force, farms, schools, and missions. They provided a legitimate avenue for further government action against the Indians and a lawful means for curbing Indian separation from the civilizing influences of American society. A legal and diplomatic line had been drawn around Indian intransigence.

For the Kiowas, their reservation life would last less than forty years—years during which whites increasingly placed pressures on their culture and made demands for their land. The proud warriors did not willingly submit to demands. From 1868 through 1875, even mere confinement to their assigned reservation took stringent government enforcement of its policies, successful military action, and the imposition of a draconian peace against the Kiowa, Comanche, and Plains Apache Indians.

4

Tears in Their Eyes

Relentless federal military action forced an end in 1875 to organized Indian armed resistance against United States government policies. To eliminate opposition leadership, army military authorities exiled Indian ringleaders. Lone Wolf was among the Indians manacled and chained and sent to prison in far-off Florida. His health deteriorated during his imprisonment, and upon his return to the reservation in 1879 he died. His demise as the leading warrior marked, in the climactic words of ethnologist James Mooney, "the end of the war history of the Kiowa."[1] Lone Wolf's death came at about the same time that other war leaders, including Satank (Sitting Bear), Kicking Bird, and Satanta (White Bear), also died, removing their influence from the Kiowa camp circle and contributing to a crippling leadership void at a crucial time in their tribal history.

Other events in 1879 made that a pivotal year for the Kiowas. Federal government actions further undermined traditional chiefs' band authority when the agency moved from Fort Sill to Anadarko on the Washita River, consolidating the Kiowa-Comanche-Apache with the Wichita, Caddo, and affiliated tribes. The move dispersed the families around the agency still farther from band chiefs. Moreover, the federal government switched from issuing rations through band headmen to the heads of families, weakening traditional Indian ties. The Indians became more dependent on the government for food supplies. Agent P. B. Hunt boasted with some success that "I have endeavored to destroy the tribal relations as much as possible, and also to destroy the influence of certain chiefs."[2]

Disappearance of the bison increased desperation on the reserve. With the end of the buffalo on the southern plains, the Kiowas had to kill and eat their horses to prevent starvation—the summer of 1879 was called the "horse-eating sun dance" time on their calendars.[3] Dietary changes under the ration system altered the nutritional balance of the Kiowas' diet and lowered their resistance to white man's diseases. The government ration system too often bordered on outright robbery. Corrupt agents stole supplies and sold them to local merchants, or doctored agency requisitions to falsify orders so as to ensure extra supplies which could be turned to a ready profit.

Plains hunters did not understand the ration system when it first began. Indians at the start could find no use for government flour or bacon. They emptied the flour on the ground and used the sacks. On ration day, the field near the agency looked like a light snow had fallen as a result of the discarded flour. The Indians threw the bacon to their dogs. Sometimes the agent with-held rations to force recalcitrant Indians to conform to government edicts. Other times, Congress failed to appropriate money for rations. Beginning in 1877, Indian Service regulations reduced rations in an attempt to coerce Indians to work at wage labor, and in 1881 rations were cut one-quarter. The only result was increased hardship. In 1888, one Indian Office inspector during his visit found that some Kiowas "were actually starving."[4]

The Kiowas had been aware of the white man's diseases since trade intro-duced their various forms long before the white man arrived on the reserva-tion. Now that they were penned into a defined space, the Indians could not move away as readily from the sources of contagion. The Indians were even more vulnerable. One inept agent failed to quarantine school children who had measles, and they infected even more Kiowas. Some 221 Kiowas, most of them children, died in the summer of 1892 from the epidemic. Measles, whooping cough, and pneumonia hit the Plains Apaches. Smallpox returned to the Kiowas in 1899, in 1900, and again in 1901. A member of a railroad construction gang and a bootlegger spread the disease across the reservation in 1900.[5]

The invidious charge of corruption clung to the agency system. National attention focused for a short while on agency affairs. The Fort Sill agency and its predecessor Camp Wichita were the featured topic of a meeting of Friends of the Indian in 1869, at Cooper Union in New York City, dealing with the whole Indian Service. A representative of Cooper Union, Vincent Colyer, visited the agency to gain personal knowledge of its operations. Colyer's observations after his visit fed reformers' insistence that religious denominations handle Indian agency administration rather than military officers. Quaker agency employees lessened problems of corruption for a decade. When the Quakers departed in 1878, agency management returned to a level of controversy unknown for nearly ten years. Agents altered vouchers, diverted public funds to private use, sold supplies to local merchants, profited personally from leasing agreements through kickbacks, and most often successfully persuaded their political sponsors to help them cover up their activities.

Government agents attempted to turn their charges into farmers in spite of a dry climate subject to violent changes in weather. At the start of the experiment, the idea had some appeal because of the extermination of the bison, the Indians' main commissary. With the loss of their normal staple, the buffalo, the Kiowas could be expected to take up the alternative, farming. However, horticulture traditionally was a female role among the Kiowas, and males resisted the plan at every turn. Returned students who had been instructed in farming techniques were disillusioned upon their return to the reservation. Few Kiowas took up farming, and even those who did found that the government did not fully support their endeavors. The United States supplied only one plow for every three farmers. Implements and seed arrived late or not at all. Farming supervisors were inadequately trained, and in the case of agent George Day, the supervisor was his brother, an individual known among the Kiowa for his absence rather than agricultural leadership. Even if the Indians wanted to farm, the government usually only provided a single farmer to instruct 1,213 Indian males (1877) in the agricultural arts. The remaining small, light Indian ponies could not pull metal plows through the tough prairie sod. There were few available markets other than the agency itself for what little the Indians produced on their farms, and the Indians had trouble competing with nearby white farmers. Most important, the climate seemed to oppose agricultural endeavor at every opportunity. Drought followed torrential rains. Insects and winter freezes assaulted the crops and the farmers.[6]

Lone Wolf the Elder before his death in 1879 passed his name, his medicine, and his shield to a younger warrior named Mamay-day-te, who became Lone Wolf the Younger, or (from his residence) the Elk Creek Lone Wolf.

Mamay-day-te in 1872 had saved the life of Lone Wolf the Elder's son during a fight with teamsters at Howard Wells, New Mexico. Two years later, Mamay-day-te counted the first coup during the raid avenging the deaths in Texas of Lone Wolf's son and of his nephew at the hands of American troops. A grateful Lone Wolf the Elder during the victory dance that followed "threw away" or gave his name to Mamay-day-te. Lone Wolf the Younger received the charm of power that Kiowas believed accompanied the name. He inherited the mantle of leadership, and the obligations. He subsequently led Kiowa resistance to government influence on the reservation.[7]

He and his followers lived in the more isolated northern part of the reserve, near Mount Scott of Lone Wolf the Elder, and along Elk and Rainy Mountain creeks.[8] Agents labeled them "The Implacables" because of their implacable opposition to government policies. The Indians intimidated missionaries and tried to force them to leave the reserve. They taunted "progressive" Indians who were seen cooperating with the agents. At planting time they stood at the edge of the fields and made fun of Indians who used a plow. Medicine men would not allow the Indian farmers to plant seeds until nearly too late in the growing season. Implacables drove pony herds through planted fields. Opponents threatened to cut fences, destroy crops, and burn lumber belonging to the farmers. They proclaimed that farming was a plot to do away with the ration system.

The Implacables contemptuously referred to Indians gathered around the agency to accept government-issued sugar, coffee, flour, and other foodstuffs as "sugar eaters." When the government agent purchased sheep in a vain attempt to make shepherds of the Indians, Lone Wolf's band set the example and shot the hapless animals for sport, ate them, or simply abandoned them because the Indians knew nothing about weaving the wool. The Implacables invented other ways to outwit federal authorities: Kiowa headmen doubled the number of eligible Indians under their immediate leadership on the agent's roll as being entitled to rations; the chiefs then used the extra rations to trade for influence or goods. However, the warriors deeply resented being fed half their rations in corn, especially since that was what white men fed their livestock. Moreover, rations were often spoiled and caused illness.

The Implacables contributed to the rapid turnover of agents through their constant pressure and opposition—they frustrated nine in the decade before 1894 alone. They supported traditional religious practices, which included following a series of prophets such as Datekan (1881) and Paingya (1887), as well as fostering a Kiowa version of the Ghost Dance and the Native American Church. To cut down school attendance, Lone Wolf scheduled councils with feasts on the opening day of government school at a point like Mount Scott, far from the agency and the school. Lone Wolf visited the government mission school but was contemptuous of its education.[9] Through the 1870s, the superintendents complained that there were no Kiowa children in the agency school.[10] When government pressure increased on Lone Wolf for government education, he complied temporarily, then used any excuse and pulled his children out of school.

Missionaries formally arrived on the Kiowa reservation in 1887, the year of the last Kiowa Sun Dance. After that, the Indians requested permission to hold their Sun Dance ceremony in 1889 and 1890, but the agent called it "both demoralizing and degrading" and used troops to halt the dance.[11] Missionaries actually had been on the reservation almost since its inception. A Quaker, Thomas Chester Battey, and others left vivid descriptions of their lives on the plains and their cold reception among most of the Indians. In spite of opposition, missionaries made inroads among the Indians. When he died in 1875, Kicking Bird received the first Christian burial among the Kiowas. An Episcopal priest, J. B. Wicks, arrived at the agency in 1881 with Kiowa and Comanche assistants, but Wicks concentrated on white parishioners and the Wichita and affiliated tribes.[12]

The Methodist minister John Jasper Methvin established the first mission for the Kiowas, Comanches, and Plains Apaches at Anadarko in 1887, the same year that Baptists came. Presbyterians followed a year later, while Roman Catholics established a school thereafter. When they first began to preach their messages, missionaries found the people on the reservation unreceptive.[13] With Quaker administration in 1869 came Quaker teacher-missionaries, such as Josiah Butler, who found the defiant Indians upon his 1870 arrival "insolent and saucy."[14]

Some Indians, especially those in Lone Wolf's band, were openly hostile to missionaries. Safety demanded an Indian sponsor or protector. To survive in the face of threats against him, Thomas Battey remained under the protection of Kicking Bird's camp when he first began to teach in 1872. As she was unpacking her belongings, the Baptist missionary Isabel Crawford looked up to view a large warrior riding up to her to deliver a message. The warrior peered down and informed her that she would have to leave the reservation because the region was "unhealthy" for her. At Saddle Mountain, the Indians decided that nothing "white" could be constructed in the vicinity. When men arrived with lumber at Sugar Creek to build a government school, Pape-done and others took their guns, mounted their horses, and drove the crew away. The government moved the school site to Rainy Mountain.[15]

Medicine men particularly opposed missionary presence on the reserva-tion. Members of the Christian denominations interfered with Kiowa cere-monies and traditions. Ministers publicly disgraced Kiowa men who had more than one wife. Missionaries told their Indian listeners that "your old religions, your dances, your . . . mescal, etc., must all drop off"[16] in favor of the new god brought to them. They reminded their flock that the faster they shed old ways, the better off they would be. Time and again, missionaries ex-claimed, "How thankful I am to have been born in a Christian home instead of a savage's lodge!"[17] The presence of the missionaries directly threatened the position, influence, and power of medicine men, band headmen, and Kiowa traditional social structure.

Missionaries broke down the fabric of traditional Kiowa social relations. Instead of turning to headmen or shamans, converts looked to the mission-ary or to the agent for guidance. When they received advice, converts also gave their gifts of gratitude to others in payment for the reciprocal obli-gation. Christian denominations made gradual but steady gains among the Indians. As of 1898 there were five mission schools, three government board-ing schools, a government day school, and fourteen field workers from the various Christian faiths, as well as uncounted lay converts, present on the reservation.[18]

Southwestern Oklahoma captured the imagination of many Americans be-cause it was the nation's last contiguous frontier in the Lower Forty-Eight with potential land openings. Land seekers viewed the area as a nearby American Canaan, a place of promise, prosperity for the taking, and a final chance for a piece of land of their own. Policy makers anxiously looked to the region for new settlement areas for homesteaders. First, though, the region had to be secured from the Indians who occupied it. National political leaders turned to allotment as one solution. Lone Wolf offered his greatest resistance to allotment. His way of life was at stake. The Kiowas led anti-allotment sentiment on the reserves.[19]

Lone Wolf realized from his past experience with settlers, from events throughout Indian Territory, and from personal observation of recent Cheyenne-Arapaho land losses that preserving the land base was vital to the future of the tribe. He had heard elders' stories of steadily shrinking hunting areas through successive treaty councils and skirmishes with United States military forces. He had witnessed the destruction of the buffalo on the plains, had fought against it, and had seen the elimination of an Indian way of life built upon that sacred animal. As a traditional religious practitioner, he was especially sensitive to the loss of a sacred relationship to the land. Veteran soldier Iseeo summarized Indian feelings when he told the Jerome Commissioners, "Mother earth is something that we Indians love. . . . We do not know what to do about selling our mother to the Government. That makes us scared."[20]

Lone Wolf's desire to preserve his old way of life for his people clashed directly with the onslaught of white assimilation. He was not blind to survival, but clearly saw that he and his followers would have to adjust to some things in order to stave off far worse. Lone Wolf pragmatically adopted those aspects of Anglo-American culture which he thought would benefit his people and himself. He compromised with change, giving up what had to be ceded in order to save what he considered to be essential. Eventually, Lone Wolf would bow to the inevitable. Not ironically, within a decade he would be counted among the "white man's road" Kiowas.

Frustrated government officials had recommended formation of a Court of Indian Offenses to introduce Anglo-American legal concepts and law enforcement onto Indian reservations. Under earlier regulations, the court settled minor on-reservation disputes, separated rival claims to livestock, and oversaw an Indian police force. They tried also to deal with white intrusion onto the reservation but had limited success. However, the most despicable aspect of the new institution was that the courts enforced arbitrary federal prohibitions against Indian ceremonies and other traditional cultural practices. The Indian judges and police, in effect, were made to jail and punish their fellow tribespeople for participating in traditional activities that Christian missionaries and government agents found offensive. The opponents of the cultural practices thought that confinement and punishment would force Indians to assimilate even faster.

In the early 1880s a court was set up for the Kiowas, Comanches and Apaches. Lone Wolf (Kiowa), Quanah Parker (Comanche), and White Man or Tehuacana (Plains Apache) served as the first judges, representing the major tribes on the reserve. In 1888 Kiowa Indians in council voted to replace Lone Wolf with his brother, John Chaddlekaungky, and three years later the Caddo George Parton replaced White Man on the court. The court carried out its duties until the 1901 enactment setting up the land lottery abolished it.

Lone Wolf opposed farming but supported stock raising. Kiowa bands could migrate with their herd across a portion of the reservation in a circumscribed imitation of their former buffalo existence. Stock raising also was a means for survival, necessary because the government inadequately aided agriculture on the reserve and periodically cut off rations, especially to the Lone Wolf group.

Conditions discouraged tribal stock raising. Climate worked against both human and beast. Culture worked against any schemes. Many Kiowas contemptuously viewed government-sponsored plans for changes as conspiracies designed to harm them. Some Indians preferred to put their favored horses and cattle in government-built houses while they continued to live in tipis until well past 1900. Government emphasis on farming took resources and interest away from cattle. Low rations led many Indians to eat their breeding cattle, so herds did not grow.

Chronic lack of capital among the Indians prevented any ventures into ranching as a business enterprise. In spite of all the factors working against cattle raising on the reserve, government agents persisted in requesting that Medicine Lodge Treaty annuities be ended and the money used to buy cattle for stock raising. Climatic, cultural, and policy factors combined by 1885 to terminate attempts to form a government herd on the reserve.

Cattle readily grazed on the blue stem sage, grama, and buffalo grasses of the region, along with mesquite. Cattlemen nearby in Texas and within the neighboring Chickasaw domain wanted to feed their herds reservation grasses and fatten their cattle before shipping them to Kansas, Missouri, and Illinois markets. Intermarried whites, mixed-bloods, and interpreters provided the bridge for cattlemen to gain leases with the Indians on the reserve. Full-bloods already leased their farmlands to whites, and it was a small step to leasing pasturage. Some of the Indians, like the Comanche Quanah Parker, quickly grasped the potential for themselves in leasing lands. For many Indians the income overcame the disadvantages of leasing, namely breaking up Indian holdings, hampering Indian farming and ranching efforts, increasing economic divisions among the bands, and corrupting Indian politics, while at the same time it damaged Indian resolve to resist changes within Kiowa society.[21]

Leasing yielded "grass money," which provided regular income for necessities and for bonuses to headmen, who could use the money to help maintain cultural relationships. Following the American Civil War, the range cattle industry grew into a major enterprise feeding a rapidly industrializing nation. Increasing demand for beef necessitated larger grazing areas. In 1885 some 908,000 acres were under lease at six cents per acre, yielding about $55,000 per year, rising to about $75,000 for 1892 and on to $230,000 in 1900 as more acres and higher rentals went into effect.[22] By 1890, seven cattlemen leased nearly 1.2 million acres of the nearly 3 million-acre reservation.

Activities in 1890 among the neighboring Cheyennes and Arapahos alarmed the Indians on the Kiowa reserve. The Cheyenne and Arapaho Reservation had just been opened to whites in April 1892. The Kiowa warrior Big Tree remarked that after the Cheyenne-Arapahos mistakenly sold their lands to the Jerome Commissioners, the Kiowas "saw tears in their eyes." [23] Rumors circulated about moving the Cheyennes and Arapahos from their reserve to the Anadarko Agency in order to open the former to white settlers. Missionaries noted that as 1890 approached, the Kiowas were especially agitated over the issue of their land base. A field inspector for the Indian Office who visited the Kiowa Agency in 1889 reported that the "Indians are uneasy about their lands." [24]

During repeated meetings, Kiowa leaders stressed that they did not want to deal with the Cherokee Commission formed for negotiating land cessions and expressed their desire "that this talk of cutting up the country will be stopped." The Indians of the Kiowa, Comanche, and Apache reserve unanimously opposed allotment in severalty as well as any further railroad rights of way through their lands. Furthermore, there was a widely held view that the Medicine Lodge Treaty was to run until 1897, that its terms would not end at the whim of Congress. Kiowa Indian court judge Chaddlekaungky summed up their views when he stated, "We want our land [left] as it is." [25] The Kiowa Anko monthly calendar for April 1892 noted a blooming tree with foliage above two wagons and a graded road, denoting the white settlement of the Cheyenne and Arapaho Reservation.[26] Kiowa opponents did not want a similar experience.

All the fears and hopes regarding retention of Kiowa land peaked with the appearance of the Cherokee Commission, established in an amendment successfully attached to the 1889 Indian Appropriation Act by Illinois Congressman William M. Springer.[27] It provided for the opening of the so-called Unassigned Lands to settlement and for three commissioners whom the president would appoint to negotiate the cession of Indian Territory west of the 96th degree of longitude and the opening of the ceded land deemed "surplus" to white settlers. In explaining his motives, Springer told an audience the year before his amendment that "no portion of this continent can be held in barbarism to the exclusion of civilized man."[28] When it was first organized in June 1889, the Cherokee Commission, as it was then called as a result of its first tribal target, consisted of General Lucius Fairchild from Wisconsin as chairman, General John F. Hartranft from Pennsylvania, and Arkansas's Alfred M. Wilson. The stubborn intransigence of Cherokee Nation representatives during prolonged negotiations for cession of their Outlet, fed illicitly from the coffers of the cattle syndicate, Fairchild felt, undermined his health. Fairchild resigned in disgust before any Indian agreements were made, and David Howell Jerome, former governor of Michigan, replaced him as chairman. Hartranft had died earlier, and Warren G. Sayre of Indiana took his place. Sayre and Wilson were both attorneys and judges who had reputations as tough and skilled negotiators. Jerome had served for five years on the Board of Indian Commissioners as an advocate of Indian assimilation. Secretary of the Interior John W. Noble approved of the Republican Party majority on the Commission and looked forward to a series of new land cessions to be added to the public domain as a result of their work.

The commission was one of fifteen similar ones working throughout Indian Country to effect the allotment of Indian lands and to open the last remaining continental frontier to white settlers. The Cherokee, now the Jerome, Commission proved to be the most important ingredient in the opening of Oklahoma Territory lands. Commissioners concluded a total of eleven agreements with tribes for dissolution of Indian reservations totaling over 15 million acres. Indians of the Kiowa, Comanche, and Apache Reservation were the last Indians of the two Southwestern agencies to face the Jerome Commission.[29] When they arrived at the reservation, the commissioners had successfully concluded nine cession agreements and wanted to close out their work quickly.[30] The commissioners anticipated that their skill gained from earlier tribal encounters across the negotiating table would lead to an early, successful conclusion to their assignment. If the Indians proved to be difficult, then the commissioners expected they would rely on coercion and browbeating to pressure the Indians into an agreement. Jerome Commission members did not anticipate trouble in their next council. They would be surprised as their deliberations fell apart in the face of intractable Indian opposition at the Kiowa, Comanche, and Apache agency.

5

The Jerome Negotiations

The terms of the 1867 Treaty of Medicine Lodge confined Indians to their reservation in western Oklahoma and permitted the federal government to supervise their activities and to provide military forts and roads through the region for protection. Various agents and teachers were to be furnished to the Indians, who, for their part, agreed to cease depredations and tend to crop-raising on their reserved lands, which could be individual parcels if the Indians chose farmsteads. The Indians accepted federal legal jurisdiction. Article 12 pledged that no more cessions of Indian land would be made without the consent of at least three-fourths of the adult male Indians on the reservation.

To persuade the Indians to cede further lands, the federal government often used specially appointed commissioners as negotiators. Commissioners in many earlier negotiations established their strategy when dealing with Indians. They began mildly by explaining that they had come to befriend the Indians and offer the best terms possible. Commissioners knew that Indians in council acted unanimously, so the federal representatives tried to separate the group into more manageable smaller blocs. They attempted to find interested individual Indians and work with them toward agreement. As deliberations continued and Indians showed reluctance to part with their homelands, commissioners hardened in their stance. If cattle leasing interests were involved, government prohibitions against cattle illegally grazing on Indian land were put into effect, thereby cutting off a primary source of Indian income and undermining opposition to cessions. Finally, the commissioners dictated terms to their wards and gained consenting signatures through intimidation, coercion, and bribery.

Commissioners came with fixed conceptions regarding private ownership of land, the democratizing effects of yeomanry, and the necessity for American Indians to enter the national marketplace of competitiveness for private gain. Individual initiative, to the commissioners, was the premise on which American welfare rested. Their remarks in councils with tribes and their correspondence reveal that the commissioners shared the fundamental tenets of turn-of-the-century American society. To them the Indian land monopoly of common ownership was unworkable and had to be altered. Tribal governments had to be abolished, the reservation system eliminated, lands allotted in severalty, and the Indian had to join mainstream American society. The tribal Indian body had to be broken up to save the individual Indian. Commissioners emphasized that Indians must act as individuals, not as a common group. Secretary of the Interior Ethan Allen Hitchcock stated the federal government viewpoint:

> To educate the Indian in the ways of civilized life, therefore, is to preserve him from extinction, not as an Indian, but as a human being. As a separate entity he can not exist as encysted, as it were, in the body of this great nation. The pressure for land must diminish his reservations to areas within which he can utilize the acres allotted to him, so that the balance may become homes for white farmers who require them. To educate the Indian is to prepare him for the abolishment of tribal relations, to take his land in severalty, and in the sweat of his brow and by the toil of his hands to carry out, as his white brother has done, a home for himself and his family.[1]

Kiowa Indians came to the negotiating table with their own well-established opinions regarding the course of action to be followed. The Kiowas approached the councils collectively, with little thought of individual initiative in the face of what many considered their common foe. The Indians already knew why the commissioners were coming and what they wanted. Commissioners had already visited in council with the neighboring Cheyenne, Arapaho, Wichita, and affiliated tribes. Most of the Kiowas shared the sentiment that the great chief Dohasan left with them when he told his nephew, "I must not give my country to the whites."[2] The Indians knew they faced the inevitable sooner or later, and some favored allotment but wanted it postponed until the Indians were better prepared.

A few of the old warriors who had sat through the Medicine Lodge treaty council in the fall of 1867 were still alive and recalled the pledges made and solemnized in Kansas then. They focused on the thirty years that the treaty was to run. Frizzle Head, a Kiowa elder, reminded listeners, "When the council was assembled at Medicine Lodge, 23 years ago, I was there. . . . At the time of the treaty, thirty years was given to us to live in these mountains to do for ourselves." He stated that the time had not yet expired on the pledges. It was a refrain that was often repeated. Comanche leader Quanah Parker agreed, saying that President Grover Cleveland's first Secretary of the Interior John W. Noble himself had assured the Indians on the reservation that the Medicine Lodge Treaty would be allowed to run its course and "nothing would be done till the treaty expired."[3] Before the Jerome Commission proceedings got under way, the aged Comanche Howea (Gap in the Woods), one of two living Indian signers of the Medicine Lodge Treaty, painfully made his way to the negotiators' tent and presented a printed copy of the treaty to the commissioners.

Beginning in September 1892, the commissioners attempted to gain Indian consent to change Medicine Lodge Treaty guarantees and Indian acquiescence to the opening of the reserve to whites. Commissioners came to dictate terms to the Indians without regard to treaty guarantees. When they arrived at Fort Sill on September 19, the commissioners came from successful negotiations with the Wichita and affiliated tribes, who shared the same agency with the Kiowas, Comanches, and Apaches. Negotiators held councils in the vicinity of the Fort Sill railroad station, just east of the Comanche Indian Mission, at Anadarko next to the building where rations were stored, and at the Red Store just southeast of the fort. The first and longest councils were held near Fort Sill in the region of the more cooperative Comanches. The federal negotiators carefully avoided holding the proceedings in the region of the reservation that Lone Wolf and his supporters occupied. They also believed it would be easier to bring together a large group of Indians near the fort and agency where they were accustomed to come for meetings and annuities and where facilities existed for communication with Interior Department officials in Washington. Besides, troops would be nearby if the rumored opposition of the Kiowas flared into open and violent defiance.

After doing paperwork from earlier meetings and visiting progressive

Indian farms and homes—on October 1 they dined with Quanah Parker and his family during an evening break in negotiations—the Jerome Commission set about its mission. The negotiations took place amid stiflingly hot weather, with only a rare gust of wind for relief. During opening comments to the assembled Indians on September 26–27, the commissioners expressed their expectations and stated that they had come as friends to obtain excellent terms for the Indians which would guarantee for the native "a home that can never be taken away from him." It would be the Indian's home "forever." Commissioners falsely emphasized that they had no secret instructions and desired that everything be done openly. David Jerome briefly went over the terms of the congressional instructions that established the Commission and national policy aimed at assimilating the Indian. In an unsuccessful attempt to allay Indian fears, he added, "I want you to remember that the Government wants nothing from you," except to give to the individual Indian something with a value greater than land, namely money. He noted that the Indians possessed three million acres, and that for their own individual needs forever in the future they only required about a half million acres. They must sell the remainder. He assured them that living on allotments would be no different than residing on their reservation.

Judge Sayre's stern opening remarks pointed out that in the past, the president forced allotments upon reluctant Indians and could do the same for the ones before him if they were not cooperative.[4] Aged war leader Stumbling Bear replied for the Kiowas with great solemnity, "We are not desirous of selling our country now,"[5] and strongly suggested that the commissioners return in four or five years after the Medicine Lodge pledges had run their course. Jerome responded that it could well take four years for any agreement they made at Fort Sill to be approved and the money successfully appropriated to pay the Indians.

Kiowas who spoke during the negotiations included Big Tree, Iseeo, Stumbling Bear, Komalty, Tohauson, Apiatan, and many lesser leaders. Lone Wolf attentively waited for two days to hear what the commissioners had to say about their task. Lone Wolf replied for the Kiowas on September 28. He represented those who wanted nothing to do with the proceedings. Lone Wolf stood and addressed the commissioners. He explained that the tribes were striving to change their old way of life, and they had made "rapid progress." He requested that the Commission not "push" the Indians, though. "Should they [the Kiowas, Comanches, and Apaches] be forced to take allotments it means sudden downfall for the three tribes." Because of that fact, all the tribes had decided "not to sell the country," and Lone Wolf repeated the phrasing with each tribal name for emphasis, underscoring his statement that they did not want to sell. Noting that the allotment policy would "be disastrous," he again asked that the government not "force" the Indians into anything they did not readily consent to do.[6]

Quanah Parker spoke for the Comanche Indians. He, too, called for the commissioners "to hold up a little" and not press forward too fast. Since the Commission brought no money to pay the Indians directly for the land, the commissioners obviously wanted to purchase the land with "mouth-shoot," and Quanah demanded to know how much they were going to offer per acre.[7]

The commissioners offered the Indians 160 acres each, suggesting that half be for crops and half be for grazing. They pointed out that the amount was double what the original Dawes Act and also the Medicine Lodge Treaty provided for Indians who were not heads of families. Commissioners injected the false threat that if the Indians did not accept their generous offer of 160 acres, the federal government would force them to take only 80 acres under the Dawes Act.

The federal negotiators evaded exact answers as to price and payment. They delayed giving details. Instead of divulging a per acre price, they held out a lump sum of $2 million, stressing that they could get 5% interest, well above the 3% the Dawes Act stipulated, and that the sum would be available at least in part to each individual Indian instead of going into the United States Treasury. The $2 million worked out to $665 per capita, or, attempting to appeal to ardent horse traders, thirty ponies for every Indian on the reserve.[8] In an attempt to dazzle their Indian listeners, the commissioners pointed out that $2 million would fill two thousand money boxes and would require 26 six-mule-team wagons filled with silver dollars to haul all that sudden wealth.[9] When pressed on the subject of a per acre amount, they said it was between $1.00 and $1.10,[10] which was well below the amount recently paid to the Wichita-allied tribes.

Various Kiowas spoke against the proposed agreement. Iseeo, an elderly Kiowa Indian cavalryman at Fort Sill, stressed the poverty of the Cheyennes and Arapahos as an example of the debilitating results of allotment. Commissioners retorted that the Kiowas' neighbors exaggerated their plight; the Cheyennes and Arapahos had never been wealthier. The old Kiowa war leader Komalty (Big Head) perceptively observed that it was not possible to raise crops on an arid 80 acres or even raise livestock on 160 acres.[11]

Land prices and payments dominated the proceedings. The Cheyennes and Arapahos had agreed in October 1890 to 50 cents an acre for their three million acre surplus. The Wichitas and their affiliated tribes refused the same amount for their 574,000 acres. Their 1891 agreement with the same Commission stipulated that Congress would set the price later, eventually $1.25 an acre. Quanah led the commercial viewpoint that pressed the commissioners for a good price, and he observed that at $1.25 the deal would yield $2.5 million to the combined tribes. Not to be outdone, the Comanche leader Tabananaca urged $1.50 per acre.[12] Commissioners deceived the Indians when the negotiators claimed that by signing the document the Indians would receive much more money than if they retained their reservation and leased the land as they had done in the past. The commissioners lied. The Jerome Commission offered $2 million, with $500,000 to be paid in two years and $1.5 million to draw interest in the federal treasury, yielding about $25 per person. The Indians had already leased a portion of their reservation for $100,000, which averaged about $33 per person. The lease amount gradually rose during the following years to $225,000 in 1899, which averaged about $75 per capita or approximately three times the amount the commissioners held out to them.[13]

Choctaw and Chickasaw rights to the Leased District clouded the negotiations. The two tribes claimed the area out of which the United States had created reservations for the Cheyennes and Arapahos, the Kiowas, Comanches, Plains Apaches, and the Wichitas and affiliates. The Choctaws and Chickasaws pressed their title vigorously. Litigation involving them continued until the turn of the century. Before the Jerome Commission arrived at Fort Sill, the federal government paid almost $3 million to settle Choctaw and Chickasaw claims to the Cheyenne and Arapaho reserve, more than double what the Cheyenne and Arapaho tribes themselves had received for the same land. The Indians who assembled at Fort Sill knew well what had transpired among the Cheyennes and Arapahos and the prices paid for nearby lands.[14]

Quanah continued his leadership of the Indian side when he surprised the council on October 3 with the request that negotiations be postponed for two months while the Indians brought in an attorney of their own to assist them. He had probably been influenced by the shadowy John T. Hill, a white man who worked for the commissioners but ingratiated himself to Indians during negotiations as he had already done with the Kickapoos when they had been hoodwinked into concluding a bad agreement with the Commission. After meeting unsuccessfully with the Kickapoos in the field, back in Washington Hill exercised a bogus power of attorney and signed fifty-one Kickapoo signatures to their allotment agreement. In spite of the notoriety of his actions, many Indians considered him sincere. Hill's personality won over some at the council ground. The Comanche White Wolf referred to Hill as "a friend of ours" who "can do something for us." [15] Rumors circulated about large sums of money for attorneys and for chiefs who agreed to cooperate with the attorney named Asp, who came from Guthrie to assist the Indians and who just happened to be an acquaintance of Hill. Lieutenant Hugh L. Scott, stationed at Fort Sill since 1889 and an admirer of the plains Indians, credited himself with informing the Indians at the ground of the conspiracy. Asp showed up the night of October 3, talked with several people including the agent, concluded that since Congress did not convene for two full months and nothing would happen until Congress acted, he could accomplish little, turned around, and left. [16]

Quanah during the October 5 parley announced that he had a new proposition. He suggested that the Commission take back to Washington the Indians' asking price of $2.5 million for the surplus lands and the Commission's own offer of $2 million and let Congress decide, as it had done recently in the case of the Wichitas. The following day the commissioners announced that leading chiefs Lone Wolf for the Kiowas, Tabananaca of the Comanches, and White Man for the Plains Apaches agreed to Quanah's proposal. The commissioners cleverly stated they would include the $2 million figure in the written agreement for the Indians to sign, and that the Indians could send a delegation to ask for $500,000 more if and when the time came for a hearing on the topic. [17] Big Tree of the Kiowas and several lesser Comanche chiefs such as Cheever and White Wolf, as well as the Plains Apache leader Chewathlanie, spoke in favor of making an agreement if it did not take effect for three years. Commissioner Sayre commented that it might well take Congress that long just to ratify the agreement, echoing Jerome's earlier reply.

The Indians furnished a list of white men and women whom they wanted included in the allotting process, and the commissioners added their own choices to the list. Article 12 of the Medicine Lodge Treaty required that three-fourths of the resident males on the reservation agree to any further land cession. The commissioners worked diligently behind the scenes through John Hill, the interpreters, and government employees to secure signatures for their document. The attempted addition of twenty-five whites to the document could only help their endeavor to gain consent of the Indians, especially since Indian opponents would make the effort difficult. Tohauson had reminded the Indians in the council of the words his father had spoken about not selling land to whites. He concluded his remarks by announcing that "half, and maybe more, have decided not to sign the paper."[18] Commissioners knew they would have a hard time gaining consent, much less unanimity, from the Indians before them, and, if people whom the Indians favored were included, it was a small price to pay for acceptance of the whole document.

Among the eighteen entitled to all benefits of land and money were whites intermarried among the Comanches George Conover, William Deitrick, interpreter Edward Clark, and Quanah's son-in-law Emmett Cox. They also included Mabel, the wife of the Kiowa interpreter Joshua Givens. Seven others, including the interpreter Emsy Smith; Quanah's tenant farmer David Grantham; the missionary John Methvin; the baby daughter of Charles Adams, who had served as agent from 1889 to 1891; the current agent George Day; the soldier Hugh Scott; and the omnipresent John T. Hill, were entitled to land. Joshua Givens added Methvin's name to the list without the minister's knowledge because the Kiowas greatly admired him and wanted him rewarded for years of dedicated service.[19] Agent Day and Lieutenant Scott both spoke during the negotiations in neutral terms for the record but privately worked for Indian consent to the final agreement.[20] On October 7, Jerome reported that he had obtained 193 out of 450 required signatures on the document.[21] After nearly a week of effort, he announced over half the Indians had signed, 342 signatures.[22]

Opposition strengthened as the council began on October 11. Chairman Jerome denied that his aides had "tried to bulldoze" any Indians into signing, and as soldiers deployed around the grounds, he called on Lieutenant Scott to remind the Indians present of the punishments for threatening and violent behavior. Kiowa trooper Iseeo observed that for the first time in a very long time he had heard a disrespectful remark from his nephew aimed at him for signing the Jerome document.[23] As a result of various pressures and inducements from the Commission, the fabric of Kiowa society was already beginning to tear.

Jerome announced that the Kiowas had invited the entire Commission to come to Anadarko for a council with the leaders and people of their tribe. The final week of the Commission's work would be by far its hardest. They encountered so much opposition that the proceedings in Anadarko rapidly grew confused, turned to turmoil, and finally degenerated into outright fraud. As the council ended in Fort Sill and before they adjourned, Indians charged deception and coercion on the part of the Commission and their interpreters. There were accusations that the headmen who earlier signed the agreement were tricked. In spite of lengthy discussions, Indians stated they did not understand what took place and that one thing was stated during daytime councils, while something entirely different occurred at night when individual Indians were approached about signing the document. After hastily conferring to discuss how to approach him, Indian leaders confronted interpreter Joshua Givens in the camp of Troop L, which was under the command of Hugh Scott. They discovered that Givens sat at the entrance to the troop quarters, and as each Indian soldier entered, Givens requested his signature. Givens lied and explained to them that they were only signing a petition asking for $2.50 per acre in accordance with what Quanah Parker and other headmen desired. Other times, Givens threatened the trooper until he gained a mark. A few times the soldier was simply ordered to sign. When a soldier refused to sign, Givens made his mark for him anyway. Givens defiantly told James Ahatone and George Poolaw he was going to secure the Jerome Agreement, as it was called, no matter what the opposition.[24] As a result of the uproar and the threats against Givens, a guard had to be posted to protect him. He was a bright returned student from Carlisle, a Presbyterian missionary, and the principal of an Indian school near Anadarko whom the government looked to as the model for the future generation of Indians. He was also the son of the great Kiowa warrior Satank and as such was a Tai-may keeper and brother of the Kiowa prophet Paingya, who lived in Lone Wolf's band.[25]

Apiatan (who was also called Wooden Lance) served as the spokesman for the Kiowas when the Commission began its October 14 council in Anadarko. The year before, a tribal council had chosen him to travel west to locate the new messiah of the Ghost Dance, interview him, and report back to the Kiowas on the authenticity of the dance. Apiatan reported in the negative, but some Kiowas did take up the Ghost Dance. For leading his people away from the Ghost Dance, the Department of the Interior had built a new house for him. Facing the commissioners, Apiatan appealed to the Great Spirit to lend weight to his words. He stated that the Kiowas were not going to depart from Medicine Lodge Treaty terms for the "new road" the commissioners advocated. When he asked those Indians in favor of his remarks to stand, almost all did so.[26] Big Bow noted that the words from the commissioners disturbed the Kiowa "like an enemy coming to camp among the people." [27] Jerome responded that the agent would issue beef and other food to the Indians so they would feel better for the following day.

Discussion turned even more explosive the next day. Big Tree released pent-up tensions from opponents of the proceedings when he confronted and publicly denounced Givens for misrepresenting what had been said, forging Indian signatures, and acting without Indian consent. Givens shot back to Big Tree, "You just like a married woman that got caught into adultery and trying to deny out of it. You *did* sign agreement." Indians demanded two additional interpreters of their choosing be added so that Givens's work could be closely checked. Sam Quoetone, who had had some schooling and understood English, was one of the added Indians. Quoetone already had shouted to the Indian leaders that Givens was not translating correctly what the commissioners, or even the Indians, were saying. A vexed Chairman Jerome dropped any pretense of negotiating with equals and forcefully reminded his audience, "Congress has full control of you, it can do as it is a mind to with you." He decreed, "Congress has determined to open this country." Either take the agreement offered, he reminded his audience, or get half as much land when the president imposed the Dawes Act on the reservation and seized the land, and as a result, obtain no money.[28] He repeated his comments about congressional power over Indians on October 17, the final day for the Commission's work.

Lone Wolf, Big Tree, Komalty, and others demanded that their names be stricken from the agreement. Apiatan denounced the deceit, cheating, and "fraud" the Commission used, and Jerome indignantly retorted, "I will not be talked to that way!" [29] He threatened the Indian leaders with jail and dismissed them. Only a few Comanches and even fewer Kiowas remained. U.S. troops moved quickly into closer position.

After the melee of shouting, gesticulating, and movement cleared, an elderly Kiowa named Waterman stood and calmly explained that the Kiowas would not harm the commissioners, that the Indians had left only to register their opposition to the agreement and not to secure weapons. Jerome and Wilson then spoke at length for the official record to the nearly empty council ground, making certain Givens recorded their words, about how solicitous and generous the commissioners had been, and then they formally concluded. Givens went back to his work of adding names and marks to the document.

The Jerome Commissioners departed. Once safely in Washington, D.C., the commissioners switched versions of the agreement, substituting their altered copy for that which had been partially signed at the councils (see appendix 2). The changed agreement in the commissioners' hands, which went through several permutations, ultimately contained only counterfeit signatures. It was a tactic in keeping with their handiwork during their negotiations with the Kiowas.[30]

The Commission not only left bitterness and anger behind them, they also left behind Joshua Givens. Even though there were other interpreters present at the council, blame rested on Givens for willfully misdirecting the Indians into signing the document. Some Indians sought revenge for Givens's actions which betrayed his people. Either a Comanche or a Kiowa medicine man made an effigy of Givens and made medicine against him. Givens was informed that in a short period of time he would begin to hemorrhage before he died. Missionaries vainly tried to convince Givens he had nothing to worry about from the "witch doctor." Shortly thereafter—the agent officially called it consumption—Givens steadily worsened and, in spite of all the medical attention missionaries and the agency physician could provide, Givens died.[31] Many Kiowas agreed with Big Tree that it was divine retribution.

Some four hundred Kiowa Indians gathered at Fort Sill to discuss the aftermath of the Commission's activities. Indians met with sympathizers in an effort to compose letters and memorials of protest. Hugh Scott, who conveniently overlooked his own participation in attempting to sell the Indians on the cession, took credit for pointing out that Lone Wolf "had sold out his people" when he signed the earlier version of the Jerome Agreement. After long discussion, the assembled Indians voted to oust Lone Wolf as chief and eventually chose Apiatan as their leader. Scott boasted that he had dethroned Lone Wolf. Scott failed to realize that Apiatan was Lone Wolf's nephew, the son of the first Lone Wolf's "brother" Red Otter, so political influence remained within the Lone Wolf extended family. Scott had not been present earlier when Lone Wolf sided with Apiatan against the Ghost Dance.[32]

The rancor Indians harbored following their experience with the Commission poisoned further Indian negotiations. As a direct result of Kiowa embitterment and their comments to other Indians of the territory, the Osage Commission two years later utterly failed in its mission to clarify false Osage enrollments and title fraud that had resulted from shoddy Cherokee Commission work among those Indians earlier. Osage mistrust regarding any further concessions and manipulation stymied attempts to correct past abuses.

Commissioners were confident that they had obtained the signatures of three-fourths of the male Kiowa, Comanche, and Apache residents of the reservation as required for a legal land cession under the terms of Article 12 of the Medicine Lodge Treaty. Agent George Day himself falsely certified that the 1892 Agreement had the necessary signatures to be legitimate. Questions dogged the document and the agent. The commissioners were to have left an official copy of the agreement with the agent for the Indians or their attorneys to examine at will. The agent "lost" the original version for eight years when controversy arose, even denying to Congress that he had it. Even with the alterations to it, the Jerome Agreement was between 21 and 91 signatures short of the needed three-fourths, depending on whether age 18 or age 21 was the cutoff for adult status.[33]

CHAPTER

6

The Kiowas Lobby

For eight years the Indians and their lobbyists delayed congressional ratification of the Jerome Agreement in spite of settlers' advocates and their
repeated attempts to enact it. When the Commission concluded its work on
the reservation, Indians and their supporters immediately began organized
opposition to the negotiations and their outcome. Friends of the Indian wrote
federal authorities protesting the agreement. Board of Indian Commissioners
member Charles Painter visited the reservation on the heels of the Commission and echoed the Indians' refrain that they had been "outrageously defrauded."[1] Ethnologist James Mooney wrote that the agreement would lead
to the "destruction" of the tribes, while Lieutenant Hugh Scott wrote the
Secretary of War that the agreement if implemented would rob wards of their
last land and would convert useful Indians "into a band of miserable and
degraded beggars."[2] Missionaries on the reserve like John Methvin helped
formulate petitions and affidavits stating that the Indians misunderstood the
1892 agreement. Petitions circulated among congressmen and the Indians'
friends.[3]

Supporters of the Indians called for a new commission to negotiate fairly
with the Indians, who were said to be ready to listen to reasonable offers for
their surplus lands. Memorialists asked for an increase in the size of allotments so Indians could eke out a living, stating that the 160-acre parcels
were too small for the arid grasslands to be usable as they currently stood.
Petitioners invoked treaty promises and cautioned that the agreement vio-

lated contracts signed for grazing leases. They appealed to the conscience of legislators, pointing out the fraudulent nature of the signatures on the 1892 document. They underscored the inability of the Kiowas to deal with a land opening. They also pleaded for fair treatment for the nation's wards. The memorials from the reservation Indians carefully contained all the adult male signatures available, more than appeared on the 1892 agreement.

Christian missionaries on the reservation and in nearby towns reported that the Indians were increasingly agitated over the looming opening of their lands. Indian Christian converts like the Kiowa Heenkey brought the issue into reservation chapels, asking as early as 1897:

> One thing I want to know. Does the Jesus Book say any place that the Kiowa Indians are to have one hundred sixty acres of land apiece? Jesus never told us this. It is the white men. The Great Father made the land and put us on it and we love the land our Great Father gave us.
>
> It makes my heart sick when we hear that white men want to come in here. . . . Pray for us that we may keep our land.[4]

The Indian Rights Association took up the call for fairness in its pamphlets, which were circulated on Capitol Hill and among its subscribers.[5] Even Office of Indian Affairs officials came to oppose ratification of the 1892 agreement because they felt it was improperly foisted upon the Indians, it had false signatures, in effect the lands were being taken without compensation since payment was indefinite, and the size of the allotments was wholly inadequate for the support of the Indians. They substantially agreed with the Indians' arguments. Hitchcock's predecessor as Secretary, C. N. Bliss, believed the agreement wronged the Indians and should not be ratified. Kiowa Agent Frank Baldwin pleaded with Congress to allow the Indians five years (to 1901) before opening their lands to give the Indians time to adjust to a new way of life. When Lieutenant Colonel James F. Randlett first came to the Kiowa, Comanche, and Apache reserve in 1899, he worried that he would find a divided and contentious group of Indians. Instead, he discovered they were all united against the Jerome document and he believed that to open the reservation would be a "calamity."[6]

Much of the argument over ratification centered on leases for cattle and the suitability of the land for farming. Since the end of the Civil War, Indian agents had maintained that the reservation was not suitable for farming and, therefore, could not be allotted and opened to whites. Proponents for opening the region to whites stated that the lush prairie grasses lent themselves as readily to the plow as to the merchant. Each side to the controversy spent much time gathering affidavits to support their appraisal. Indians complained that intermarried squaw men and other non-Indians had already settled the fertile Washita Valley from Chickasha to Anadarko, leaving only the dry uplands to the Indians in the event of allotment. Special Agent Gilbert Pray and Agent Randlett took testimony in the region, testimony that was heavily weighted in favor of cattle interests, and informed the secretary of the interior that as a result of low rainfall and frequent droughts the reserve was unfit for agriculture but excellent for grazing, supporting Indian claims.[7] During every session of Congress between the conclusion of the Commission's work in 1892 and the final passage of the 1900 Act implementing the agreement, Indian delegations appeared before Congress and held audiences with the commissioner of Indian affairs seeking drastic modifications to the agreement. Hugh Scott usually accompanied the Indians. In 1894, Scott and Mooney met with Commissioner of Indian Affairs Daniel Browning. Mooney's constant advocacy of the Indians' causes in western Oklahoma shortly led to his banishment from the reserves. After one particularly emotional meeting which Apiatan and Scott led in the office of Commissioner Browning, the commissioner slammed his fist down on his desk and exclaimed, "I will not permit it. I will see justice done to those Indians as long as I am in power!" Secretary Hitchcock met two different times with Indian delegations on the subject. Similar exchanges between Quanah Parker and President Grover Cleveland, between other Indians from the reserve and members of the congressional committees on Indian affairs, and effective Indian Rights Association lobbying helped delay ratification.[8]

Beginning almost immediately after the Jerome Agreement was submitted to Congress, congressmen John H. Stephens (Texas), Dennis T. Flynn (Oklahoma), and Charles Curtis (Kansas) and senators Horace Chilton (Texas), James K. Jones (Arkansas), and Henry L. Dawes (Massachusetts) introduced bills to ratify the agreement. In 1898 Stephens introduced HR 10049, just one of his attempts at ratification, and the bill passed the House with a provision to speed the settlement of Choctaw and Chickasaw claims to the Leased District; but the Senate passed a resolution asking for more information regarding the signatures appearing on the Jerome document.[9] Undaunted, Stephens introduced HR 905 shortly thereafter for ratification, but protests sidetracked it, too.

Early in 1900, Stephens reported S. 255 out of the House Committee on Indian Affairs with extensive amendments, including a rewritten Senate version of his earlier HR 8590.[10] A Kiowa and Comanche delegation traveled to the capital to protest the measure. The Indian Rights Association worked against it and appealed to the president not to approve it. The Association had lobbied hard against previous bills and helped table Stephens's HR 8590 in favor of an amendment that Orville Platt of Connecticut offered in the Senate, which called for a clarification of Choctaw and Chickasaw rights and depredation claims against the Kiowas, while confirming the Kiowas in their rights to payment for their title.

Founded in the home of philanthropist and former ambassador John Welsh of Philadelphia, where about forty prominent residents gathered in 1882, the Indian Rights Association grew into the nation's leading Indian reform organization. Its membership advocated Christian missions to Indians, rapid assimilation, and protection of the Indian's individual rights. John Welsh's son Herbert became the group's corresponding secretary, a position that dominated the body's deliberations and shaped its policies. The workload in the Philadelphia office expanded so that before the end of the decade the Indian Rights Association opened a Washington, D.C., office. When journalist Francis E. Leupp stepped down as the full-time Washington lobbyist for the Assocation, he recommended and obtained the appointment of Kansan Samuel M. Brosius as his replacement. Brosius eagerly set about investigating abuses of the nation's wards and focused his attention in 1900 on the Kiowa reserve.

Brosius favored enlarging the amount of land for Indian allotments on the semi-arid reserve. Association lobbying encountered stiff opposition from the Rock Island Railroad attorney, who wanted to limit the size of Indian allotments in order to increase railway landholdings on the reserve for use in luring and transporting potential home seekers to the region. Brosius finally was able to obtain double the original 160-acre amount for allotments when sponsors tacked on a 480,000-acre Big Pasture to be held in common that could be used in the future to compensate Indians born after the enactment of the measure. The bill also raised the amount to be paid the Indians to $2 million.[11]

In 1900 Congress added a heavily amended Jerome document as Section 6 to the Fort Hall Agreement of June 6 and passed the legislation allotting the Kiowa, Comanche, and Apache reserve and opening the reservation's surplus land to settlement.[12] Defenders of the bill cleverly turned Indian protest around and pointed out that the act was passed only after the fullest possible hearings from the Indians involved. Brosius published an account of the entire issue that laid the blame for passage of the final act at the feet of Chicago, Rock Island, and Pacific Railroad officials. He denounced their malevolent influence in terms designed to appeal to reform sentiment during the Progressive era. His attack received much coverage in newspapers devoted to national administration opposition. With no little irony, Brosius accused the officers of "railroading" the legislation through Congress.[13] Vainly, the Indian Rights Association appealed to the president not to sign the act, pointing out that it was "void" because three-fourths of the tribesmen had not signed it and it would set the precedent of trampling on treaty pledges to Indians.[14] In spite of the pressure against it from reformers, the president signed the measure.

Under the terms of the Act of June 6, 1900, the United States took possession and title to 2,991,933 acres of the Kiowa, Comanche, and Plains Apache Reservation. Omitted from the total were 23,000 acres of the Fort Sill Military Reservation that federal officials treated as part of the surplus lands. The United States set apart 480,000 acres as common grazing lands in four numbered pastures and allotted in severalty 445,000 additional acres. The 1900 Act made no provision for dividing allotted land into grazing and grain-growing land as the 1892 agreement required. Later, national officials allotted 100,000 more acres from the pasture lands. The 1900 Act incorporated a suggestion Quanah Parker had made to Commissioner Warren Sayre and provided that when allotted land contained mineral deposits, the land was open to entry under existing mineral laws of the United States, but in its final version without any compensation to the Indian allottee. The federal government further set aside 10,310 acres for agency, school, religious, and other purposes, which left 2,033,583 acres, for which the government paid out $500,000 for per capita payment and deposited the remainder in the national treasury with the interest distributed to the tribes. Eventually the national treasury paid the three tribes the last of their $2 million under a tribal roll closed in late 1920.[15] However, the $1.5 million had to be held until Congress settled Choctaw and Chickasaw claims to the leased district. Those claims were finally concluded through court orders and later payments.

Overall, Brosius thought the measure "quite good"[16] given the pressure for ratification of the agreement, the behind-the-scenes maneuvering for amendments, and the clamor from white constituents for an immediate opening of the land.[17] The original agreement with the three tribes had been extensively amended, but the additions had not been submitted to the tribes for their consent as the terms of the original Springer Amendment in 1889 had specified. Given the climate of opinion on the reservation in the wake of the Commission, there was little possibility that consent could have been obtained successfully. In a letter printed in the *Washington Post*, Brosius thought that the June 6 Act was "the first instance in which Congress has amended an Indian agreement without the changes being submitted for agreement of the tribe interested." Indian Rights Association staff believed that this signaled a new and alarming Indian policy. They feared pressure for allotment would lead to confiscation of Indian lands and wholesale violations of Indian rights. The Act had overthrown a custom of long standing and had tarnished the nation's pledged word.[18]

Under the Act of 1900, the federal government paid the Kiowa Indians just over 93 cents per acre for the land acquired. The United States had paid the Cheyennes and Arapahos 60 cents an acre to extinguish their claim to their reservation, and in 1893 the government had paid the Choctaws and the Chickasaws $1.25 for each acre they claimed within the very same lands because of their prior and paramount title. In effect, the United States paid $1.85 per acre for Cheyenne/Arapaho land adjacent to the Kiowa reserve for which the government only paid the Kiowas 93 cents an acre. Eventually, the national government sold the remaining 1,807,630 acres of Kiowa, Comanche, and Apache lands under the Jerome Agreement for entry under the public land laws. None of those proceeds went to the Kiowas. While they may not have been aware of the actual figures involved, the Kiowas well understood that the land had changed hands many times and that they had realized little gain from the transactions.[19]

Charles F. Nesler led the team that surveyed and allotted the Kiowa reserve. Nesler came from Washington, D.C., to supervise the actual subdividing of the reservation in his role as the special allotting agent. During mid-1900 through early 1901 he and his small staff made 2,759 allotments over an area encompassing 4,000 square miles and 111 townships. The haste under which railroad surveyors, local amateurs, and the government survey crew team worked, often at cross purposes, inevitably created confusion and led to mistakes, forcing later adjustments that added to the anger of the Indians involved. The number of allotments finally grew to 3,444 to provide for adjustments. However, considering the difficulties under which he worked, the special allotting agent accomplished an amazing feat in a remarkably short time.[20]

7

The Lone Wolf Movement

During the spring of 1901, Lone Wolf and his nephew Delos Knowles Lone Wolf visited the nation's capital and spoke with several people about helping them. Delos, a Carlisle-educated Methodist missionary, worked on the reserve as district farmer and as a government interpreter. Anadarko and El Reno lawyers had mentioned names of those whom the Indians could approach in the capital for assistance. Prominent among the names was that of Democratic Party regular William McKendree Springer. An attorney, William Springer aided the writing of a memorial to the president protesting the 1900 Act. He obtained a contract with the two Indians to hire him to work for the defeat of the act and handle litigation for a $5,000 fee.

William Springer is one of the keys to the litigation involving the Kiowas. His entire adult life had been devoted to the dual professions of the bar and politics. Born in Indiana in 1836, Springer had moved to Illinois in 1848. He had been chosen secretary of the 1862 Illinois constitutional convention at the surprisingly young age of 26 and briefly served as assistant secretary of the state's senate. He represented that state for two decades in Congress. During his service in Congress, Springer was prominently involved in the investigation of election frauds during the disputed Hayes–Tilden campaign and in legislative battles over the Wilson tariff, Speakership rules under Thomas B. Reed, and territorial admissions. While chairing the committee on territories, he framed the bills that organized Oklahoma Territory and created a federal judicial system for the Indian Territory. It was his Springer Amendment that created the mechanism for the Jerome Commission in 1889. When he was defeated in 1894 for reelection, President Grover Cleveland named him the first appointee to the federal district judgeship for the Northern District of Indian Territory in Muskogee. Later, Springer became chief justice of the United States Court of Appeals for the Territory, serving until 1899. While in the Creek Nation, he worked diligently to abolish tribal courts and the "anomaly" of their "crude" justice to make way for statehood. Springer strongly supported the Curtis bill in 1898 and other measures to end tribal court jurisdiction. In 1900 Springer left his judicial post to establish law offices in Chicago and Washington, D.C. He was especially successful before the Court of Claims dealing with territorial litigation. He also worked for the National Livestock Association as their lobbyist, which had exposed him to the Kiowa reserve grasslands. In addition, he lobbied for and served as chief counsel for the Cherokee Nation and other members of the Five Tribes in Oklahoma. As a lifelong Democrat, he was close friends with such party luminaries as William Jennings Bryan. He very likely knew Chief Justice Melville Fuller from immersion in Illinois Democratic Party politics, as well. His law practice represented a wide spectrum of clients, ranging from the federal government, cattle leasing investors, oleomargarine interests, Democratic and Republican politicians, to Indian nations.[1]

From Washington, D.C., Springer sent Delos back to the reservation in 1901 with the memorial to bolster Lone Wolf's suit. Delos and Big Tree established a camp two miles from the agency and sought signatures for the memorial and the contract among the Indians on the reserve. Indian leaders earlier had assured the agent that they opposed Lone Wolf's actions and would not attend the council. Springer and Indian Rights Association staff felt the majority of the reserve's Indians had been unduly influenced through railroad corporation money, but in spite of that, Delos and Big Tree persuaded many of them (but fewer than 100) during the June 3–7 council to agree to the documents. Comanches Eschiti, Nar-wats, and William Tivis were chosen along with Delos to represent the tribes as parties to the impending legal action. The Comanches joined Delos for the return trip to Washington. Their names were added to the court action through an amendment to the original suit on June 17. Earlier that month Lone Wolf himself headed an Indian delegation presenting President William McKinley with the memorial against the threatened opening of the reservation. Federal authorities believed that the signatures on the memorial had been forged and quickly made certain that friendly newspapers carried the innuendo.[2]

The entire affair was popularly called the Springer Movement, or in Agent Randlett's contemptuous phrase, the "Springer combine." Kiowa band headmen traditionally acted independently, except in ceremonial matters during the twice-yearly gatherings of the entire tribe. Raiding or hunting parties often acted on their own initiative. Lone Wolf acted independently in beginning legal action against the government, and only after discussions in council did others join him. Lone Wolf was a headman of his band, and as a leader of opponents of government plans on the reserve, he took appropriate action to continue the struggle for his lands and tribal ways. He sought the advice of local attorneys whom he had used periodically in the past to investigate agents and agency affairs, to embarrass agents, to supervise annuity payments, to arrange pasture leases, as well as to try and hold off white encroachments and thefts of Indian property.[3] The Indian Service steadfastly refused to supply legal counsel to Indians, so they had to go to private attorneys for assistance. The author prefers to call the genesis of litigation over the Jerome Agreement the "Lone Wolf Movement" to give credit to the person who began it.

Historians also have not recognized the role of Lone Wolf. Historians give cattlemen credit for being the major motivating force behind Kiowa resistance to allotment.[4] In effect, they see cattlemen cynically manipulating Lone Wolf and other Indians, since range cattle industry influence helped delay the opening.[5] Cattle interests, they say, provided most of the money to fuel obstructionism, and Lone Wolf and his followers were government wards with severely restricted incomes. Lone Wolf received a small amount of grass money as his share from pasture leasing. The sum was often barely sufficient to sustain his family and was not nearly large enough to initiate adjudication or lobbying efforts. He *was* used, but his opposition was not the product of cattlemen's manipulation. The Kiowa leader's self-interest and the desire of cattlemen to retain their profitable leasing arrangements coincided. Lone Wolf had consistently distrusted government blandishments long before cattlemen appeared on the reservation.

The estimated $2 million and more that cattlemen contributed from 1885 to 1906[6] bought a lot of resistance. However, much of that income went for living expenses, local and national attorneys' fees, stock purchases, unauthorized travel away from the reservation, and other costs, and never found its way into the hands of lobbyists working for the cattlemen. The Kiowas used income from sources other than cattlemen, too. Sales of agricultural produce, livestock, rights of way, easements, prospecting leases, collected donations, and even federal government appropriations went toward funding Indian protests to delay allotment. The Indians received much free assistance as well. Missionaries and church aid societies wrote memorials and letters and carried on fundraising throughout the nation. Lawyers provided work on behalf of the Kiowas' cause for which they complained loudly they were never paid. William Springer repeatedly approached potential sources for payment of his fees, varying from the Kiowa Indian council to the Indian Rights Association, even to the federal government, and including cattlemen's associations. All of them professed a chronic lack of money that prevented them from paying his high fees.

Moreover, at different times in the saga, corporate forces contended against each other. In an earlier period of sparse frontier settlement, railroad officials were only too anxious to obtain lucrative contracts to transport cattle to market. Cattle and railroad interests merged over the issue of using prairie grasslands. Later, railroad officers were even more desirous to transport settlers into newly opened reservation lands in direct opposition to range cattle profits. Railroad influence deflected or negated much of the leverage that the range cattle industry possessed over the issue of opening the Indians' lands. Funding for Kiowa resistance to the threatened opening of their lands remained hidden from view, and charges and countercharges flew back and forth over who was providing money to which side. Cattle industry money certainly helped fuel opposition to any land opening, but cattle interests were not the sole major influence favoring the Indians in the conflict.

The Indian Agent determined that Indians' journeys to the District of Columbia and the signature council, which were carried out in the face of Indian Office opposition, would be punished. Agent Randlett was already exasperated with Lone Wolf's continual opposition and interference in agency affairs. Both Lone Wolf and Delos had traveled to Washington, D.C., without official authorization. The agent retaliated when he relieved Delos of the Indian's remunerative positions as main agency farmer and interpreter in May 1901. Randlett replaced Delos as farmer with Apiatan's brother-in-law, William E. Pedrick. The attorney William C. Shelley countered for the Lone Wolf group with the charge that Apiatan should be ousted from the reservation's Court of Indian Offenses because of his polygamy. Further accusations against Laura Pedrick (To-what-ta-mah, or T'ow-hadle, Limping Woman), Apiatan's sister and William Pedrick's wife, calculated to obtain her dismissal as a government employee, were unsuccessful. Shelley and his associates failed in their effort to embarrass the government-approved leader, Apiatan, and his extended family, including the Pedricks. Neither the attorneys nor the Indian Agency staff realized during the controversy and finger-pointing that there was an underlying connection among the Kiowas. The lawyers and agency staff failed to perceive the Kiowa kinship relationship. Laura Pedrick was the niece of the elder deceased Lone Wolf, so a family connection continued albeit by adoption.[7]

Randlett lectured Delos Lone Wolf that Springer was only hustling the Indians for "fat fees" and would not materially aid their doomed cause. Randlett believed that Easterners only raised false hopes among the Indians and greatly complicated his work as agent. He especially resented the lies he believed Lone Wolf, attorneys, and Indian Rights Association investigator Samuel Brosius spread about him. During more than one outburst of temper, Randlett penned vituperative letters accusing his enemies of a host of vendettas against him personally and of scheming against the Indian Office with the result of having "seriously retarded the advancement of the Indians." In response to the mutual hostility between the agent and the Indian Rights Association staff, that organization had approached Senator Matthew Quay, who directly contacted President Theodore Roosevelt. The latter began an investigation of Randlett's administration. That further infuriated the agent. Another investigation exonerated his management, even though some of his actions and his personal comments were criticized. Indian Office investigator Francis Leupp came away from meeting with Randlett even more convinced that the agent's viewpoint regarding a self-serving William Springer in the employ of cattlemen was accurate.[8]

William Springer worked with the lawyers Hays McMeehan, William C. Reeves, and Charles Porter Johnson to represent the Kiowa and Comanche Indians. Through his attorneys, on July 22 Lone Wolf sought a temporary restraining order and a permanent injunction halting the cession and the opening of the surplus lands. Eschiti, White Buffalo, Ko-koy-taudle, Mar-mo-car-wer, Nar-wats, Too-wi-car-ne, William Tivis, and Delos K. Lone Wolf joined Lone Wolf as plaintiffs. Eschiti or White Eagle was a Comanche who had often sided with Lone Wolf against government agents and frequently was on the opposing side of issues from his fellow tribesman Quanah Parker. Nar-wats was a Mexican captive among the Comanches. William Tivis, a Comanche returned student from Carlisle, worked in concert with Eschiti. Together through their counsel, they sued William A. Richards, Assistant Commissioner of the General Land Office, who was in charge of platting and opening the surplus lands. A Canadian County probate judge granted the restraining order to halt the disposal of individual Indian tracts until the matter could be legally clarified. Canadian County Judge Clinton F. Irwin in a preliminary opinion July 29 and a final decree on August 17, 1901, turned down the request and refused the temporary restraining order by the probate judge—beginning the long odyssey for the Indian case through the appeals process.[9]

At the same time, a group of Caddo Indians in the Young family filed suit in the same court to obtain allotments for their minor children. Simultaneously, William Shelley started a suit in the capital to compel the Department of the Interior to award an allotment to Emmett Cox, brother-in-law of Quanah Parker. The litigation is often confused with the Lone Wolf case even though they were for different purposes. Assistant Commissioner Richards usually referred to the suits as being synonymous. The Rebecca Young suit dragged through Canadian County District Court proceedings almost until statehood. Other land rights suits at the same time or shortly thereafter involved claims for allotments, title to townsite tracts, and access to rights of way to improve the marketability of tracts. Richards went about his official duties undeterred. He commented in his official report at the conclusion of his endeavors that the Indian suits "temporarily prevented the disposition" of a portion of the lands only.[10]

Lone Wolf's attorney on June 6 had filed a special appeal in the Supreme Court for the District of Columbia, since the issues involved American Indian rights. Springer requested that the court bring an injunction against Secretary of the Interior Ethan Allen Hitchcock, Commissioner of Indian Affairs William A. Jones, and Commissioner of the General Land Office Binger Herman. Willis Van Devanter, attorney for the Department of the Interior, represented the federal officials. Van Devanter responded on June 12 with a motion of his own to block the Springer injunction.

In spite of Lone Wolf's eloquent personal appeal, Justice A. C. Bradley turned down the special request for an injunction on June 21. He issued an interlocutory decree on June 26. Justice Bradley's opinion reviewed the facts of the case, then dismissed allegations that the act of 1900 had been amended without Indian consent when he stated that the United States government was the superior power and could do as it deemed proper with its wards. He stressed American Indian "dependence" on the United States, citing *Kagama,*[11] *Cherokee Tobacco,*[12] and *Foster v. Neilson.*[13] He further noted that once Congress had acted and ratified the Jerome Agreement, even if it were fraudulent, the courts could not interfere because such matters were within the political domain that belonged exclusively to Congress. Indians held only a possessory right of occupancy to their land, and the United States Congress could legislate for the nation's wards under its authority as the political branch of the government. Furthermore, enforcement of treaties also fell under the control of Congress, a realm that was likewise beyond the reach of the judiciary.[14] Van Devanter had printed copies of Bradley's decision and the full proceedings mailed to every Oklahoma judge. Springer also asked the Oklahoma Territory Supreme Court in September to halt the opening of the reservation but lost. After Bradley blocked his injunction, Springer immediately asked a special appeal to the District of Columbia Court of Appeals and paid the $100 deposit on June 27 to initiate the action. Once again, Kiowa, Comanche, and Plains Apache delegates and Oklahoma Territory journalists were present in the courtroom for the proceedings. Chief Justice R. H. Alvey turned down the case on December 4 but reheard motions before rendering his opinion on March 4 of the following year that resoundingly rejected the Indians' claims for their requested injunction. After Springer's motion for reargument was filed, Alvey issued his final decree on March 14, 1902:

> [R]eservations are held by the Indians subject to the control and domin-
> ion of the United States, and such Indian tribes are subject to be changed
> from one locality or reservation to another, as may best serve the pur-
> pose and policy of the government . . . . They have no title in the lands
> which they occupy.[15]

Judge Alvey did delay the proposed opening of the lands to enable Springer to take the litigation on to next the higher court. Two weeks later, Springer and Brosius called on Senator Quay in an effort to influence Attorney General Philander C. Knox to advance the *Lone Wolf* appeal rapidly to the Supreme Court because of its importance for Indian policy.[16]

Lone Wolf, Delos, Eschiti, White Buffalo, Ko-koy-taudle, Mar-mo-car-wer, Nar-wats, Too-wi-car-ne, and William Tivis formed an Indian contin-

gent in the appeals courtroom for the arguments. Indians in the group who
had been in the capital before served as guides for those new to the hustle
of the metropolis. Commuters' eyes immediately looked in their direction
when they boarded trollies in the city. Even though the Indians wore Anglo-
American attire, their braided hair set them apart from the other passengers.
The Indians were all, of course, intensely interested in the outcome of the
case and its implications for their lives.[17] Springer, Lone Wolf, White Buffalo,
and Ko-koy-taudle called at the White House in an attempt to gain a presidential delay or cancellation of the slated land opening. The Indian visitors
were severely restricted in their travel because they lacked sufficient money
and had to rely on the help of a variety of supporters. Secretary Hitchcock
refused the use of any Indian Office or trust funds for them, so they were on
their own, and they received the largess of the hard-pressed Indian Rights
Association Washington office.

The sweeping nature of the opinions of the lower courts that left the
Kiowas powerless in the face of the federal juggernaut and the popular clamor
to open the reservation to white settlement alarmed Indian Rights Association personnel and led to Indian Rights Association involvement in the case.
Lone Wolf and others had written letters to Springer and to other supporters trying to enlist their aid in reaching the secretary of the interior and the
president in hopes of stopping the land opening. Springer had in his turn
corresponded with Herbert Welsh of the Indian Rights Association about the
Kiowas, Comanches, and Apaches. The Association had sent an investigator
to examine the local situation. The lawyer, in contacting the Association, also
sought contributors to pay his fee.

Springer's early correspondence with that organization termed the land
opening that violated treaty pledges made to the Kiowas "the worst piece of
business in which the Government ever engaged in order to rob Indians of
their lands."[18] Springer stressed that the case would have to go all the way to
the highest court in the land if necessary because the issues involved would
be "far-reaching" in their "consequences."[19] Herbert Welsh took up the refrain when he addressed the Indian Rights Association executive committee
on the issue of congressional members who as a general rule ignored treaty
guarantees.[20]

The Association's executive committee decided to retain Springer in
spite of Francis Leupp's vigorous remarks against him. Springer had served
as counsel for the Cherokee Nation in its suit against Interior Secretary

Hitchcock earlier the same year and represented that Indian nation and the Creeks in their efforts to alter Dawes Commission agreements for allotment. Springer represented Lone Wolf in an appeal to the United States Supreme Court, but the lawyer clearly needed help because of his age, his workload, and the potential enormity of the impact of any decision. Members of the Indian Rights Association discussed several attorneys who might be brought in to assist. Samuel Brosius favored Walter A. Logan, president of the New York Bar Association and chief counsel for a Delaware tribal case. However, Indian Rights Association staff members were confident the suit would be strengthened when Pennsylvania Attorney General and Indian Rights Association founder Hampton L. Carson joined Springer.[21] Carson officially notified the clerk of the court he would appear as counsel on March 24. Because of his professional experience, Carson would give the oral argument before the Supreme Court.

Hampton L. Carson ranked among the most prominent members of the Indian Rights Association. Carson had been a long-time friend of the Welsh family. He had attended the University of Pennsylvania with Herbert Welsh. Together in 1871 they had shared the university prize in declamation for their public speaking. Carson had joined other prominent Philadelphians in John Welsh's home in late 1882 as part of the initial discussions which led to the founding of the Association. Hampton Carson's Indian reform credentials extended as far back as anyone cared to search.[22]

His opposite in the litigation was Willis Van Devanter of Wyoming. He served as Assistant Attorney General for the Department of the Interior, handling a variety of cases for the federal government. He left his position the year of the Lone Wolf decision to be a judge for the United States Circuit Court of Appeals for the Eighth Circuit sitting in St. Louis. In 1911 President William Howard Taft would appoint Van Devanter to the Supreme Court, where he was to sit for 26 years until 1937. Van Devanter joined the remaining justices such as Edward White, before whom he had argued the Indian case in 1902 and 1903. Still later, in 1921, former president Taft would join Van Devanter on the High Tribunal.

While the appeal was pending, President McKinley issued the Proclamation opening the ceded and surplus lands on August 6, 1901.[23] Unlike earlier methods of settlement, officials decided to hold a preliminary registration and then a lottery instead of a land run to lessen the chances of injuries to claimants and to lower the level of confusion among those seeking land. A land run favored the speculator, but critics charged that the lottery would be more speculative still than an open auction.[24] Under pressure of demands for immediate action, constant intrusions, Indian intransigence, and the general excitement attending an impending land opening, the federal government moved swiftly to survey, prepare, register, and enter claims for homesteads on the surplus lands. A former governor of Wyoming, Assistant Commissioner Richards accompanied thirty-three clerks from Washington, D.C., to supervise the entire operation. Richards kept former fellow Wyoming resident Van Devanter informed of his progress.

After allotting Indian lands, two million acres remained as surplus. Land agents estimated that the region would yield 12,500 to 13,000 claims, and they quickly set about establishing the structure to handle the large number of expected registrants. Richards placed eight of his clerks in Lawton and twenty-five in El Reno in official land offices, with another registration station in Fort Sill. He divided the region into two land districts.[25]

Excitement grew as anticipation built. People eagerly gathered for the lottery registration. Lone Wolf looked on with dismay at the over ten thousand people camped along Cache Creek near Fort Sill for the start of the registration process. Chicago and Rock Island Railroad laborers had feverishly worked to complete a line from El Reno to the fort. During just two hours of one day, eight heavily loaded trains dropped off their passengers anxious to join the registration line. The railway took in over \$2 million from ticket sales to passengers headed for the land offices. As a result of the influx of people, virtual towns sprang up overnight. Suddenly, Lawton had a population of 4,500. The second day of registration at the fort witnessed over seven thousand people waiting their turn at the tables.[26] Hopeful people made a total of over 165,000 registrations from July 10 to 26 for the 12,500 possible parcels. The number of registrants greatly exceeded the expectations and prediction of a pleased Willis Van Devanter.[27] In spite of oppressively hot weather, fifty thousand people observed the drawing for land rights in El Reno alone. The dust and crowded conditions provided a scene of unrivaled commotion for the region. Hucksters and hustlers of every description worked the throng, selling bogus land chits and false claims. Officials worked hard to maintain order. During a two-month period, 11,638 homestead entries were made at the two land offices. The secretary of the interior carved three new counties out of the reserve, naming them Comanche, Kiowa, and Caddo. Anglo-American society surrounded and engulfed the Kiowa and other Indians.[28]

8

Kiowas before the Supreme Court

On October 23, 1902, the suit at last reached the High Bench. Lone Wolf would have his chance to persuade the Supreme Court of the United States. Appearing for the appellants, Lone Wolf and the other Indians, were William M. Springer and Hampton L. Carson. Appearing for the government side and the Secretary of the Interior was Assistant Attorney General Willis Van Devanter.

Friends of the Indian approached the court appeal buoyed with an air of positive anticipation. They wrote that never before had the executive, legislative, or judicial branches seized Indian property and thrown it open without at least the tacit consent of the Indians involved. They thought the June 6, 1900, Act was the first instance. For the first time the High Court would directly address the question of treaty-recognized property rights.[1] Reformers were certain Supreme Court justices would bar the taking of property without compensation, especially since the property was protected under a treaty. On the thirteen reservations established after the Civil War in Oklahoma Territory, only the Kiowas, Comanches, and Apaches occupied lands which a ratified treaty defined.[2] There was not a single case on record and certainly no precedent where treaty lands had been taken without Indian consent.

Advocates pointed to the Court's own opinion in the 1873 case of *U.S. v. Cook*, which stated "that the right of Indians to their occupancy is as sacred as that of the United States to the fee."[3] The clear provision in the 1867 Medicine Lodge Treaty requiring Indian agreement bolstered their appeal. Only during the passion of the 1862 Sioux uprising in Minnesota had the government taken Indian property in clear violation of the sanctity of a contract (or treaty)[4] and then only as a result of open warfare. Another favorable precedent was the Cleveland administration's 1885 reversal of an executive order opening a part of the Crow Creek Reservation in South Dakota because officials decided that treaty lands were "inviolate." The inviolability of the contract in American law portended a favorable hearing. The blatantly deceitful nature of the 1892 agreement also argued in favor of the Indians' cause.[5]

The Indians' attorneys argued, as well, that the 1892 agreement had been unilaterally changed through amendments to the 1900 Act. Signatures on the original document had been obtained through subterfuge, and even if they were not fraudulent, the signatures did not constitute three-fourths of the adult male tribal membership, as Article 12 of the 1867 treaty required. The federal government was going to pay only a fraction of the land's value to its Indian wards, and the remaining land could not support them because it was unfit for cultivation. Since the acts implementing the Jerome Agreement violated the property rights of the Kiowa, Comanche, and Apache Indians, they would deprive the natives of their lands "without due process of law" in direct defiance of the 5th Amendment to the Constitution. Such matters to the Indians' attorneys were within the protection of the judicial branch of the government. Brosius had announced months earlier that since there existed a preponderance of law favoring "due process," "I do not see how they [the justices] can take away the rights of the Kiowas under these decisions."[6] To the Indians' advocates, all these points clearly violated Medicine Lodge Treaty Council pledges on the part of the federal government.

Assistant U.S. Attorney Willis Van Devanter represented the government defendants. He had argued the government's side opposite William Springer in the Cherokee Nation case against Secretary Hitchcock.[7] He had been helpful in getting the Lone Wolf suit onto the crowded Supreme Court docket as quickly as possible in spite of the summer recess. On April 7 the court clerk scheduled arguments for October. Van Devanter borrowed heavily from earlier opinions in the appeals and maintained that a lengthy series of judicial decisions acknowledged that the federal government possessed paramount authority and could do as it pleased with Indians. He pointed out in his brief that more than the required three-fourths of signatures were on the Agreement and the agent in charge of the Kiowa, Comanche, and Apache Agency had officially certified them, making the signatures and the document itself legal within the strict terms of interpretation. The 1900 Act, he noted, was duly modified to accord with Indian wishes regarding grazing land both as to individual allotment tracts and for a large common pasturage. He further argued that the Indians had already accepted the $50 per capita government payment for the ceded surplus land and had taken allotments, including Lone Wolf and his family.

Courtroom observers in October contacted the Indian Rights Association and informed them that Carson presented his arguments to the Court without notes or memoranda, giving his statements one by one in clear and concise tones. Washington, D.C., attorney William Shelley, who heard the proceedings, found Carson's closing remarks "by all odds the finest argument he . . . ever heard before the Supreme Court of the United States."[8] The same observers noted that in sharp contrast to Carson's animated presentation and the justices' rapt attention, Van Devanter read his arguments in a dry tone and the justices appeared "listless." They kept interrupting Van Devanter with questions and comments. On the basis of elocution, Springer felt "perfectly confident of success."[9] Brosius listened to both sides in the courtroom and stated that he was "inclined [to believe] . . . that Lone Wolf will win the suit."[10]

Each side also carried on its struggle in newspapers, planting appropriate articles in an attempt to gain a public relations advantage and to sway legislative opinion. Brosius for the Indian Rights Association skillfully utilized his contacts in Washington and New York to continue the pamphlet war that marked so many Association appeals. Herbert Welsh in Philadelphia made use of his ties to journalists in that city and others in the East to serve as an outlet for the organization's views. Letters to the editor from Association members added to the chorus. Department of the Interior staff were equally conscientious. They placed articles of their own in newspapers, such as the "Washington Telegram" series in the *St. Louis Globe-Democrat* and the *Cincinnati Times Star,* to offer their side of the controversy and to boost prospects for the land opening. Cooperative congressmen and local interests also argued in print for the land opening, usually maintaining that it would in the long run benefit the Indians. The land opening was a part of the inevitable progress of the nation. An example of the newspaper opinion is the *Kansas City Star* for July 1, 1901, which remarked that it was utterly "inconceivable" that duly sworn federal authorities would violate law in opening the reservation to settlers. Any attempts to block it in court were "unsound."[11]

The Supreme Court justices had received the Lone Wolf case and its preliminary arguments in October 1901. To allow both sides to present additional evidence, they continued the case to the following term in October 1902. In response to Van Devanter's documentation that Indians had accepted money for the purchase of the lands, thereby in effect ratifying the 1900 Act, the justices gave the appellants one week to file an additional brief in response. Carson believed that the Indians had a solid case before the Court if the justices did not accept the government motion that as a result of the Indians' accepting a portion of the money from the sale of the lands they had consummated the entire transaction. Lone Wolf contended that the Indians had been tricked by the ruse that they were only receiving grass money. He further alleged that there were many more allotments made than there were Indians on the reserve, the purpose being to fatten the agency roll and thereby increase appropriations which the agent pocketed.

Springer, Carson, and the Indian Rights Association worked hard to forestall losing the case in midstream. The necessity for quick action and the pressure to obtain fast results created resentment among senior Association staff members. At one point, Association executive member Edward Wistar was to go with Springer to visit President Roosevelt, who was vacationing at Oyster Bay, in an attempt to block the per capita payment to the Kiowa, Comanche, and Apache Indians. When he was unsuccessful in obtaining an audience with the president, Springer proposed that Brosius gain a signed protest from the Indians as they received their payments. Brosius did secure affidavits from Lone Wolf's followers that they took the money under duress. The Indian Rights Association also persuaded Senator Quay to intervene with Roosevelt on behalf of the Indians and ensure that the federal government did not take advantage of its wards. In spite of hasty measures to convince the Supreme Court justices that government claims were false, Carson did not succeed in his argument because the Indians had, indeed, accepted payments for the land, whatever deceit had been involved.[12]

The Indian Rights Association delayed the publication of its annual report for 1902, waiting for the court ruling. On January 5, 1903, Justice Edward Douglas White announced the Court's opinion (see appendix 3). The portly justice looked every bit the part of a Chief Justice, which he would become in 1910. His physical size mirrored that of William Howard Taft in girth. Massive, tall, yet personable, White also epitomized the social background of a justice. He represented the Louisiana planter class that had bitterly opposed post–Civil War carpetbag rule with night riding escapades in the resurgent Democratic Party of the South.[13] In *Lone Wolf* he presented one of the most famous Indian decisions to come from the Court.

A recent jurist termed the fifth of January "one of the blackest days in the history of the American Indian," because Justice White announced "the Indians' Dred Scott decision." [14] Justice White had also read the High Court's decree earlier in *Cherokee Nation v. Hitchcock. Lone Wolf v. Hitchcock* is the Court's strongest statement about the Indians' place in American society, proclaiming that Congress may abrogate an Indian treaty at will, that Congress held plenary power over native peoples beyond the control of the judiciary, and that Indian reservation land could be seized while the Indian had little recourse for legal redress except to protest. The decision maintains:

> The power exists to abrogate the provisions of an Indian treaty, though presumably such power will be exercised only when circumstances arise which will not only justify the government in disregarding the stipulations of the treaty, but may demand, in the interest of the country and the Indians themselves, that it should do so. . . . [I]t was never doubted that the *power* to abrogate existed in Congress, . . . particularly if consistent with perfect good faith towards the Indians.

The justices overturned the Court's earlier post–Civil War ruling that held Congress's plenary authority over tribes could not justify confiscation of Indian property in Kansas.[15] Justice White established a "good faith effort" standard for taking Indian land that later courts elaborated upon. The justice maintained that the public record had "purported" to demonstrate that Congress had made a "good faith effort" to give the Indians full value for their land through an "adequate consideration" involving an exchange of lands. In the case of the Kiowa Indians, Congress responded to their earlier complaints and materially improved the final act to the Indians' benefit. While not full market price at 93 cents per acre for land valued at $2 an acre, at least Congress made an effort which did not violate the 5th Amendment guarantee for "just compensation" for takings. A mere change in the form of investment of Indian tribal property from land to money, even well below the full market price, was clearly not expropriation.[16]

Justice Edward Douglas White relied on the last-in-time rule,[17] under which a congressional statute that is the latest enactment may supersede a prior treaty, as the excuse for abrogating the 1867 treaty. In addition, the Court justified the seizure of Kiowa property through the implication that fundamentally changed circumstances necessitated a different course of action, leading one party to an earlier treaty to terminate that treaty. The doctrine is called *rebus sic stantibus* in international law. The justice said, "[I]n a contingency such power might be availed of from considerations of governmental policy."[18] He went on in the hope that he could find a national emergency that would serve as the basis for altering the treaty. In the end, he could not find one and satisfied himself that there was really no treaty violation, since the confiscation of Kiowa land was only another form of investment for the Indians. For Justice White, the issue was one of occupancy and use, not ownership. Only the use changed, because the ownership remained with the United States.

The Indians' state of pupilage in the eyes of the justices necessitated the congressional guardian's use of stern measures to lift the Indian charges out of barbarism. The justices were reluctant to interfere:

> Plenary authority over the tribal relations of the Indians has been exercised by Congress from the beginning, and the power has always been deemed a political one, not subject to be controlled by the judicial department of the government. . . . [A]ll these matters . . . were solely within the domain of the legislative authority and its action is conclusive upon the courts.[19]

> [A]s Congress possessed full power in the matter, the judiciary cannot question or inquire into the motives [however admittedly fraudulent] which prompted the enactment of this legislation.[20]

The justices faced a dilemma in their holding because of the obviously fraudulent nature of the signatures on the 1892 agreement. The justices also confronted an irony in the case. Would they turn down the majority-approved 1892 agreement, however it may have been achieved, in favor of the three-quarters proviso and risk being undemocratic? They took shelter in the political question doctrine. Justice White avoided the issue of fraud, bribery, and chicanery regarding the agreement with the reservation Indians and the alterations involved in the 1900 Act when he stated that all such matters belonged to Congress: "[A]s Congress possessed full power in the matter, the judiciary cannot question or inquire into the motives which prompted the enactment of the legislation."[21] If the Indians felt injured by action of Congress, "relief must be sought by an appeal [directly] to that body for redress and not to the courts."[22] The justices dismissed cries of fraud and deceit over the 1892 Agreement, stating, "We must presume that Congress acted in perfect good faith" in dealing with the Indians. In the same breath, White rejected Carson's argument that the abrogation violated the Kiowas' due process.[23] White pointed to his recent opinion in *Cherokee Nation* and said that "the controversy which this case presents is concluded by the decision" earlier.[24]

Justice White cited a number of cases that dealt with congressional authority over Indian affairs by way of reference for his remarks. He invoked *Kagama*[25] for authority to abrogate provisions of an Indian treaty, as well as *Cherokee Tobacco*,[26] the original post–Civil War opinion on the subject. He also looked to *Ward v. Race Horse*[27] for congressional authorization to admit a state equally to the Union in violation of treaty-guaranteed Indian hunting rights. *Beecher v. Wetherby*[28] further pointed to the temporary status of Indian occupation of lands historically theirs but held by the federal government and subject to the will of Congress. *Stephens v. Cherokee Nation*[29] approved congressional power to determine tribal membership, while leasing of Indian lands through congressional delegation of administrative action to the secretary of the interior was recognized as a part of congressional paramount authority in *Cherokee Nation v. Hitchcock*.[30]

Shortly after the decision, Samuel Brosius matter-of-factly and without comment returned in the mail the deposit William Springer earlier had made through the Indian Rights Association for the Supreme Court appeal. Lone Wolf lost his case and his cause. Documentation does not exist detailing how Lone Wolf and his neighbors in the courtroom received the Court's pronouncement, but they must have taken the information with calm resignation. The verdict added to their depression. They had already seen and been told stories about land lotteries and forced allotments, as well as survey teams swarming over their reserve.

Clerk of the Supreme Court J. H. McKenney complained that demand for the Court's printed decisionquickly depleted the available copies. Regretfully he could not fill the request from the Indian commissioner for more copies.[31] Through their decree, the justices permanently opened Indian lands to thousands of whites, towns sprang up, and the bustle of a new way of life engulfed Indians. And, courts appeared to have closed their doors to solemn treaty rights as an avenue for justice.

The Supreme Court opinion "came with startling significance to the friends of the Indians."[32] Indian Rights Association members at first were stunned, and pamphlets from that organization alarmingly announced a "new" and "discouraging" Indian policy of wholesale confiscation and robbery.[33] Samuel Brosius earlier wrote that if the appeals court decision stood, then "we may look forward to the early confiscation of the remaining reservations" without any compensation to Indians.[34] "[N]o tribe of Indians in the United States have any title to lands" any longer, Brosius claimed in the aftermath of the decision.[35] One writer echoed the same thought but took it even further, stating that the case "will mark the beginning of a new departure in our Indian policy. There will then be no legal bar to the removal of all the American Indians from their reservations and the banishment of every man, woman, and child of them to Alaska or Porto Rico." The same writer borrowed the famous title of a reform volume and announced that "we have ended one 'Century of Dishonor,' and are . . . about to begin another."[36] He later stated in the same magazine that since the Supreme Court "has virtually given Congress full power to take Indian lands without the Indians' consent," there will begin in the American West a final, inexorable scramble for desirable Indian reservation land.[37]

Another commentator on the Court's opinion noted that the justices virtually "pronounced the death sentence" on tribes. Indian land was firmly placed under the control of members of Congress, who were always anxious to dispose of others' property for profit.[38] Sympathetic writers proclaimed that what had been previously considered secure Indian allotments were now jeopardized, and aboriginal title was not forfeited.[39] In their immediate despair many agreed with Samuel Brosius that the justices left the Indians powerless, "for the Indians have no rights which command respect."[40] The refrain reverberated well afterward into the 1920s and 1930s. Friends of the Indians worried that the powers of the Indian agent drastically increased over lives of his wards and that *Lone Wolf* left Indians permanently in "a critical position of disadvantage" in regard to the federal government.[41]

As time intervened and Indian Rights Association members' attention turned to other problems, attitudes of the staff changed to one of resignation and then confident acceptance of the outcome. Time itself was a factor. So much Indian Rights Association energy and effort had been expended during the decade of lobbying against the Jerome and other agreements and in the appeals process that there was little left after the initial shock of the decision wore off. Other concerns regarding national Indian policy, new crises on the northern plains, Brosius's uncovering of allotment scandals in the Indian Territory, continued questions about agents' use of government funds, overseas territorial possessions, and a host of other challenges soon took reform attention away from the effects of *Lone Wolf*. Herbert Welsh's declining health diminished his direct involvement in the Indian Rights Association.

After all, Indian Rights Association personnel rationalized, the inundated Kiowas, Comanches, and Plains Apaches would be forced to assimilate even faster, and the Association's work of uplifting the Indian would be completed even sooner.[42] The Executive Committee of the organization reported shortly after the events that they looked forward to the day when the Indian's "island reservations will be merged in the *saving* sea of white civilization that surrounds them."[43] After visiting the Kiowa reserve on the heels of the court decision, Francis Leupp felt it was far better that Lone Wolf went to court and now realized "his pitiful status" than to continue to live in a fool's paradise under the delusion of Indian independence.[44] Author and long-time Indian advocate Hamlin Garland, who had spent extended periods visiting the Cheyennes, thought it was high time that the Indians of western Oklahoma became full citizens, and he called for federal officials conclusively to "abolish the reservation line in Oklahoma" once and for all.[45]

The Lone Wolf decision also came at a crucial time in the Indian Rights Association's history of supporting Indian litigation. Two years before *Lone Wolf*, the organization had lost the substantial sum of $4,200 on a surety bond when the Warner Ranch Cupeño Indians of southern California lost in court. Their loss in *Barker v. Harvey* prompted the reform group's leadership to reconsider its approach of using the judiciary to win Indian rights.[46] The defeat particularly stung the Association because it not only reversed the Association's very first outing into the higher court appeals process in 1888, but the decision obliterated California Mission Indian land titles and claims. In their May 1901 decree in *Barker*, the justices ominously foretold their holding in *Lone Wolf*, restating a harsh mid-century opinion that the United States government had given a tribe only "a temporary occupancy" of land and that the Court had "no power to set itself up . . . for enforcing a treaty . . . which the Government of the United States . . . chooses to disregard."

Association leaders believed that individual Indian rights could still be secured through use of the judicial system in the case of the plains Indian, since the allotted native was very nearly a full-fledged citizen in their view. Since legal status was "the crucial point in the Indian problem,"[47] the Indian

Rights Association by 1902 emphasized the use of courts for Indian rights.[48] However, the expense involved and the repeated judicial defeats for their causes led Indian Rights Association leaders to alter their approach. Herbert Welsh himself warned that "in view of the uniformly unfavorable decision[s] rendered on the Indian cases," the Indian Rights Association "ought to be very cautious about further appeals to the courts." [49]

Only once more—five years after *Lone Wolf*—did the Association single-handedly sponsor Indian litigation before the United States Supreme Court. The last attempt the organization sponsored, the case of *Quick Bear v. Leupp*, involved government trust funds for mission instruction on reservations. Hampton Carson acted for the Association before the High Court and opposed the expenditure of public funds for Roman Catholic mission schools on the Rosebud Sioux Indian reservation. The issue of sectarian education was a major national controversy during the era of assimilation of European immigrants. The historian Francis Paul Prucha has detailed the reformers' pamphlet war over the conflict. Protestant reformers did not want government Indian funds going to Catholic Indian mission schools. The Supreme Court in *Quick Bear* held that tribal treaty and trust funds, public funds in the government treasury, could be used for sectarian Indian education because the money belonged to the tribes, which could specify how those funds might be used. While a victory of sorts for Indian tribal rights, the decision was a sound defeat for the Indian Rights Association. Thereafter, the reform group encouraged Indians to seek protection in state courts. The Assocation, in effect, abandoned natives to local legal systems that were anti-Indian.[50]

9

More Indian Land Lost

The Supreme Court's decision affected how the Indian Office dealt with its wards. Indians on the Sioux reserves in the northern plains immediately felt the opinion's effects. However, the Kiowa, Comanche, and Apache Indians on the southern plains faced the immediate and harshest impact.

SIOUX LAND CESSIONS ON THE NORTHERN PLAINS

In the wake of *Lone Wolf,* Indian Rights Association confidence in the commissioner of Indian affairs, William A. Jones, and his policies greatly declined. Indian office staff responded to the message contained in the early decisions involving Lone Wolf and increased paternalistic control over their Indian wards. Moreover, Samuel Brosius attributed sinister motives to a series of grazing lease changes in the Dakotas following the court decrees. After its blow to the Kiowas, *Lone Wolf* had its second most immediate impact on the Sioux of the northern plains. The decision became an integral part of the federal government attitude toward Sioux reservation land policies. Officials quickly used the opinion to legitimize their actions on northern reserves. Since the government so easily defrauded the Kiowas, humanitarians reasoned after the opinion, the government was about to do the same thing to the Standing Rock Sioux.[1] At one time, Brosius placed an article in the *New York Evening Post* that proclaimed the Lone Wolf decision "threw down all the bars and left Congress [free] to do what it pleased" with Sioux reservation lands.[2] On the heels of the Lone Wolf decree, Brosius announced that such a "precedent" meant all other Indian cases were endangered in the nation's court system.

The whole issue of Standing Rock leases was especially alarming to the Association's Washington watchdog.[3] Brosius believed the Sioux "held their lands by almost the identical words used in the Kiowa treaty."[4] In fact, he believed that the Sioux case was far stronger than either the Cherokee or the Kiowa case of the same year because, in the Standing Rock instance, the Department of the Interior had acted without any congressional authorization to violate treaty guarantees. During a lengthy dispute over leasing on the Standing Rock Reservation, staff in the Office of Indian Affairs in mid-1901 decided, after the first court rejection of the Kiowas', Comanches', and Apaches' claims, that Indian consent was no longer needed to lease reservation lands and resources. The Indian Office started to contract for much of the unused reservation pasturage in spite of strong Sioux objections that the contracts were much too generous to cattlemen, favored only a very few mixed-bloods and intermarrieds, and threatened Sioux treaty and land rights.

In an October council, the Standing Rock Indians overcame misgivings about any land transaction with the government and agreed to a fixed rent leasing system that would insure all of them at least some steady income. Pressures of desperate poverty, the effects of assimilation policies, and lack of a unified leadership in opposition to the grass leasing persuaded many of the reservation residents that there really was no alternative to the government demand. The Indians wanted assurance that they would have oversight over the leasing of their lands. They acquiesced in the leases provided that three of their own would mark the area off with the agent and that no existing allotted Indian land would be included or endangered. The final, written version of the agreement left out the latter two parts and inserted only their consent to the contracts. The G. E. Lemmon lease embraced almost 800,000 acres, while the W. I. Walker lease included nearly 500,000 acres of reservation land. The combined acreage of the leases dominated nearly the entire western two-thirds of the reserve. While reluctant to agree to any rental, the Indians in their council finally decided that they had to have some sort of leasing arrangement to head off the threatened government plan for a permit system that was in reality unenforceable and would generate little real income for the tribe.[5]

1. Pictographic representation of the 1867 Medicine Lodge Treaty Council from the Kiowa Set-t'an Calendar history. At the time in October termed A'ya'dalda Sai, "Timber-hill winter," on the A'ya'dalda P'a, "Timber-hill River." A white man, probably a U.S. Army general, grasps the hand of a seated Indian. The location is indicated by the wooded hill above the solid bar denoting winter for the Kiowa. From Mooney, "Calendar History of the Kiowa Indians," p.320.

INDIAN LODGE AT MEDICINE CREEK, KANSAS—SCENE OF '

2. *Medicine Lodge Treaty Council, 1867. Sketched by John Howland for* Harper's Weekly, *16 Nov. 1867, p.724. Courtesy National Anthropological Archives, Negative No. 55,947, Kiowa.*

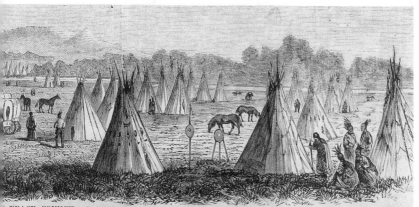

PEACE COUNCIL.—Sketched by J. Howland.—[See Page 725.]

3. *Members of the Jerome Commission.*
Upper left: *David H. Jerome. Courtesy of*
State Archives of Michigan, Negative
No. 02886. Lower left: *Warren G. Sayre.*
Courtesy of Indiana Historical Society
Library, Negative No. English 72.
Above: *Alfred M. Wilson. Courtesy of*
Special Collections, University of
Arkansas Libraries, from John Hallum,
Biographical and Pictorial History of
Arkansas *(1887), 282–83.*

4. Above: *Ethan Allen Hitchcock.*
Upper right: *Samuel Brosius.* Lower right:
Binger Herman. Hitchcock photo from
The Literary Digest 27 *(29 August 1903);*
Brosius photo courtesy of The Historical
Society of Pennsylvania; Herman photo
courtesy of the National Archives
(49-CP-21).

5. Left: *Delos K. Lone Wolf by Gill, ca. 1910. Courtesy of the*
National Anthropological Archives, Negative No. 1415-c.

6. Above: *Kiowa Delegation to Washington, D.C., in October 1902, by Gill.*
Seated, left to right: *Lone Wolf and Kiowa Bill.* Standing, left to right: *Little Bow,*
brother of Big Bow, and Asah-quo or Daniel Boone, first son of Luther Sahmaunt.
Courtesy of the National Anthropological Archives, Negative No. 1434-a.

7. Anadarko Townsite Auction, August 6, 1901.
Courtesy of the National Archives,
No. 48-RST-7B-83.

8. Upper left: *William Springer.*
Lower left: *Hampton Carson.*
Below: *Willis Van Devanter. Springer
photo by M. B. Brady, courtesy of the
Chicago Historical Society; Carson photo
courtesy of The Historical Society of
Pennsylvania; Van Devanter photo
courtesy of theNational Archives,*
No. *48-PLS-1.*

9. *Herbert Welsh. Courtesy of The Historical Society of Pennsylvania.*

10. *United States Supreme Court, 1899. Seated, left to right: J. David Brewer, J. John Marshall Harlan, Chief Justice Melville Weston Fuller, J. Horace Gray, J. Henry Billings Brown.* Standing, left to right: *J. Rufus Wheeler Peckham, J. George Shiras, Jr., J. Edward Douglas White, J. Joseph McKenna. From the Collection of the Supreme Court of the United States.*

In response to an article in *Outlook* magazine, the Indian Rights Association examined the leasing issue and once again hired William Springer as the attorney to represent the Sioux in their effort to block the leasing and prevent what the Association viewed as another government outrage in its treatment of the Indian.[6] Springer succeeded in obtaining a temporary injunction that halted any leasing pending the outcome of the *Lone Wolf* appeal.[7] Brosius briefly held the view that the Standing Rock injunction would come in front of the justices before the Kiowa case and would become the more important precedent when the Indian Rights Association side won.[8] The justices, however, postponed the full hearing while the Lone Wolf suit was before the Court. At the same time the Sioux council blocked fencing the Lemmon tract while awaiting the court order.

On April 15, Springer lost the court fight to gain the injunction in the same District of Columbia Supreme Court that earlier had turned down Springer on behalf of Lone Wolf. Undaunted, the Indian Rights Association diligently turned to political lobbying to preserve Sioux pasturage income and Indian rights.[9] The Association appealed directly to President Roosevelt. A short time later, Commissioner Jones canceled the Walker lease agreement, ending the court appeal and halting the judicial conflict. As a result of the Association's urging, Roosevelt asked a friend, the writer George Bird Grinnell, to investigate the Lemmon lease on Standing Rock. Grinnell probed the issues firsthand, heard considerable testimony against historic government mistreatment of the Sioux, and then had the fence line moved to rectify the boundary and preserve some Sioux landholdings.[10]

Lone Wolf also dominated government attempts to alter the land area of the Lower Brule and Rosebud reservations at the same time as the Standing Rock leases. Since allotment in 1889, the government had attempted to adjust the Rosebud reserve's boundaries, shrink reservation land area, and open the surpluses to white settlers. The current controversies carried with them the residue and resentments from earlier government attempts to alter Sioux Indian lives. A concerted effort to remove the Lower Brule Sioux in 1892 to the Rosebud Reservation and cede Brule and Rosebud lands had utterly failed to obtain the required consent of three-quarters of adult male Sioux; and eventually the Office of Indian Affairs, which disliked the scheme from the beginning, succeeded in killing the plan.[11] The commissioner of Indian affairs at the time was "unwilling to sanction any transfer that lacked the 3/4ths agreement because it would not be in good faith." [12] The three-fourths rule had been written into the 1868 treaty, as well as into the Sioux Act of March 2, 1889, and had been included in 1891 Indian appropriations act provisions. No such qualms arose three years later when South Dakota Senator Richard Pettigrew, newly appointed chair of the Senate Indian committee, skillfully maneuvered passage of an amendment to the Indian appropriations bill in the face of weak Indian Rights Association opposition that permitted Lower Brule Sioux to take allotments on Rosebud, thereby opening more Brule land to eager white settlers.[13]

In a council concluding on May 6, 1901, Brule Sioux agreed to cede to the United States a tract at the time thought to contain 56,560 acres that comprised the western portion of the reservation, for a sum of $70,700. Later it turned out that the ceded area actually consisted of 59,400 acres. Along with the money, the Brule insisted on obtaining a wire fence that would enclose the entire reservation area not bounded by the Missouri River. Intrusions onto the reservation and controversies over stock ownership fed the Indians' insistence on fencing. Money was also to be used for an equal distribution of grazing cattle among tribal members. Through patient effort and not a little cajolery, Indian Service Inspector James McLaughlin obtained over three-quarters of adult male Indian signatures on the agreement document.[14]

Pressure to open the "surplus" to whites also led the federal officials to seek Rosebud Indian consent to a further cession of land in 1901. The negotiations dealt with 416,000 acres that lay entirely within Gregory County, South Dakota, for which the government negotiator offered $2.50 an acre, for a total of $1,040,000. McLaughlin traveled to the Rosebud Agency to gain the agreement of three-quarters of the adult male Indians to yet another cession. He urged them to comply, unctuously stressing that the Indians would be brought into beneficial contact with whites who would teach them how to farm and advance in American society. He forcefully informed his listeners that he was not obligated to obtain their agreement under the terms of the Lone Wolf ruling, but that he wanted to persuade them to accept. At first Mclaughlin encountered Indian recalcitrance, then a delaying ploy with a demand for quadruple what he was authorized to offer to pay for the land, and finally the Indians' resignation to the inevitable opening of their lands to whites. While many of the Indians were not actively opposed to cession of the unallotted portion, they demanded almost $8 an acre at the start of the negotiations before finally agreeing on September 14 to McLaughlin's offer of $2.50 an acre. McLaughlin was especially sensitive to the contro-

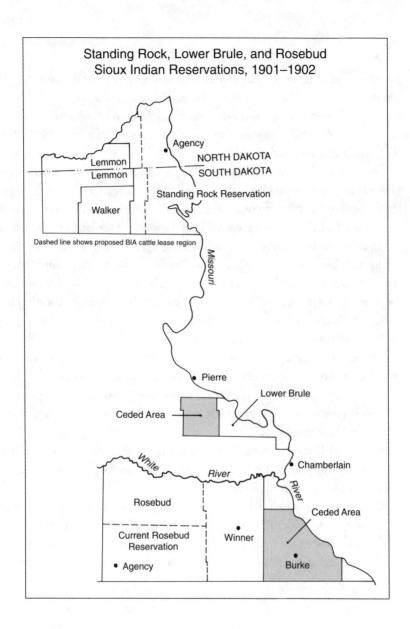

Map 2. *Standing Rock, Lower Brule, and Rosebud Sioux Indian Reservations, 1901–1902.*
Sources: Standing Rock leases: Clow, "Cattlemen and Tribal Rights," 27; Lower Brule:
Sen. Doc. No. 28, 57th Cong., 1st Sess., Serial No. 4220, 5 December 1901; Rosebud:
Sen. Doc. No. 31, 9 December 1901; as well as CIA Annual Reports, 1901–1905.

versy surrounding the lack of adequate signatures on Indian documents. The inspector used behind-the-scenes maneuvering and managed to get twelve more signatures than the three-fourths required on the final agreement.[15]

The very first bill introduced in the wake of *Lone Wolf* to take Indian land without Indian consent was HR 10418, which dealt with Rosebud lands. As sponsor of the bills to implement the altered 1901 agreement terms, South Dakota Representative Charles H. Burke played the leading role in the legislative opening of the surplus to whites. Burke believed that Congress could act without waiting for Sioux consent and simply take the land and transfer it to settlers. Burke castigated the Indian Rights Association for its opposition to his bill. He voiced sentiments widely shared in the two legislative chambers. Burke introduced bills in 1903 and 1904 to approve a modified Rosebud agreement.[16] In an attempt to get around earlier objections, the 1903 bill unsuccessfully tried what he termed "a new policy" of opening the land under homestead laws and paying the Indians as the land was taken up to avoid lump sum payments. He pointed out during the debate on the measure that while over three-quarters of the Rosebud Indians had consented to the 1901 agreement, over a majority had agreed to the stipulations of the 1904 bill and that was more than sufficient for enactment.[17] In his view, the unilateral congressional cession of Rosebud lands was "exactly identical" to the Lone Wolf decision and Congress ought to act swiftly to satisfy settlers' demands.[18] In defense of his position, Burke had printed in the congressional proceedings significant portions of the Lone Wolf decision.[19]

Commissioner of Indian Affairs Jones believed that Sioux and Kiowa treaty lands were held under the same tenuous rights of Indian occupancy, which the Department of the Interior could ignore with impunity.[20] Shortly after the peak of the controversy, Jones impaitently pointed out to his field negotiator:

> If you depend upon the consent of the Indians as to the disposition of the land . . . , you will have difficulty in getting it, and I think the decision in the *Lone Wolf* case, that Congress can do as it sees fit with the property of the Indians will enable you to dispose of that land without the consent of the Indians. If you wait for their consent in these matters, it will be fifty years before you can do away with the reservations.[21]

He announced that, henceforth, in every instance he planned to report on any bills pending before the national legislature in favor "of Congress taking the property of the Indians without their consent." He claimed his measure would be "a pioneer bill" for relieving Indians of lands "for which they have no use."[22]

Congressional debate over the Rosebud bill focused on whether Congress should dispose of the land without Indian consent in the aftermath of the Lone Wolf court opinion. Various measures which had been introduced on the subject differed only over the question of Indian consent. The 1904 House report recommending ratification of the land transfer included a copy of the Lone Wolf decree, while committee members recommended passage of HR 10418.[23] Committee members noted that Congress and the Indian Service could do with native peoples and their property as they deemed necessary without consulting Indians, but suggested that gaining Indian consent would be useful.

Brosius drafted a bill of his own, even before the Rosebud sale, that would guarantee land title to allotted Indians unless the reason for cancellation was clearly and specifically stated.[24] In response to encroachments on Kiowa, Sioux, and Chippewa lands, he worked with George Grinnell and President Roosevelt for a legislative solution that became law. Brosius believed that his bill, in effect, nullified the Lone Wolf decision through protection of an Indian's allotment, making the allotment safe from congressional and secretarial cancellation. The enactment embodied Indian demands, Bureau desires, and Indian Rights Assocation caution into a measure that was designed to quell the disputes at both the Standing Rock and Rosebud reservations.[25]

The controversy flared briefly again in 1907 when a bill was introduced to open the surplus yet another time on the Rosebud Reservation and to authorize a payment of $5 an acre. The Indians insisted on $7 and once again appealed to the Indian Rights Association. Brosius worked with congressional members of the committees on Indian affairs and obtained a compromise provision that provided for payment of $6 an acre for only the first three months of the sale, after which homesteaders paid $4.50 until the sixth month of the sale, then only $2.50 an acre. The bill became law.[26] Overall, it was only a partial victory for the Indian Rights Association, while white settlers obtained more coveted acreage, and the Sioux lost more land in exchange for monetary reward that was too quickly spent.

TURMOIL AT THE KIOWA, COMANCHE, AND
APACHE RESERVATION

National publicity that focused on Lone Wolf's litigation, regional interest in
the possibility of more available land, and local demand for an opening of the
Kiowa, Comanche, and Plains Apache Reservation brought large numbers
of people to the area anticipating a land run. Whites who streamed into the
region looked forward to quick profits and easy money to be gained from exploiting Indians and a speculative real estate market. An example of the local
opinion favoring immediate opening of the area is the editorial comment in
the *Chickasha Express:*

> They [full-bloods] are first-class citizens at a shooting-match or at a
> game of monte or make a full hand at loafing, but as a benefactor in
> making two spears of grass grow where one grew before they are a fail-
> ure.
>   Let them go. Let the government buy their land it gave them and then
> drive them to some other country. . . . They have been pests and scabs
> long enough.[27]

The Indian agent estimated in mid-1900 that there were as many white
trespassers in the Wichita Mountains as there were Indians under his charge
on the reservation.[28] Many of them slipped in to prospect under the 1900
act's provision allowing mineral exploration. Through 1902–1903 there was
a small gold rush in the mountains, even though the rumor was false. For a
brief time, the communities of Meers and Mountain View in the northern
part of the reserve took on the bonanza atmosphere of boom towns. A federal official encouraged the gold rush. Indian Office Special Agent Gilbert B.
Pray conspired with others to mine the gold in a fashion similar to illegal
Osage Indian leases he had made earlier.[29]

In 1901 Randlett estimated that more than fifty thousand intruders were
on the reservation.[30] That was only one part of a larger population explosion
in the region. A population of seven thousand whites in the territory in 1880
skyrocketed to one million by the turn of the century, increasing fivefold
in the previous decade alone. Randlett even accused some whites of trying
to sneak onto the reservation disguised under shawls and blankets in an attempt to be mistaken for Indian women. As anticipation of a land opening
increased, whites entered the reserve under the excuse of finding work when

they actually were gaining a foothold and the advantage of selecting the plot they wanted well in advance.

"Sooners" included illegal homesteaders keen on a land run, bootleggers, cattle and horse thieves, legitimate businessmen, whites anxious to appropriate Indian livestock and property to satisfy alleged debts, loan sharks, and all manner of hustlers. Contractors dealt in stolen permits to sell hides of the beef issued to the Indians.[31] White squatters' hogs ate Indian crops in gardens, Anglos' cattle grazed freely and at will, trespassers illegally took Indian timber and livestock, prospectors and laborers openly defied federal authority. Indians who protested infringements were threatened and beaten. Local juries acquitted whites who violated federal laws. Many whites when faced with an agent's eviction order, usually in the form of a personal letter to the individual, were determined enough to file lawsuits in local courts to enjoin the Indian agent from using Fort Sill troops and federal marshals from evicting them.[32] Territorial jurists like Clinton F. Irwin in El Reno readily accommodated the whites. Soon, the agency was virtually clogged with court injunctions.

Randlett wrote that so many non-Indians flooded the reservation that to curb the influx, he would have to resort to "drastic measures."[33] The much-tested agent faced an unprecedented challenge. He relied on authority granted him under an attorney general's ruling in 1891, based on the 1879 decision in *U.S. v. Crook,* that gave the Indian agent the power to oust non-Indians from reservation lands. However, seeking legal rulings on each incident from the Department of the Interior legal staff in Washington was time-consuming, cumbersome, and ineffective.[34]

Even when Randlett utilized United States cavalry to evict white intruders, the troops quickly returned to their barracks, and the intruders just as readily came back to the reservation, since open highways crisscrossed the reserve. Many of the whites who were escorted off the reserve became agitators for a land opening so their activities would no longer be subject to federal authority. Following a territorial supreme court decree against trespassers in the Cherokee Strip, the agent successfully forced trader Henry Huston to depart. Huston became an outspoken leader in the Boomer movement to open western Oklahoma and painted in many speeches and letters to newspapers a glowing portrait of the region to encourage settlers.[35]

Only after the agent repeatedly reminded his superiors that the 1893 appropriations had authorized an additional assistant U.S. attorney for the region was one assigned to Anadarko to help defend the Indians. The new appointee faced extortionate tax levies, unjust prosecutions of Indians, appropriations of Indian livestock under the territorial herd law, unfair contracts involving Indians, suspicious probate proceedings, and other devices to obtain Indian property. Adding to the pressure was the fact that the government payment in late 1902 was not made on time and some Indians were destitute. To prevent their ponies from being stolen, Indians sold them for whatever they could get. Randlett called the entire situation "systematic robbery" of his Indian charges.[36]

Randlett sought prosecution for white loan sharks who preyed on Indians who needed to feed their families but had no land rental, surplus payment, or grass money available. On occasion culprits were actually convicted. In 1905 one Gotebo banker in the county was found guilty and fined $1,000 for assessing Indian debtors interest of up to 3,360 percent.[37] Bank officials in Anadarko were similarly charged. Still other Kiowa, Comanche, and Plains Apache Indians fell victim to gamblers, pimps, and whiskey peddlers, who indebted the Indians through loans only to take Indian property for payment shortly thereafter. In most instances, local courts offered no protection to the Indians.

Some whites filed on Indian allotments believing that Section 6 of the 1900 act permitted mineral claims on allotments. Randlett accused them of "plundering the Indian allotments" and sought their eviction from the reservation, but Department of the Interior superiors cautioned him to move slowly, use proper notification, and abstain from any forceful eviction.[38] Other squatters intruded on the allotments of whites intermarried among the Kiowas and Comanches or Mexican captives. Some interlopers even challenged victims of the Comanche smallpox epidemic of 1900–1901, hoping the weakened or deceased sufferers and their heirs would not be able to defend their title before compliant local justices. In some instances, special congressional acts permitted restricted Kiowa allottees to sell portions of their allotments under carefully regulated conditions.[39]

Agent Randlett also strongly urged the federal government to stop interference in Indian affairs from groups like the Indian Rights Association. He accused the Association and the Board of Indian Commissioners of "being bent upon robbing the Indians of the magnanimous provisions made for them by the Act of . . . June 6, 1900." Randlett blamed the humanitarians for unsettling the Indians with nonsense about legal rights and treaty obligations.

After all, the agent tried hard to convince his charges that they ought to accept their fate and that they had no rights beyond what Congress wanted to grant to them.

What really galled Randlett, moreover, was the Indian Rights Association's interference in his duties in the face of what he himself considered his best efforts under extremely difficult circumstances. The agent felt he had been unfairly singled out for reformers' attention. He believed he had been maligned by implication in front of a 1901 Lake Mohonk audience during remarks about the problem of public drunkenness in Anadarko and that Albert K. Smiley of the Lake Mohonk Conference had made personal allegations against his administration. Randlett cited the incidents as examples of the Indian Rights Association membership's "reckless statements."[40] Samuel Brosius wrote Welsh urging the latter to use his influence to insist that the federal government delete the section of Randlett's annual report stating that the Association had begun the Lone Wolf suit solely to establish the right of the government to take Indian land without native consent.[41] The Assocation insisted that William Springer respond in an attempt to remove the organization from the protest. Randlett had attacked the Association and "grafting attorneys" for meddlesome scheming against the United States government and its Indian wards. According to the agent, the outsiders only caused agitation leading to disturbances that gained nothing. In the strongest terms— and Randlett often drew from his military and frontier background for some barbed language—he urged the secretary of the interior to terminate all independent contracts between Indians, the Indian Rights Association, and attorneys.[42]

William Springer worked diligently to undermine the agent. Indians on the reserve who opposed Randlett kept up their pressure. On January 27, 1903, fifty to seventy-five Indians gathered fifteen miles south of the agency in the community of Apache under the guidance of a local attorney working in concert with Springer. A few Indians, Randlett said only ten, signed a memorial, and several more (six according to Randlett) signed the document in the Anadarko law office of Baker & Vaughan. The memorial,[43] forwarded to Springer, who presented it to the Senate, requested that an attorney be appointed to oversee Agent Randlett's handling of tribal funds and that Congress investigate agency fiscal management. Earlier, some of his opponents had called for his prompt ouster from office.

The memorial document is interesting because of what it reveals about

the complex forces at work on the reservation in 1903. The memorial requested an investigation into agency management, but for the reason that
Randlett was too restrictive. The Indians protested the ratification and implementation of the Jerome Agreement because the Indians had not been told
whether money paid to them was from interest due on trust fund deposits
in the United States Treasury, was part of the principal on those deposits,
or was grass money. The Indians suspected fraud on the part of the agent
and appealed to Congress to inquire into his monetary activities. Furthermore, the Indians wanted to rent their infants' restricted allotments simply
by appearing before the local agent—they hoped a new and more cooperative
one—without waiting for the time-consuming and bureaucratic approval of
the secretary of the interior. They ended their memorial with the request that
all Kiowa, Comanche, and Apache Indians be "placed on a footing upon an
equality of [sic] the other citizens of the United States." Little Bum signed
as council president. Yellow Face served as secretary. Lone Wolf's signature
is on the document.

The Indian council mixed longtime opponents of Randlett with his some-
time supporters in order to gain economic advantages for allottees. In the
absence of documentation, Lone Wolf's motives can only be the subject of
speculation, but perhaps he sought to embarrass an agent whom he had re-
lentlessly opposed since the start of his administration. The Indians repeated
charges that federal officials sold allotted land to whites or kept land only to
sell it to whites during the land lottery confusion. Land title frauds plagued
Indian Office officials in the eastern part of the region, called Oklahoma Territory. The Kiowa, Comanche, and Plains Apache Indians in their memorial
against Agent Randlett hoped to paint his administration with the same taint
of scandal that hung over the eastern superintendencies.

At the insistence of the Indian Rights Association and with continuing
Indian protests, Senator Quay requested that the Department of the Interior look into Randlett's administration. The secretary of the interior had
approached George Grinnell to look into Kiowa Agency affairs, but Grinnell was unable to do so. In January and February 1903, Inspector James
McLaughlin visited the reserve. After he talked only with cooperative Indians
whom Randlett personally selected, McLaughlin's report praised the agent.[44]
Protests and Senator Quay's concern only grew stronger. President Roosevelt helped arrange for another investigation of Randlett's tenure. In late
1903, Francis E. Leupp spent six weeks at the agency as a special supervisor

of Indian education under an arrangement worked out by Assistant Secretary of the Interior Thomas Ryan. Leupp, a journalist from New York, was a personal friend of Roosevelt's and had been a Washington lobbyist for the Indian Rights Association at Roosevelt's recommendation. Leupp replaced the deceased Charles Painter in the national capital in 1895, preceding Brosius in that position. Roosevelt thought enough of Leupp's abilities that in 1905 he would make him his commissioner of Indian affairs.

Leupp was charged with finding out if Randlett or allotting agent Charles Nesler had accepted bribes during reservation allotment, as some Indians like Lone Wolf insisted.[45] The Indians had hired local attorney E. F. Baker to examine charges against Randlett and Nesler, but the agent threw Baker out of his office and slammed the door on him, all to the accompaniment of a stream of invective from the outraged agent. The federal investigator interviewed agency personnel, Indians, and local citizens. Leupp searched agency books and observed operations on a daily basis. He personally talked with Lone Wolf and the latter's followers to get their views. Lone Wolf questioned the agent's disbursement of Indian payments.

Leupp arranged for Lone Wolf and his followers Little Bow, Big Tree, Saddle Blanket, and the Comanches Eschiti and Per-mam-su (also called Comanche Jack), as well as the attorney Baker, to sit at the agency pay table to oversee the disbursement of an installment payment on the $500,000 due the Indians under the Jerome Agreement, to observe that the agent did not pocket the money, and to correct any errors in the agency roll of Indians eligible for payments in order to learn if the agent had padded the official roll for personal gain. Leupp forcefully persuaded reluctant Indians to speak to him at the table through threats of imprisonment at hard labor and withholding their payments until they grudgingly cooperated with him.

Eschiti informed Leupp that the Indians would sell the 480,000-acre pasture to the United States for $25 per acre, the resulting $12 million compensating the Indians for the Jerome fraud. The investigator also looked into Lone Wolf's charge that Randlett had blocked a lease made for an orphan ward of Lone Wolf. The documentation, it turned out, had been sent back from Washington because the agency staff had forgotten to include all the guardianship papers in the lease packet. It was quite easy for Lone Wolf to believe the agency staff purposely misplaced the papers as retribution for his latest mischief-making.

After all questions had been answered through painstaking research and

interviewing, Leupp concluded that Lone Wolf and his followers had created false accusations against the agent. In the polite language of the day,
Leupp stated that Lone Wolf performed "something perilously near perjury."
However, Leupp never took into consideration the overwhelming factor of
poor communication between Indians and the agent. Leupp's report absolved
Randlett of wrongdoing but noted that the agent's frustrated and angry out-
bursts aggravated his already sharp tongue and compounded many of his
problems. Leupp's report mirrored the agent's attitudes, sympathized with
Randlett's "unremitting grind," and had only contempt for Lone Wolf and his
followers. Leupp wrote that they were mescal-eating, disaffected, lost souls
who were chronic anti-government agitators. The special supervisor felt that
ill will over the loss of Lone Wolf's court suit motivated the Indians to cause
the entire episode.[46]

In the meantime, whites continued their push for Indian land and believed
that Congress should open remaining acreage without delay. They first sought
the land within the Big Pasture, which under the 1900 Act was held in common for the tribes. For three years after the opening, 400,000 acres of it
brought an average of 31 cents per acre for cattle-grazing leases.[47] In 1903
those leases brought $128,000 into the agency coffer. Lawton reporters called
for the land to be opened to whites, since in their eyes the Indians were not
using the land.[48]

By 1904, strong rumors circulated in Lawton and other towns that the
acreage would soon be thrown open to homestead entry. One outspoken pro-
ponent of opening the land was Texas congressman John Stephens, whose
sponsorship of the 1900 Act benefited his own home town of Vernon just
across the Red River from the most recent area to be opened, which stood
to profit directly when prosperous farmers and ranchers improved the now
idle land.[49] Stephens stated that the total 505,000 acres would provide 3,200
homes for families and that "stopping these annual payments [to Indians] will
be quite a saving to the Government, as no appropriations will have to be
made for them in the future."[50] Agent Randlett responded that the sale sum
deposited in the Treasury at the going rate of interest would yield only one-
quarter of the amount that the region's annual leasing brought the Indians.
The Indians already were hard pressed and would lose fifty thousand acres
reserved for their stock, placing them into even greater dependence on their
inadequate allotments.

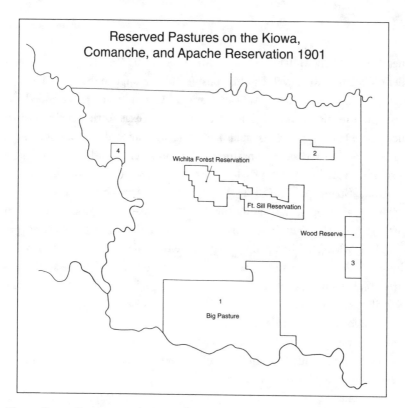

Map 3. Reserved pastures on the Kiowa, Comanche, and Apache Reservation, 1901. From CIA Annual Report for 1907 in Dept. of the Interior Annual Report, 1907, pp. 113–14.

To counter proposals for opening Big Pasture, Randlett suggested that all tribal children born since the opening receive 160-acre allotments, while the remaining land would continue to be leased to whites as before. The agent underscored the government's role:

> Since the decision of the Supreme Court in the *Lone Wolf* case, . . . Congress, the guardian, may deal with the lands of the Indian wards of the nation precisely as an individual legal guardian would deal with and dispose of the lands of an infant or other incompetent person, being careful at all times that no injustice is visited upon the ward.[51]

A senator who questioned the wisdom of opening the land agreed with Randlett and Stephens that the United States had the power to open the lands but ironically stressed that "as their guardians we have the right [responsibility] to open it in a fair way."[52]

For the first time, a United States president visited the territory. During a nearly week-long wolf-hunting expedition across Big Pasture in April, President Theodore Roosevelt lent his considerable prestige to the issue. Colonel Cecil B. Lyon, Texas Republican National Committeeman, extended the invitation to the president. His hosts included Texas cattlemen Burk Burnett and Dan Waggoner. Quanah Parker accompanied the entourage. They camped on Burnett's leased pasturage. The president let it be known that he strongly favored public disposal and opening of the pasture land.[53]

A new Stephens bill (HR 431) swiftly moved through Congress the following year to open the Big Pasture tract, as well as a 25,000-acre timber preserve for Fort Sill. The legislation set a minimum price of $1.50 per acre but lacked Randlett and Quanah Parker's earlier suggested proviso that Indian children born since the 1900 act be included. The bill passed Congress on March 20, 1906, but vigorous protest from Agent John P. Blackman, Randlett's former chief clerk and chosen successor in 1905, and from the commissioner of Indian affairs persuaded President Roosevelt to insist on reconsideration of the bill.[54] Roosevelt on June 5 signed into law a revised measure that included 517 Indian children born since the land opening and raised the minimum price to $5 per acre.[55]

Oklahoma Territory Senator Thomas P. Gore and Representative Scott Ferris, both from Lawton, pushed special legislation dealing with pasture number three. Because it was actively farmed, pasture number three was not included in the general land opening of the remaining pasture and wood reserve. Instead of permitting Indians to select children's allotments from the fertile 22,500-acre third pasture next to the town of Duncan, the president next signed legislation granting white lessors a preference right to buy the land their farms occupied.[56] A short controversy flared over the method that should be used to sell the opened lands. Eschiti spoke for Indian sentiment, particularly among the Kiowas and Comanches, that favored a public auction. Eschiti claimed that a public auction would yield a million more dollars over any other means of disposal.[57] Many people had come to believe since 1901 that a lottery only favored the hustler and gave advantage to the gambler-speculator. Secretary Hitchcock chose sealed bids as the method of sale and issued regulations in October.

A presidential proclamation on September 19, 1906, exposed 2,531 tracts of Kiowa, Comanche, and Apache Reservation land for sale through bids. Officials extended the time one week to secure adequate offers, yielding

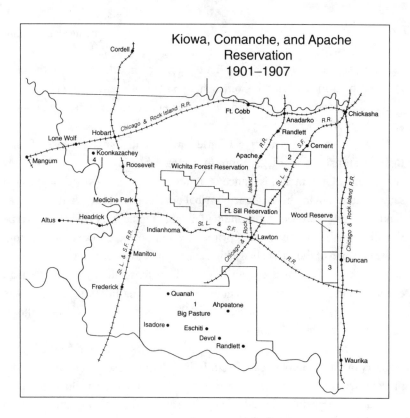

Map 4. *Kiowa, Comanche, and Apache Reservation, 1901–1907. From CIA Annual
Report 1907 in Dept. of the Interior Annual Report, 1907, pp. 113–14, for town sites
within pastures; Gov. of Okla. Annual Report 1902 in Sec. of the Interior Annual Report,
House Doc. No. 5, 57 Cong., 2 Ses., Serial No. 4461, vol. 22, p. 496, for railroads.*

nearly 250,000 separate bids. Averaging $10.54 per acre, the bidding brought
in $4,015,785 from the sale of the tracts. The sum averaged about $1,200
per capita for the Indians. The amount covered 380,790 acres out of the total
396,139 acres for sale. Officials either withdrew the remainder or had no bids
on them.[58]

A separate act provided for 1,841 acres to be set aside for the establishment
of townsites on former Kiowa, Comanche, and Apache pasture lands.[59] Five
towns, named Randlett, Eschiti, Quanah, Isadore, and Ahpeatone, were set
up in Big Pasture. Isadore was named for a local missionary priest. One community was formed in the northwest part of pasture number four and called
Koonkazachey, after a man referred to as a "notable" Indian leader who encouraged and took part in the opening of the reserve. Sale of the three county

seat town sites brought the government $737,000, one-third of what the government paid for all Kiowa, Comanche, and Apache lands under the 1900 act. The episode formed the last Oklahoma land opening before statehood, achieved November 16, 1907.

In late 1910 Representative Charles Burke and Senator Moses Clapp (Minnesota) sponsored legislation, following a hearing into the matter, revoking the allotment and issuance of a patent to James F. Rowell and at the same time removing his name from tribal enrollment. Rowell had misrepresented his intermarried status and had obtained temporary title to an exceptionally valuable allotment in a prime location on the outskirts of Lawton. The net worth of the parcel had a high appraisal of $100,000 in value.[60] Minor adjustments to Big Pasture lands were made in subsequent years through an enactment in 1908, its amendment in 1910, and a measure in 1912, while acts in 1911, 1913, and 1915 disposed of small pieces or allowed selected illegal claimants to retain their holdings.[61]

The events entered tribal folklore with a bitterness that marked the Indian memory of the Lone Wolf case itself. Indians harbor resentment down to the present as a result of the Big Pasture opening, over their feeling that they were denied rightful proceeds from the sale of the Pasture and its town sites. That anger, coupled with frustration over the whole opening process, bred the Indians' assessment in following years that they had been "cheated" and "tricked" out of their lands. Big Pasture became another in a series of unfulfilled promises.[62]

10

The Legacy of *Lone Wolf*

The Supreme Court's 1903 order placed the Indian allottee as well as the allottee's tribe firmly under the domination of the United States Congress. "*Lone Wolf* brought the process of tribes' legal incorporation to completion."[1] Proponents of allotment in severalty viewed the decision as a green light for increased division of tribal holdings and the destruction of tribal governments. Subsequent edicts built on *Lone Wolf* and greatly expanded federal legislative and judicial control over the Indian and Indian resources.

Aside from the look on the faces of the Friends of the Indians in the courtroom when Justice White read his pronouncement on January 5, the most visible effect of *Lone Wolf v. Hitchcock* was on Kiowa landholding. The decree had a profound impact on acres under Indian control as well as all aspects of the Indians' lives which the unseen hand of poverty touched.

For the Kiowa, Comanche, and Apache reserve the average per capita holding of land during the 1880s was just under 160 acres; by 1934 it had plummeted to 17 acres; today it is about 10.5 acres each for tribal members.[2] Kiowa reservation landholdings dropped over 90 percent as land ownership passed out of Indian hands. From its preallotment total of 2.9 million acres, the reservation land base shrank by the end of the allotment era to just above 3,000 acres. Increased federal expenditures for Indian projects did not much affect the individual Kiowa because land administration costs steadily rose and consumed any extra dollars. At the Kiowa and Comanche Agency in 1934, exclusive of schools, the federal government spent $80,000. Of that amount, $65,000 went toward estate operations concerned with leasing and fractionated inheritances. Only $15,000 remained for tribal agriculture, health, and other services.[3]

Land sales to provide home improvements during the wintertime or for needed surgery, as well as fee patents forced on the Indians, including within Lone Wolf's own family, drastically diminished Kiowa landholdings in the aftermath of the Lone Wolf decision. More than normal attrition and sales contributed to the loss. Bureau of Indian Affairs personnel in charge of Indian allotted land management for the Kiowa reserve were encouraged through Department of the Interior policies to divest Indians of their holdings at the very time that federal officials had imposed legal restraints preventing them from exploiting their dependent wards. Government policy assisted the Indians in conveying their lands to non-Indians. Forced fee patents resulted in "heavy losses" from land transactions. The agent only implemented official policy that declared that all "surplus" Indian lands ought to be leased or sold "for the benefit and in the interest of all the people of the country" instead of being kept for the individual Indian.[4] Agents also aided private economic interests in gaining valuable concessions from allottees. Board of Indian Commissioners informants offered evidence that confirmed for the Board investigator that there was "something radically wrong in the leasing business" at the Kiowa Agency in the period after World War I, hinting that local bankers were in collusion with real estate speculators buying Kiowa Indian allotments under the guise of "leases" anticipating an oil boom, which ultimately did not materialize.[5] Rumors and investigations into allegations of leasing improprieties at the agency have persisted down to the present time.[6]

Loss of land, lack of rental and lease income, and few marketable skills left the Kiowa deeply impoverished by the 1920s, with an unemployment rate among Kiowa males above 60 percent,[7] establishing a pattern that persists down to the present. The Lone Wolf decision cast a whole people into an economic coma. All the Indians became a casualty. Allotment proved too successful in individualizing Indian holdings at the same time that it individualized Indian poverty. Without a tribal land base, they were economically paralyzed. It was not possible to develop tribal capital through collateral to invest in the future. Dependency, much like poverty, fed on itself in stubbornly persistent ways.

The case is of major importance in the development of federal–Indian law. *Lone Wolf* was as much a watershed for American Indian legal rights as was

President Andrew Jackson's 1832 determination, however implicit, that he would not enforce federal law regarding removal of native peoples against states where Indians were concerned. *Lone Wolf* climaxed a century of accumulating opinions on the Indian's place within the national legal structure as well as within American society. The decision served as the cornerstone of both the "plenary power" authority and the "political question doctrine" of Indian law. The High Court did accept Hampton Carson's argument that there was a distinction between treaty-recognized property rights and the mere right of occupancy under aboriginal title to lands within an executive order reserve.[8] Under the *Lone Wolf* doctrine, federal power over Indians "is paramount to treaty or state law" and Congress could deal with Indian property as it saw fit.[9]

Jurists used the decision in subsequent years to justify taking Indian land, including allotted and treaty land, throughout the nation. As guardian for lands held in trust, Congress could and did legislate at will regulating the disposition of Indian property. In 1909 the Court invoked the political question doctrine and applied the Major Crimes Act to an Indian who had become a citizen after receiving an allotment.[10] Congress and the courts often changed the terms of allotment agreements after they had been implemented, adding more participants, restricting individual Indian rights, and augmenting tribal holdings, as well as imposing liquor traffic control laws on tribal areas.[11] A series of decisions incorporated language about federal "paramount authority" and congressional "plenary power" over tribes.

The author has performed a search of *Shepard's Citations* for *Lone Wolf v. Hitchcock* and found it one of the most cited cases in all of federal–Indian law. The Shepard's series cumulatively lists United States Supreme Court cases from 1900 to date by the name of the case and the volume citation. *Lone Wolf* is the most important turn-of-the-century case to which federal judges repeatedly turned for justification of later influential opinions in federal–Indian law. *Lone Wolf* dominated Indian legal decisions after the turn of the century. The ruling proved useful to justices who sought a decree that would aid their opinions dealing with postallotment issues of leasing, inheritance of petroleum rights, and assumed disappearance of tribes and of a tribal land base.

One of the early influential cases relying on the Kiowa decision involved Albert Heff,[12] a mixed-blood Indian convicted of selling beer to another Indian in violation of liquor control laws. The Supreme Court justices held in 1905 that Indians were "under the care and control"—emphasizing that the American Indian was under "the full control"—of the United States, especially congressional plenary authority, pointing to their decision in *Lone Wolf.* The justices surprised nearly everyone when they stated that the United States "may at any time abandon its guardianship"[13] of Indians and leave them to fend for themselves as ordinary citizens. The Indian in question had been allotted land in Kansas and was, therefore, a citizen. The justices re-iterated, "It is not within the power of the courts to over-rule the judgment of Congress" where Indians were concerned.[14] For a time, the decree of the Court threw those concerned about Indians into a dither. Many people in-terpreted the opinion to imply that allotted Indians were no longer wards under federal government protection, even to the extent that it was "beyond the power of Congress" to interfere.[15] Some even feared that Indians would shortly thereafter fall prey to real estate sharks and other unscrupulous char-acters. Before *Heff* was overturned in 1916 in another Indian liquor case, those favoring a complete release of the Indian from federal control often turned to the Heff decision to support their claims.

North Dakota Senator Porter J. McCumber used the Lone Wolf case as his excuse and the Heff decree as his immediate reason to try to rescue what in his belief was the allotted Indian left adrift as a citizen. He also wanted to protect remaining Indian landholding rights "from the rapacity of the white man."[16] Several of his colleagues denounced his efforts on behalf of full-blooded Indians as being "absolutely worthless"[17] because his col-leagues believed that the Indians were no longer wards of the government. McCumber stubbornly defended his amendment to 1906 legislation extend-ing restrictions over the surplus of full-bloods' allotments to prevent their sale.[18] Ultimately, the assessment of McCumber's colleagues, while wrong in their assumption as to the status of wardship, proved only too correct in their prediction of the success his amendment would have in staving off the continuing loss of Indian landholdings.

Tiger v. Western Investment Company [19] is another major pronouncement that drew directly from *Lone Wolf. Tiger* built on congressional authority over "de-pendent people,"[20] set out in *Lone Wolf,* to extend federal guardianship power to restrict land conveyances over allotted members of the Five Tribes in Okla-homa. In effect, the decision regarding Creek Indian Marchie Tiger in 1912 blocked the types of sales of allotted Indian land that *Heff* seemed to imply could take place. Another important case, *Choate v. Trapp,*[21] is a landmark be-cause at the same time that it borrowed from *Lone Wolf,* the opinion was one of the few to declare a congressional enactment unconstitutional where the Indian was concerned. The justices held in *Choate* that Congress could not authorize taxation of Indian lands after previously pledging that they were tax-exempt, protecting Indian property rights lawfully vested. At the same time, the justices pointed out, "The tribes have been regarded as dependent nations, and treaties with them have been looked upon . . . as public laws which could be abrogated at the will of the United States."[22] A final example, that of *Heckman*,[23] the same year as *Choate*, also reaffirmed "plenary control of the Congress" over American Indian allottees, permitting the federal government to go to court on their behalf to prevent alienation of their lands even when Indians were not directly parties to the suits.

Tribunals only gradually recognized limitations on plenary authority through the first half of the present century. The 1913 Sandoval ruling noted that Congress could not bring a community under plenary power through the action of arbitrarily calling it an Indian tribe.[24] In a 1919 opinion dealing with the Pueblo of Santa Rosa, the justices stated that in spite of guardianship authority, the congressional grant of administrative authority for the secretary of the interior's proposed seizure of tribal land "would not be an exercise of guardianship, but of confiscation."[25] In the 1930s, judges narrowed *Lone Wolf* somewhat more. In return for guaranteed ownership of remaining tribal lands, the Creek Nation much earlier had ceded half its tribal lands to the United States. Later, the Creek Nation sued the federal government under a special, restrictive claims act to gain compensation for a survey error. In 1935 the Court ruled in favor of the Creek Nation, holding that the federal trust responsibility did not permit the United States to take Indian land without assuming "an obligation" for just compensation. Justice Van Devanter read the opinion and pointed out that plenary power was not unlimited.[26] Most notably, Chief Justice Fred M. Vinson, in an important 1946 Indian claims decision, limited plenary authority with his statement that the "power of Congress over Indian affairs may be of a plenary nature; but it is not absolute."[27] Chapter 11 addresses contemporary survivals of the threat inherent to tribal sovereignty within the Lone Wolf case.

Further restrictions on the decree took place in the following years. After the Lone Wolf decree, federal courts announced that Indian lands could be taken from tribes as long as the public record of debates, reports, and discussions of the action showed that Congress had made a good faith effort to provide just compensation to the Indians for their land under the 5th Amend-

ment. Justices of the United States Supreme Court in 1912 halted the state
taxation of previously restricted Indian lands in Oklahoma, with the notation
that the drastic change from nontaxable to taxable status would constitute a
seizure of Indian property which the Court ruled was protected under the
5th Amendment of the United States Constitution.[28] The Court in 1937 further narrowed the issue of taking property rights under *Lone Wolf,* saying
in *Shoshone Tribe v. U.S.* that the federal government should not have expanded the Shoshone Reservation in Wyoming to make room for the Arapaho
Indians. By doing so, the United States owed the Shoshone "just compensation" under the 5th Amendment because the federal government confiscated
Indian property for its own use.[29]

In his study of nineteenth-century federal–Indian law, Sidney L. Harring
pointed out that most cases that shaped federal–Indian law in that century
dealt with criminal questions. Up to the Dawes Act in 1887, the largest number of Indian cases in the court system were criminal cases. In large part,
those early foundational cases were criminal because of the violence atten-
dant to American legal incorporation of American Indians. *Crow Dog* and
Kagama attest to the criminal law involved in incorporation.[30] In addition,
criminal cases predominated because there were few governmental regulatory functions in that century to serve as the basis for civil suits, and because
American Indians lacked the money to initiate court suits even if they had
wanted to do so. After the Dawes Act and the allotment of Indian lands,
criminality still played a role to be sure, but the proportion of criminal cases
dropped in relation to other issues. In the aftermath of allotment, more complicated conflicts over leasing, inheritance of oil rights, and disappearance
of a land base loomed ever larger in the court system. After *Lone Wolf* there
was greater emphasis on civil or economic incorporation dominating federal–
Indian law. The Kiowa case's emphasis on land and resources signified a shift
in federal–Indian law away from criminal to civil issues that would dominate
the twentieth century.

The Kiowa case is also important because it approximately divided the
years in which allotment dominated national Indian policy. The Kiowa litigation came roughly halfway between the twenty-one years before 1900 in
which allotment took shape and the thirty-four years after the turn of the century during which reform sentiment grew for a halt to the allotment of Indian
reserves, culminating in the Indian New Deal. *Lone Wolf v. Hitchcock* served
as the legal yardstick for the progress of the allotment policy nationwide.

One of the cornerstones of allotment was the attainment of individual competency, enabling the Indian to act for him- or herself. That was the pinnacle of citizenship.

Under *Lone Wolf*, no tribe or Indian individual could prove competency. Incompetency and the necessity for restrictive oversight was presumed from the mere fact of "Indianness." Only Congress authorized itself to remove restrictions, which separate measures could establish. Congress granted authority to the secretary of the interior under many enactments to speed the granting of fee simple patents to individual Indians, and many secretaries vigorously pursued the goal of releasing the Indian ward from restrictions against selling property. The courts only rarely interfered.[31]

Lone Wolf is also a significant decision because it dealt with issues before the Supreme Court that preceded allotment. Lone Wolf and his supporters attempted to uphold tribal and band sovereignty, albeit without success. They also tried to make a statement regarding the solemnity of treaty pledges between governments. That was the cause that brought the Indian Rights Association into the litigation on the American Indian side. The Kiowa, Comanche, and Plains Apache parties to the suit wanted to retain their former reserved land base in the face of enormous pressures to force them to relinquish it. Successive courts chose to emphasize Indian dependency rather than self-government in their opinions, because that approach was much more useful than supporting Indian sovereignty and treaty rights under the weight of popular clamor for more Indian lands.

Nineteenth-century attitudes toward paternalistic rule over Indian property continued on the High Court well after the turn of the century. President William Howard Taft appointed Willis Van Devanter to the United States Supreme Court in 1911. Van Devanter carried with him many of the notions regarding Indian rights that he had expressed before the court in the *Lone Wolf* appeal. In one of his early decisions from the Supreme Court dealing with Indians, he emphasized the duty that befell "a superior" when overseeing "dependent Indian communities."[32] Van Devanter and other jurists continued a paternal attitude toward wardship and federal tutelage over Indian affairs well into the twentieth century.

Lone Wolf occurred just at the peak of American patriotic fervor over acquisition of new overseas territories from Spain as a result of the Spanish-American War. The decree summarized America's approach to island peoples acquired in the takeover of Spanish colonial possessions after 1898. The subject status of the ward in *Lone Wolf* became the colonial status of the overseas dependent of the Insular Cases just at the time Uncle Sam "found new wards appealing to him for protection" during the same period, when the United States reached across the ocean for additional territory and subjects in the aftermath of the Spanish-American War.[33] Humanitarians concerned with overseas natives in 1904 changed the title of the Friends of the Indian organization to the Lake Mohonk Conference of Friends of the Indian and Other Dependent Peoples. The latter name signified their enlarged interest a year after the Lone Wolf decision as a result of the wartime extension of United States authority. A process of colonial political incorporation and land expropriation on ocean possessions such as the Hawaiian Islands similar to the American Indian experience rapidly took place, leaving the native populace subordinate and increasingly landless.

Lone Wolf placed colonial peoples in clear subject condition. One editorial remarked favorably that America was "taking on so many more 'wards of the Government' in different parts of the world."[34] Henry Cabot Lodge, during Senate debate on the legal foundations for American colonial governance, summarized imperialists' views when he stated that national Supreme Court decisions declared "the United States could have under its control . . . a 'domestic dependent nation,'" thereby solving for all time in his mind "the question of our constitutional relations to the Philippines" and other territories.[35] Guardianship over "dark skinned people"[36] brought new obligations and stern responsibilities which called for severe policies. Aguinaldo's claims to independent sovereignty and self-government in the Philippines were tolerated no more than were Lone Wolf's on the Kiowa Indian reserve. Secretary of War Elihu Root, noted for forcing a thoroughgoing Army reorganization, commented that it would be as "preposterous" for Aguinaldo's men to exercise sovereignty over the Philippines as for Indians who aided the United States during the Indian wars to lay a claim of sovereignty over the vastness of America's Far West.[37]

Judicial action, particularly the Lone Wolf case, also offered precedents. The decision itself reads like the summary of a patriotic Fourth of July oration, filled with rhetoric about "justice" by "a Christian people in their treatment of an ignorant and dependent race."[38] The emphasis was on "the relation of dependency . . . towards the government of the United States," "the paramount power" that the legislative and judicial branches possessed over natives, as well as the untutored condition of peoples deemed by their very "weakness and helplessness" in questions of self-rule to require the guidance of a superior power. Secretary Root drew from Indian case law for legal assurance on the subject status of Filipinos. President McKinley's instructions of April 7, 1900, to his Philippine Commission stressed that United States officials there "should adopt the same course" America used in dealing with Indians, permitting local limited tribal self-government that was carefully regulated and closely supervised.[39] The United States did not recognize native governments in its new possessions, only American colonial regimes. Philippine Islands law officer Charles E. Magoon, in the Division of Insular Affairs, looked like the quintessential administrator. He was a corpulent attorney who was also an able overseas manager. He, too, quoted Supreme Court statements on Indians as guiding standards for Filipino rule.[40]

In the Insular Cases, courts accepted expanded congressional power to control possessions just as the judiciary had done in the Kiowa case. American case law at the turn of the century set the legal stage for American overseas rule. American jurists drew a distinction between American Indian rulings and court decisions involving overseas possessions. In *Cariño v. the Insular Government of the Philippine Islands*,[41] justices of the Supreme Court noted that domestic United States Indian policy was for the sole purpose of obtaining Indian lands, but that Philippine policy was in no way meant to exploit the Filipinos or their lands. The case of *Downes v. Bidwell* decided the question of American overseas rule under the United States Constitution. Territories abroad belonged to the United States, but their inhabitants possessed only the rights of natural law. They were not subject to Bill of Rights guarantees, a part of the ruling that quickly upset an advocate of black civil rights like John Marshall Harlan on the Court. Colonials' lives and commerce were "absolutely subject to the will of Congress." According to a dissenter on the High Court, Justice Edward Douglas White had argued in the majority opinion that Congress possessed the fullest power over the new territory "to keep it, like a disembodied shade, in an intermediate state of ambiguous existence for an indefinite period" of time.[42]

Justice White championed the Insular Doctrine on the Supreme Court. His concept of "incorporated" and "unincorporated" territories in the cases comprised his most notable constitutional contribution to the law.[43] As long as the newly acquired peoples were not citizens and none of the new territories were incorporated directly into the United States system, then Congress could dispose of the new territories more readily in the future. White made a distinction between areas annexed (unincorporated) and areas that were properly territory (incorporated). Citizenship and territorial status would not hamper congressional action. The new lands and their peoples were not under the Constitution's numerous restrictions dealing with new territories and citizenship. In chambers, it may have been Justice William Moody's lurid story graphically depicting the consequences of twelve tattooed savage chieftains filing into a jury room, resting their spears and war trophies against the wall, and deliberating evidence in a jury trial that swept the other justices along into supporting White's Insular Doctrine. The Doctrine provided a solution to the dilemma of how to deal with new peoples overseas without at the same time jeopardizing what they viewed as a precarious social and political balance at home.[44]

Political leaders and legal scholars discussed the theoretical, moral, and practical problems of governing overseas possessions. Indian policy provided a domestic guide to overseas rule. The climate of opinion within the American nation regarding paternalistic treatment of "lesser" peoples created a popular acceptance of island possessions once American leaders determined that to be the proper national course of action. Some of the same rhetoric about guardian–ward relationships found its way into the debate regarding annexation of such insular areas as the Philippines. Even though it preceded the Kiowa case slightly, one magazine editorial argued in a similar vein of paternalistic obligation that United States soldiers in the Philippine archipelago were themselves faced with "the case of a child found upon a doorstep," since American troops were forced to govern a childlike tribal people.[45] The national literary figure Mark Twain, known particularly for his humor, used stark anti-imperialist language in rebuttal to the editorial and pointed out that the United States "beguiled" Filipinos in the name of "civilization" in much the same fashion that government agents and missionaries had hoodwinked American Indians years before in a sleight of hand policy that had pledged great benefits to the Indians but in reality brought only misery and degradation.

Former president Theodore Roosevelt drew from his study and travels in western America for his observation that, like American Indians before them, Filipinos could only partake in self-government "under a wise supervision" that the United States firmly administered over them. The United States could not turn its back on the national necessity of bringing order to chaotic tropical lands. America could not turn away from its overseas duty any more than it would be "incumbent upon us to leave the Apaches of Arizona to work out their own salvation, and to decline to interfere in a single Indian reservation" at home.[46] Philippine Governor William Howard Taft informed his island audience at Union Reading College in late 1903 that since "civilization follows material development," it was clear that the Philippine Islands and other American possessions "needed the helping and guiding hand" of the Americans who knew how to instill "popular rule" after generations of experience as pioneers battling hostile forces.[47] Indiana Senator Albert J. Beveridge impressed his audience with the observation that God "has made us [English-speaking peoples] adept in government that we may administer government among savage and senile peoples" in the Almighty's attempt to redeem the world. Moreover, another speaker assured listeners in upstate New York that dependent peoples did not automatically have the "capacity for self-government." It "is a result to be achieved by patient and persistent endeavor" on the part of those who were willing to make the sacrifice to show how to develop self-government.[48]

Imperialists resorted to the same smug phraseology the Supreme Court justices employed in their discussions of why the United States could seize Kiowa land. The High Court declared that the disposition of Indian lands would only be permitted when it was clearly "in the best interest of the Indians." Considerations of "justice," the jurists claimed, would govern all dealings "with backward races."[49] It was America's mission "to establish . . . good government among less-favored nations."[50] New subjects among island tribes would be treated like "tribal Indians" and as "wards" or "dependent nations."[51] Advocates of national overseas dominion evoked nearly the same wording as the justices had used in the Lone Wolf decision when they talked about an overseas rule which "would be governed by such considerations of justice as would control a Christian people in their treatment of an ignorant and dependent race."[52]

Indian Rights Association founder and leader Herbert Welsh turned much of his reform zeal toward anti-imperialism, devoting nearly all his energies after 1898 to opposing overseas dominion. He also drew his examples from Indian policy: "If upon the verge of a colonial policy we make stronger the precedent we have established of dealing with the Indians unjustly . . . so as to make vagrants and paupers of them, . . . our management of outside dependent peoples will be conducted in the same unhappy way," he wrote at the start of the nation's imperialistic adventure.[53] Other anti-imperialists shared his views. One newspaper editorialized, "With the experience of the Indians . . . before us, is it not the height of folly for Americans to reach out after eight millions of aliens [overseas] . . . with mixed races, half-breeds, and blacks?" The paper asked, If Americans could not successfully rule other cultures at home, then how could the United States do so abroad in faraway places like the Philippines and Cuba?[54] Still others raised questions about the unbridled power of Congress to deal with foreign nationals, a power that appeared to be "without any constitutional limits whatever."[55] To them, imperialism raised unsettling questions of constitutional law. Ironically, imperialism involved for some writers more secure relations than had been operating for United States interaction with American Indians, because the new relationship would be based on the recent United States treaty with Spain concluding hostilities. They presumed American Indians no longer had any treaty relationship left.[56]

11

Conclusion

The major legal premises of *Lone Wolf v. Hitchcock* dealing with confiscation of Indian lands under unrestrained congressional plenary authority and denial of judicial review of Congress's decisions regarding Indians and their property are currently largely outmoded and rejected in America's federal courts. Justice Harry Blackmun underscored the fact that the rationale behind *Lone Wolf* was "discredited" and "had little to commend it as an enduring principle" in a major opinion in 1980.[1] One scholar of federal–Indian law in the twentieth century deems it "outmoded"[2] today.

That assessment is prematurely optimistic, because the 1903 opinion is still frequently cited among references and precedents in court opinions dealing with Indian affairs. The Lone Wolf decree, unfortunately, continues to sit there, like a dark, lurking presence just out of sight, all the more menacing because it can be vaguely and disturbingly sensed even though it is only rarely directly observed. Like the beast chained in the dungeon and all but forgotten, it potentially can be used in the future, brought out from where it is kept hidden and harmless to renew its swath of destruction.[3]

Justice Edward White in the Lone Wolf opinion had stated that Congress's plenary power exercised over Indian tribes was a political question and was not a subject for judicial review. Courts have used the political question doctrine to refuse to interfere in sensitive areas, deemed to be purely political in nature, that are better left under the separation of powers to the will of Congress and beyond the reach of the courts.[4] In the 1935 Creek Nation case, they slightly lifted the veil of immunity from judicial review of congressional actions regarding the federal trust responsibility to Indian tribes. The Creek Nation case, detailed in the previous chapter over the issue of property seizure, noted that Congress could not completely shield itself from judicial review under the political question doctrine if congressional actions were in violation of constitutional guarantees. During the late 1970s, in a dispute involving Delaware Indian Business Committee authority, the High Court again narrowed the doctrine in property seizures and hinted that it would no longer follow *Lone Wolf*. The Court would not any longer refuse judicial review to Indians who challenged a congressional act, saying that separation of powers and plenary power over tribes did "not mean that all federal legislation concerning Indians is . . . immune from judicial scrutiny." [5]

The Supreme Court partially laid the issue to rest in 1980, holding that no more would the Court be barred from judicial review of congressional Indian legislation. The justices found that the congressional obligation to compensate Indian tribes under the 5th Amendment for takings of tribal land bound the United States to make a good faith effort only to compensate the Indians with property of equivalent value, and not the land's full value as the Indians had claimed. In phraseology that directly addressed *Lone Wolf*, the justices stated that no longer could they conclusively presume congressional good faith "based on the idea that relations between the Nation and the Indian tribes are a political matter not amenable to judicial review" because that view of plenary power "has long since been discredited in takings cases, and was expressly laid to rest in [the] *Delaware*" case.[6] The justices restated the fact that the Supreme Court continued to recognize congressional "paramount power over the property of the Indians." However, the justices said that the political question doctrine cannot any longer forbid courts from determining whether Congress acted as a trustee for Indians under constitutional requirements, claiming that the body merely abrogated Indian treaty rights under plenary power. Finally, they stated that Congress could not take away treaty rights in the future without providing tribes with "just compensation" under the 5th Amendment.[7] Recently, Justice John Paul Stevens in a concurring claims opinion involving the Oglala Sioux, reiterated that although Congress possessed plenary power in Indian affairs, such power was no longer total and absolute because it was subject to constitutional limitations.[8]

A significant further recognition of the limits on plenary power, this time at the executive level, came during the peak of the most inflammatory Indian controversy of the 1980s, the relocation of Hopi and Navajo Indians from their disputed lands in the Southwest. The assistant secretary for Indian affairs specifically rejected invoking congressional plenary authority as a possible solution because he felt that it was an outmoded approach and no longer helpful, in that it was an expensive and straight path toward more litigation.[9]

In spite of judicial whittling away at it, plenary authority remains one of the cornerstones of federal dominance of Indian affairs. Courts currently recognize that plenary power extends over Indian affairs,[10] regulation of liquor traffic,[11] disposition of tribal property[12] and trust funds,[13] and federal intervention in tribal activities through secretarial discretion,[14] as well as Congress's action,[15] and in the exercise of Indian sovereignty.[16] Contemporary statements of the doctrine demonstrate that it remains alive within the court system. In 1978, the landmark decision of *Santa Clara Pueblo v. Martinez,* which upheld tribal sovereign rights, included the often overlooked statement that "Congress has plenary authority to limit, modify, or eliminate the powers of local self-government which the tribes otherwise possess."[17] Again that same year, the Supreme Court's *Wheeler* opinion underscored the Court's feeling that tribal sovereignty exists "only at the sufferance of Congress."[18] In the tribally favorable tax judgment involving the Jicarilla Apaches of New Mexico in 1980, the ruling noted the superior–inferior relationship of tribes to the federal government. A dissenter from the opinion conjured up the ghosts of both *Kagama* and *Lone Wolf* to remind readers that "[t]he U.S. retains plenary authority to divest the tribes of any attributes of sovereignty" at any time.[19] The dissenter failed to realize that American Indian sovereignty existed long before the arrival of Euroamericans on the shores of the continent and survives even though modified and sometimes unrecognized in a court opinion. The federal trust responsibility toward Indian tribes carried with it enormous congressional power over Indians' lands and lives, power that could in the future ride roughshod over ordinary constitutional guarantees and carried with it a great potential threat to American Indian tribal sovereignty.

A scholar has aptly phrased ongoing plenary authority in federal–Indian law: "The music has stopped, but the melody lingers on."[20] Recent authors, including Indian leaders, have called for a complete overthrow of the plenary power doctrine and full recognition of tribal rights within the American constitutional system. "Mounting an attack on the plenary power doctrine may be the top legal priority for Indian tribes today. A victory over the doctrine may become the '*Brown v. Board of Education*' of Indian rights."[21] Elimination of the doctrine and a repudiation of the onerous aspects of *Lone Wolf* would establish the reality of the government-to-government relationship officially launched in the 1980s between the United States and tribes. No greater step toward goodwill could be taken. It will signify a major gesture toward tribal self-government and recognition of tribal sovereignty. It could serve as the start of a true working relationship between tribal and federal governments. It will be far more significant than endless rhetoric about a new relationship and benevolent government intentions.

Courts have modified but perpetuated the rule established in the Cherokee Tobacco case and underscored in the Lone Wolf determination that a congressional statute last-in-time took precedence over an Indian treaty, the terms of which were abrogated through the statute. If Congress possessed plenary power over tribal governments, then it followed that Congress could alter Indian treaties as circumstances changed. Courts continue to find that Congress has abrogated rights guaranteed in Indian treaties for specific purposes.[22] Court doctrine and congressional enactment procedures remain extremely murky as to guidelines for changing the terms of Indian treaties. There is no distinct, clear mandate that jurists can use in determining to what extent a treaty has been altered. Of the various judicial tests applied to determine whether Congress actually intended to abrogate an Indian treaty, most involve some sort of express legislative reference to the Indian treaty rights under question and a clear showing of legislative intent to modify the treaty terms.[23] Discussions over the necessity for a clear congressional statement of its intent to break an Indian treaty smack of the self-serving nineteenth-century choice of wording in the Lone Wolf pronouncement that Congress will only act when such action is "consistent with perfect good faith towards the Indians" whose treaty was unilaterally changed. Because of the sensitivity—especially in Indian religious matters—involving Indian treaty rights, the debate over treaty abrogation will only continue.

The Kiowa Indians during their history withstood military encounters, missionary pressures, agent manipulation, assimilation policies, debilitating diseases, even the malnutrition of the ration system. They could not successfully stand in the way of Anglo-American law. Law touched all aspects of their lives simultaneously and tore away their land base at the same time that it incapacitated their religious foundation. Law surrounded them and placed them in a legal straitjacket.

Lone Wolf remains today the crowning statement of federal supervisory control over colonial dependents' lives and property. It set one of the most significant Indian legal precedents and it remains the most famous declaration of federal power over tribal entities. The case provides insight into the nature of government–Indian relations as the nineteenth century turned into the twentieth. Ironically, Supreme Court justices recognized the right of Indians to sue in courts and the existence of tribes. That acknowledgment, however tenuous at first, laid the basis for steady tribal governmental resurgence beginning in the mid-twentieth century.

For the longer term, the Kiowas' case raised the persistent question: Can American society evolve means that allow tribes to remain viable, or will American institutions continue to impose assimilationist values on its wards without regard to cultural differences? Finally, the Lone Wolf case demonstrated that in spite of all of the vicissitudes the Kiowa Indians faced, the basic tribal sovereignty, cultural core, and identity survive down to the present time.

EPILOGUE

Because the Supreme Court justices specifically barred further appeals to the courts for redress of their land losses, the Kiowas returned to Congress in later years to seek legislation to aid them. Special legislation permitted their land claim to be investigated through the Court of Claims but required that the court uniquely report to Congress for a settlement.[1] The settlement effort dragged through the 1920s and 1930s. The Indians sought $3.75 per acre, while the federal government countered with an offer of 50 cents per acre. Late in 1955 the Indian Claims Commission awarded the three tribes $2,067,166 in additional compensation for the land taken under the 1900 act, amounting to about $200 per capita when it was finally paid in 1960.[2] The payment closed out for the federal government the aftermath of the lawsuit.

After eight years of service, Ethan Allen Hitchcock ended his tenure as secretary of the interior in 1907, having served the longest in that office of any secretary of the interior up to that time. Thereafter, he lived a quiet retirement existence, trying to remain active in civic and business affairs, until his passing two years later in 1909.

Lone Wolf in the years following the high tribunal's opinion continued his adjustment to the surrounding new world that had judicially engulfed him in 1903. He watched as other family members lost their allotments through sale in order to meet their health and other emergency needs, although he lived on his allotment with his family. Tribespeople continued to look to him for leadership. He joined the Elk Creek Baptist Church and to all outward appearances followed the "white man's road" until he died in 1923.

APPENDIX 1

THE TREATY OF MEDICINE LODGE
15 STAT. 581 (1867);
text from Sanger, *Statutes*, pp. 581–87

Treaty between the United States of America and the Kiowa and Comanche Tribes of Indians; Concluded October 21, 1867; Ratification advised July 25, 1868; Proclaimed August 25, 1868.

ANDREW JOHNSON,

PRESIDENT OF THE UNITED STATES OF AMERICA,

TO ALL AND SINGULAR TO WHOM THESE PRESENTS SHALL COME, GREETING:

[NOTE BY THE DEPARTMENT OF STATE.—The words of this treaty which are put in brackets with an asterisk are written in the original with black pencil, the rest of the original treaty being written with black ink.]

WHEREAS a treaty was made and concluded at the Council Camp, on Medicine Lodge creek, seventy miles south of Fort Larned, in the State of Kansas, on the twenty-first day of October, in the year of our Lord one thousand eight hundred and sixty-seven, by and between N. G. Taylor, Brevet Major-General William S. Harney, Brevet Major-General C. C. Augur, Brevet Major-General Alfred H. Terry, John B. Sanborn, Samuel F. Tappan, and J. B. Henderson, commissioners, on the part of the United States, and Satank, (Sitting Bear,) Sa-Tan-Ta, (White Bear,) Parry-Wah-Say-Men, (Ten Bears,) Tep-Pe-Navon, (Painted Lips,) and other chiefs and headmen of the Kiowa and Comanche tribes of Indians, on the part of said Indians, and duly authorized thereto by them, which treaty is in the words and figures following, to wit:—

Articles of a treaty and agreement made and entered into at the Council Camp on Medicine Lodge creek, seventy miles south of Fort Larned, in the State of Kansas, on the twenty-first day of October, one thousand eight hundred and sixty-seven, by and between the United States of America, represented by its commissioners duly appointed thereto, to wit, Nathaniel G. Taylor, William S. Harney, C. C. Augur, Alfred *S*. [H.] Terry, John B. Sanborn, Samuel F. Tappan, and J. B. Henderson, of the one part, and the confederated tribes of Kiowa and Comanche Indians, represented by their chiefs and headmen, duly authorized and empowered to act for the body of the people of said tribes, (the names of said chiefs and headmen being hereto subscribed,) of the other part, witness:

ARTICLE I. From this day forward all war between the parties to this agreement shall forever cease.

The government of the United States desires peace, and its honor is here pledged to keep it. The Indians desire peace, and they now pledge their honor to maintain it. If bad men among the whites, or among other people subject to the authority of the United States, shall commit any wrong upon the person or property of the Indians, the United States will, upon proof made to the agent and forwarded to the Commissioner of Indian Affairs at Washington city, proceed at once to cause the offender to be arrested and punished according to the laws of the United States, and also reimburse the injured person for the loss sustained.

If bad men among the Indians shall commit a wrong or depredation upon the person or property of any one, white, black or Indians, subject to the authority of the United States and at peace therewith, the tribes herein named solemnly agree that they will, on proof made to their agent and notice by him, deliver up the wrongdoer to the United States, to be tried and punished according to its laws, and in case they wilfully refuse so to do, the person injured shall be reimbursed for his loss from the annuities or other moneys due or to become due to them under this or other treaties made with the United States. And the President, on advising with the Commissioner of Indian Affairs shall prescribe such rules and regulations for ascertaining damages under the provisions of this article as, in his judgment, may be proper; but no such damages shall be adjusted and paid until thoroughly examined and passed upon by the Commissioner of Indian Affairs and the Secretary of the Interior; and no one sustaining loss, while violating or because of his violating, the provisions of this treaty of the laws of the United States, shall be reimbursed therefor.

ARTICLE II. The United States agrees that [the*] following district of country, to wit: commencing at a point where the Washita river crosses the 98th meridian, west from Greenwich; thence up the Washita river, in the middle of the main channel thereof, to a point thirty miles, by river, west of Fort Cobb, as now established; thence, due west to the north fork of Red river, provided said line strikes said river east of the one hundredth meridian of west longitude; if not, then only to said meridian line, and thence south, on said meridian line, to the said north fork of Red river; thence down said north fork, in the middle of the main channel thereof, from the point where it may be first intersected by the lines above described, to the main Red river; thence down said river, in the middle of the main channel thereof to its intersection with the ninety-eighth meridian of longitude west from Greenwich; thence north, on said meridian line, to the place of beginning, shall be and the same is hereby set apart for the absolute and undisturbed use and occupation of the tribes herein named, and for such other friendly tribes or individual Indians, as, from time to time, they may be willing [with the consent of the United States*] to admit among them; and the United States now solemnly agrees that no persons except those herein authorized so to do and except such officers, agents, and employés of the government as may be authorized to enter upon Indian reservation in discharge of duties enjoined by law, shall ever be permitted to pass over, settle upon, or reside in the territory described in this article, or in such territory as may be added to this reservation, for the use of said Indians.

ARTICLE III. If it should appear from actual survey or other satisfactory examination of said tract of land, that it contains less than one hundred and sixty acres of tillable land, for each person, who at the time may be authorized to reside on it under the provisions of this treaty, and a very considerable number of such persons shall be disposed to commence cultivating the soil as farmers, the United States agrees to set apart for the use of said Indians, as herein provided, such additional quantity of arable land adjoining to said reservation, or as near the same as it can be obtained, as may be required to provide the necessary amount.

ARTICLE IV. The United States agrees at its own proper expense to construct at some place, near the centre of said reservation, where timber and water may be convenient, the following buildings, to wit: A warehouse or store-room for the use of the agent, in storing goods belonging to the Indians, to cost not exceeding fifteen hundred dollars; an agency building for the residence of the agent, to cost not exceeding three thousand dollars; a residence for the physician, to cost not more than three thousand dollars; and five other buildings, for a carpenter, farmer, blacksmith, miller, and engineer, each to cost not exceeding two thousand dollars; also a school-house or mission building, so soon as a sufficient number of children can be induced by the agent to attend school, which shall not cost exceeding five thousand dollars.

The United States agrees further to cause to be erected on said reservation, near the other buildings herein authorized, a good steam circular saw mill, with a grist mill and shingle machine attached; the same to cost not exceeding eight thousand dollars.

ARTICLE V. The United States agrees that the agent for the said Indians in the future shall make his home at the agency building; that he shall reside among them, and keep an office open at all times, for the purpose of prompt and diligent inquiry into such matters of complaint by and against the Indians as may be presented for investigation under the provisions of their treaty stipulations, as also for the faithful discharge of other duties enjoined on him by law. In all cases of depredation on person or property, he shall cause the evidence to be taken in writing and forwarded, together with his findings to the Commissioner of Indian Affairs, whose decision, subject to the revision of the Secretary of the Interior, shall be binding on the parties to this treaty.

ARTICLE VI. If any individual belonging to said tribes of Indians, or legally incorporated with them, being the head of a family, shall desire to commence farming, he shall have the privilege to select, in the presence and with the assistance of the agent then in charge, a tract of land within said reservation, not exceeding three hundred and twenty acres in extent, which tract, when so selected, certified, and recorded in the "Land Book" as herein directed, shall cease to be held in common, but the same may be occupied and held in the exclusive possession of the person selecting it, and of his family so long as he or they may continue to cultivate it. Any person over eighteen years of age, not being the head of a family, may in like manner select and cause to be certified to him or her, for purposes of cultivation, a quantity of land not exceeding eighty acres in extent, and thereupon, be entitled to the exclusive possession of the same as above directed. For each tract of land so selected, a certificate, containing a description thereof and the name of the person selecting it, with a certificate indorsed thereon that the same has been recorded, shall be delivered to the party entitled to it, by the agent, after the same shall have been recorded by him in a book to be kept in his office, subject to inspection, which said book shall be known as the "Kiowa and Comanche Land Book." The President may, at any time, order a survey of the reservation, and, when so surveyed, Congress shall provide for protecting the rights of settlers, in their improvements, and may fix the character of the title held by each. The United States may pass such laws, on the subject of alienation and descent of property and on all subjects connected with the government of the said Indians on said reservations, and the internal police thereof, as may be thought proper.

ARTICLE VII. In order to insure the civilization of the tribes, entering into this treaty, the necessity of education is admitted, especially by such of them as are or may be settled on said agricultural reservations; and they therefore pledge themselves to compel their children, male and female, between the ages of six and sixteen years, to attend school; and it is hereby made the duty of the agent for said Indians to see that this stipulation is strictly complied with; and the United States agrees that for every thirty children between said ages, who can be induced or compelled to attend school, a house shall be provided, and a teacher, competent to teach the elementary branches of an English education, shall be furnished, who will reside among said Indians and faithfully discharge his or her duties as a teacher. The provisions of this article to continue for not less than twenty years.

ARTICLE VIII. When the head of a family or lodge shall have selected lands and received his certificate as above directed, and the agent shall be satisfied that he intends in good faith to commence cultivating the soil for a living, he shall be entitled to receive seeds and agricultural implements for the first year not exceeding in value one hundred dollars, and for each succeeding year he shall continue to farm for a period of three years more, he shall be entitled to receive seeds and implements as aforesaid not exceeding in value twenty-five dollars. And it is further stipulated that such persons as commence farming shall receive instruction from the farmer herein provided for, and whenever more than one hundred persons shall enter upon the cultivation of the soil a second blacksmith shall be provided, together with such iron, steel, and other material, as may be needed.

ARTICLE IX. At any time after ten years from the making of this treaty the United States shall have the privilege of withdrawing the physician, farmer, blacksmiths, carpenter, engineer, and miller herein provided for; but, in case of such withdrawal, an additional sum thereafter of ten thousand dollars per annum shall be devoted to the education of said Indians, and the Commissioner of Indian Affairs shall, upon careful inquiry into the condition of said Indians, make such rules and regulations for the expenditure of said sum as will best promote the educational and moral improvement of said tribes.

ARTICLE X. In lieu of all sums of money or other annuities provided to be paid to the Indians, herein named, under the treaty of October eighteenth, one thousand eight hundred and sixty-five, made at the mouth of the "Little Arkansas," and under all treaties made previous thereto, the United States agrees to deliver at the agency-house on the reservation herein named, on the fifteenth day of October of each year, for thirty years the following articles, to wit:—

For each male person over fourteen years of age, a suit of good substantial woollen clothing, consisting of coat, pantaloons, flannel shirt, hat, and a pair of home-made socks. For each female over twelve years of age, a flannel skirt, or the goods necessary to make it, a pair of woollen hose, *and* twelve yards of calico, and twelve yards of "domestic."

For the boys and girls under the ages named, such flannel and cotton goods as may be needed, to make each a suit as aforesaid, together with a pair of woolen hose for each; and in order that the Commissioner of Indian Affairs may be able to estimate properly for the articles herein named, it shall be the duty of the agent, each year, to forward him a full and exact census of the Indians on which the estimates from year to year can be based; and, in addition to the clothing herein named, the sum of twenty-five thousand dollars shall be annually appropriated for a period of thirty years, to be used by the Secretary of the Interior in the purchase of such articles, upon the recommendation of the Commissioner of Indian Affairs, as from time to time the condition and necessities of the Indians may indicate to be proper; and if at any time within the thirty years it shall appear that the amount of money needed for clothing under this article can be appropriated to better uses for the tribes herein named, Congress may by law change the appropriation to other purposes, but in no event shall the amount of this appropriation be withdrawn or discontinued for the period named; and the President shall, annually, detail an officer of the army to be present and attest the delivery of all the goods herein named to the Indians, and he shall inspect and report on the quantity and quality of the goods and the manner of their delivery.

ARTICLE XI. In consideration of the advantages and benefits conferred by this treaty and the many pledges of friendship by the United States, the tribes who are parties to this agreement hereby stipulate that they will relinquish all right to occupy permanently the territory outside of their reservation, as herein defined, but they yet reserve the right to hunt on any lands south of the Arkansas [river,*] so long as the buffalo may range thereon in such numbers as to justify the chase, [and no white settlements shall be permitted on any part of the lands contained in the old reservation as defined by the treaty made between the United States and the Cheyenne, Arapahoe, and Apache tribes of Indians at the mouth of the Little Arkansas, under date of October fourteenth, one thousand eight hundred and sixty-five, within three years from this date;*] and they, [the said tribes,*] further expressly agree—

1st. That they will withdraw all opposition to the construction of the railroad now being built on the Smoky Hill river, whether it be built to Colorado or New Mexico.

2d. That they will permit the peaceable construction of any railroad not passing over their reservation as herein defined.

3d. That they will not attack any persons at home, nor travelling, nor molest or disturb any wagon-trains, coaches, mules, or cattle belonging to the people of the United States, or to persons friendly therewith.

4th They will never capture or carry off from the settlements white women or children.

5th. They will never kill nor scalp white men nor attempt to do them harm.

6th. They withdraw all pretence of opposition to the construction of the railroad now being built along the Platte river and westward to the Pacific ocean; and they will not, in future, object to the construction of railroads, wagon roads, mail stations, or other works of utility or necessity which may be ordered or permitted by the laws of the United States. But should such roads or other works be constructed on the lands of their reservation, the government will pay the tribes whatever amount of damage may be assessed by three disinterested commissioners, to be appointed by the President for that purpose; one of said commissioners to be a chief or headman of the tribes.

7th. They agree to withdraw all opposition to the military posts now established in the western territories.

ARTICLE XII. No treaty for the cession of any portion or part of the reservation herein described, which may be held in common, shall be of any validity or force as against the said Indians, unless executed and signed by at least three fourths of all the adult male Indians occupying the same, and no cession by the tribe shall be understood or construed in such manner as to deprive, without his consent, any individual member of the tribe of his rights to any tract of land selected by him as provided in Article *III.* [VI.] of this treaty.

ARTICLE XIII. The Indian agent, in employing a farmer, blacksmith, miller, and other employés herein provided for, qualifications being equal, shall give the preference to Indians.

ARTICLE XIV. The United States hereby agrees to furnish annually to the Indians the physician, teachers, carpenter, miller, engineer, farmer, and blacksmiths, as herein contemplated, and that such appropriations shall be made from time to time, on the estimates of the Secretary of the Interior, as will be sufficient to employ such persons.

ARTICLE XV. It is agreed that the sum of seven hundred and fifty dollars be appropriated for the purpose of building a dwelling-house on the reservation for "Tosh-e-wa," (or the Silver Brooch,) the Comanche chief who has already commenced farming on the said reservation. And the sum of five hundred dollars annually, for three years from date, shall be expended in presents to the ten persons of said tribes who in the judgment of the agent may grow the most valuable crops for the period named.

ARTICLE XVI. The tribes herein named agree, when the agency house and other buildings shall be constructed on the reservation named, they will make said reservation their permanent home and they will make no permanent settlement elsewhere, but they shall have the right to hunt on the lands south of the Arkansas river, formerly called theirs, in the same manner, subject to the modifications named in this treaty, as agreed on by the treaty of the Little Arkansas, concluded the eighteenth day of October, one thousand eight hundred and sixty-five.

In testimony of which, we have hereunto set our hands and seals on the day and year aforesaid.

N. G. TAYLOR,
President of Indian Com'n.

WM. S. HARNEY,
Bvt. Majr. Gen.

C. C. AUGUR,
Bvt. Majr. Gen.

ALFRED H. TERRY,
Brig. and Bvt. Majr. Gen.

JOHN B. SANBORN,
SAMUEL F. TAPPEN,
J. B. HENDERSON.

Attest: ASHTON S. H. WHITE,

Secretary.

Kioways.

SATANK, or Sitting Bear,	his x mark.
SA-TAN-TA, or White Bear,	his x mark.
WA-TOH-KONK, or Black Eagle,	his x mark.
TON-A-EN-KO, or Kicking Eagle,	his x mark.
FISH-E-MORE, or Stinking Saddle,	his x mark.
MA-YE-TIN, or Woman's Heart,	his x mark.
SA-TIM-GEAR, or Stumbling Bear,	his x mark.
SIT-PAR-GA, or One Bear,	his x mark.
CORBEAU, or The Crow,	his x mark.
SA-TA-MORE, or Bear Lying Down.	

Comanches.

PARRY-WAH-SAY-MEN, or Ten Bears,	his x mark.
TEP-PE-NAVON, or Painted Lips,	his x mark.
TO-SA-IN, or Silver Brooch,	his x mark.
CEAR-CHI-NEKA, or Standing Feather,	his x mark.
HO-WE-AR, or Gap in the Woods,	his x mark.
TIR-HA-YAH-GUAHIP, or Horse's Back,	his x mark.
ES-A-NANACA, or Wolf's Name,	his x mark.
AH-TE-ES-TA, or Little Horn,	his x mark.
POOH-YAH-TO-YEH-BE, or Iron Mountain,	his x mark.

SAD-DY-YO, or Dog Fat,   his x mark.

Attest:

    JAS. A. HARDIE,
        Inspector Genl. U.S. Army.
    SAM'L S. SMOOT,
        U. S. Surveyor.
    PHILIP MCCUSKER,
        Interpreter.
    J. H. LEAVENWORTH,
        U. S. In. Agt.
    THOS. MURPHY,
        Supt. Ind. Affairs.
    HENRY STANLEY,
        Correspondent.
    A. A. TAYLOR,
        Assistant Secretary.
    WM. FAYEL,
        Correspondent.
    JAMES O. TAYLOR,
        Artist.
    GEO B. WILLIS,
        Phonographer.
    C. W. WHITRAKER,
        Trader

APPENDIX 2

Senate Executive Doc. No. 17, 52nd Cong., 2d Sess., Serial Set No. 3055, vol. 1, 4 January 1893, pp. 11–16:

Articles of agreement made and entered into at Fort Sill, in the Indian Territory, on the ——— ———, by and between David H. Jerome, Alfred M. Wilson, and Warren G. Sayre, Commissioners on the part of the United States, and the Comanche, Kiowa, and Apache tribes of Indians, in the Indian Territory.

ARTICLE I.

Subject to the allotment of land in severalty to the individual members of the Comanche, Kiowa, and Apache tribes of Indians in the Indian Territory, as hereinafter provided for, and subject to the conditions hereinafter imposed, and for the considerations hereinafter mentioned, the said Comanche, Kiowa, and Apache Indians hereby cede, convey, transfer, relinquish, and surrender, forever and absolutely, without any reservation whatever, express or implied, all their claim, title, and interest, of every kind and character, in and to the lands embraced in the following described tract of country in the Indian Territory, to wit: Commencing at a point where the Washita River crosses the ninety-eighth meridian west from Greenwich, thence up the Washita River, in the middle of the main channel thereof, to a point thirty miles, by river, west of Fort Cobb, as now established; thence due west to the north fork of Red River, provided said line strikes said river east of the one-hundredth meridian of west longitude; if not, then only to said meridian line, and thence due south, on said meridian line, to the said north fork of Red River; thence down said north fork, in the middle of the main channel thereof, from the point where it may be first intersected by the lines above described, to the main Red River; thence down said Red River, in the middle of main channel thereof, to its intersection with the ninety-eighth meridian of longitude west from Greenwich; thence north, on said meridian line, to the place of beginning.

ARTICLE II.

Out of the lands ceded, conveyed, transferred, relinquished and surrendered by Article I hereof, and in part consideration for the cession thereof, it is agreed by the United States that each member of said Comanche, Kiowa, and Apache tribes of Indians over the age of eighteen (18) years shall have the right to select for himself or herself one hundred and sixty (160) acres of land to be held and owned in severalty, to conform to the legal surveys in boundary; and that the father, or, if he be dead, the mother, if members of either of said tribes of Indians, shall have the right to select a like amount of land for each of his or her children under the age of eighteen (18) years; and that the Commissioner of Indian Affairs, or some one by him appointed for the purpose, shall select a like amount of land for each orphan-child belonging to either of said tribes under the age of eighteen (18) years.

ARTICLE III.

It is further agreed that the land in said reservation shall be classed as grain-growing and grazing land; and in making selection of lands to be allotted in severalty as aforesaid, each and every Indian, herein provided for, shall be required to take at least one-half in area, of his or her allotments, of grazing land. It is hereby further expressly agreed that no person shall have the right to make his or her selection of land in any part of said reservation that is now used or occupied for military, agency, school, school farm, religious or other public uses, or in sections sixteen (16) and thirty-six (36) in each Congressional Township; except in cases where any Comanche, Kiowa or Apache Indian has heretofore made improvements upon, and now uses and occupies a part of said sections sixteen (16) and thirty-six (36), such Indian may make his or her selection within the boundaries so prescribed so as to include his or her improvements; it is further agreed that wherever in said reservation any Indian, entitled to take lands in severalty hereunder, has made improvements, and now uses and occupies the land embracing such improvements, such Indian shall have the undisputed right to make his or her selection within the area above provided for allotments, so as to include his or her said improvements.

It is further agreed that said sections sixteen (16) and thirty-six (36) in each Congressional township in said reservation, shall not become subject to homestead entry, but shall be held by the United States and finally sold for public-school purposes. It is hereby further agreed that wherever in said reservation any religious society or other organization is now occupying any portion of said reservation for religious or educational work among the Indians, the land so occupied may be allotted and confirmed to such society or organization, not, however, to exceed one hundred and sixty (160) acres of land to any one society or organization, so long as the same shall be so occupied and used, and such land shall not be subject to homestead entry.

ARTICLE IV.

All allottments hereunder shall be selected within ninety days from the ratification of this agreement by the Congress of the United States, provided the Secretary of the Interior, in his discretion, may extend the time for making such selection; and should any Indian entitled to allotments hereunder fail or refuse to make his or her selection of land in that time, then the allotting agent in charge of the work of making such allotments, shall, within the next thirty (30) days after said time, make allotments to such Indians, which shall have the same force and effect as if the selection were made by the Indian.

ARTICLE V.

When said allotments of land shall have been selected and taken as aforesaid, and approved by the Secretary of the Interior, the titles thereto shall be held in trust for the allottees, respectively, for the period of twenty-five (25) years, in the time and manner and to the extent provided for in the act of Congress, entitled, "An act to provide for the allotment of land in severalty to Indians on the various reservations, and to extend the protection of the laws of the United States and Territories over the Indians, and for other purposes." Approved February 8, 1887. And an act amendatory thereof, approved February 28, 1891.

And at the expiration of the said period of twenty-five (25) years the titles thereto shall be conveyed in fee simple to the allottees, or their heirs, free from all incumbrances.

ARTICLE VI.

As a further and only additional consideration for the cession of territory and relinquishment of title, claim, and interest in and to the lands as aforesaid, the United States agrees to pay to the Comanche, Kiowa and Apache tribes of Indians, in the Indian Territory, the sum of two million ($2,000,000) dollars, as follows: Two hundred thousand ($200,000) dollars in cash, to be distributed per capita, among the members of said tribes within one hundred and twenty (120) days after this agreement shall be ratified by the Congress of the United States; two hundred thousand ($200,000) dollars to be paid out to said Indians under the direction of the Secretary of the Interior in one year after said first payment, and one hundred thousand ($100,000) dollars in the same manner in one year from date of second payment, and the remaining one million and five hundred thousand ($1,500,000) dollars to be retained in the Treasury of the United States, placed to the credit of said Indians, and while so retained, to draw interest at the rate of five per centum per annum, to be paid to the said Indians per capita annually.

Nothing herein contained shall be held to affect in any way any annuities due said Indians under existing laws, agreements, or treaties.

ARTICLE VIII.

It is further agreed that wherever in said reservation any member of any of the tribes of said Indians has, in pursuance of any laws or under any rules or regulations of the Interior Department taken an allotment, such allotment, at the option of the allottee, shall be confirmed and governed by all the conditions attached to allotments taken under this agreement.

ARTICLE IX.

It is further agreed that any and all leases, made in pursuance of the laws of the United States, of any part of said reservation, which may be in force at the time of the ratification, by Congress, of this agreement, shall remain in force the same as if this agreement had not been made.

ARTICLE X.

It is further agreed that the following-named persons, not members by blood of either of said tribes, but who have married into one of the tribes, to wit, Mabel R. Given, Thomas F. Woodward, William Wyatt, Kiowa Dutch, John Nestill, James N. Jones, Christian Ke-oh-tah, Edward L. Clark, George Conover, William Dietrick, Ben Roach, Lewis Bentz, Abilene, James Gardloupe, John Sanchez, the wife of Boone Chandler (whose given name is unknown), Emmit Cox, and Horace P. Jones, shall each be entitled to all the benefits of land and money conferred by this agreement, the same as if members by blood of one of said tribes; and that Emsy S. Smith, David Grantham, Zonee Adams, John T. Hill, J. J. Methvin, H. L. Scott, and George D. Day, friends of said Indians, who have rendered to said Indians valuable services, shall each be entitled to all the benefits, in land only, conferred under this agreement, the same as if members of said tribes.

ARTICLE XI.

This agreement shall be effective only when ratified by the Congress of the United States.

In witness whereof, we have hereunto set our hands, this sixth day of October, A. D. 1892.

DAVID H. JEROME,
ALFRED M. WILSON,
WARREN G. SAYRE,
Commissioners on the part of the United States.

1. Quanah Parker, his mark.
2. White man, his mark.
3. Lone Wolf, his mark.
4. Tabe manaka, his mark.
5. Tan-han, his mark.
6. Tabby yetchy, his mark.
7. Kom-alty, his mark.
8. Cheevers, his mark.
9. Big Tree, his mark.
10. White Wolf, his mark.
11. Joshua Given.
12. Howeah, his mark.
13. Thos. F. Wooderd.
14. Mer to hovet, his mark.
15. Da-va-ko, his mark.
16. White Eagle, his mark.
17. Attockney, his mark.
18. Tah pony, his mark.
19. Jack Mullen.
20. Jack Permamsu, his mark.
21. Po-ow-whe, his mark.
22. Ko ma cheet, his mark.
23. Tabby to savit, his mark.
24. Po hock su cut, his mark.
25. Pah-woon-ard, his mark.
26. Tah ko woonard, his mark.
27. Ne nock a vi, his mark.
28. Cha-wath-lana, his mark.
29. Lloyd Kahovorah.
30. Po ha dooah, his mark.
31. Nocktooah.
32. Red Elk, his mark.
33. Ko-mah, his mark.
34. Apache John, his mark.
35. E-sn-o-ha pith, his mark.
36. Pi-hi-pe-op, his mark.
37. Soon-tay, his mark.
38. Nan no yo ro, his mark.
39. Kos cho quitta, his mark.
40. Howard Chawhip.
41. Tis chy coddy, his mark.
42. Pies chy, his mark.
43. Woodah peop, his mark.
44. Ka-ta-po-ny, his mark.
45. Tabby Coots, his mark.
46. Tah doo a vis chy, his mark.
47. E sa doo ah, his mark.
48. O tis chy, his mark.
49. Pe ki yo va, his mark.
50. Per too ah vo ne qua, his mark.
51. Shoddy o coom, his mark.
52. Ten a ver ka, his mark.
53. Tah tay with ke ka, his mark.
54. Nappy wat, his mark.
55. Hos cho to sa vit, his mark.
56. [S]an-ka-do-ta, his mark.[1]
57. Pe ah ko do ke, his mark.
58. Po ha vox su, his mark.
59. E sa ta quon, his mark.
60. No naddy mok, his mark.
61. Ho vah, his mark.
62. Tar cy up, his mark.
63. Nan oats, his mark.
64. Wa se ke yah, his mark.
65. O ha wau di, his mark.
66. Woox see, his mark.
67. Chok po ya, his mark.
68. Ho a kog p[i]t ty, his mark.
69. Chas se nah, his mark.
70. Chee mi meah, his mark.
71. Wah hah sy, his mark.
72. Poh ho, his mark.
73. Chee woon ah, his mark.
74. Yah po yah, his mark.
75. Nah nah vite, his mark.
76. Tatcho noek i vit, his mark.

77. Mo tah, his mark.
78. Ka hin a watch it, his mark.
79. Mo so yo, his mark.
80. Tice a ki, his mark.
81. Ne hi, his mark.
82. Ate te wuth ta quon, his mark.
83. Tah ko ney, his mark.
84. Saw with ka, his mark.
85. To sa ma reah, his mark.
86. Wer wau ney, his mark.
87. Ca vey yo, his mark.
88. Nin cy, his mark.
89. Kiowa yo ko, his mark.
90. Wins chop, his mark.
91. Ho vas reth ka, his mark.
92. Acy naw, his mark.
93. Ni ye f per, his mark.
94. Cho sa qua, his mark.
95. Ah dose, his mark.
96. Ate te mi chi, his mark.
97. Tab bo her, his mark.
98. Pah ke kum ma, his mark.
99. To wak ney, his mark.
100. No yer tam a wat, his mark.
101. Pah-da-po-ny, his mark.
102. Nah watch, his mark.
103. Ah des sy, his mark.
104. Pen na teth ka, his mark.
105. Acy kau na, his mark.
106. Ko cy mood wa, his mark.
107. Perk a qua na, his mark.
108. Pueblo, his mark.
109. Nim cy, his mark.
110. Tof pah, his mark.
111. Yacky poby, his mark.
112. To cas, his mark.
113. Peach an nah, his mark.
114. Wa sis chy, his mark.
115. Boaf py bit ty, his mark.
116. Chah tammy, his mark.
117. Po e mak e ah, his mark.
118. O dy pe ah, his mark.
119. Poh ko, his mark.
120. Weath chan ne ka, his mark.
121. Nah da yeh ka, his mark.
122. Yoke s[u] wy, his mark.
123. Wy yeck we, his mark.

124. Wo quay, his mark.
125. Wer whe, his mark.
126. Tis sy wa woonah, his mark.
127. To sa woonah, his mark.
128. I-nee, his mark.
129. Po ha pat cho ka, his mark.
130. Toth ko yan, his mark.
131. Ti he vek we, his mark.
132. Kah den na, his mark.
133. Tis sy qua va, his mark.
134. To a nef per, his mark.
135. Frank Mo e ta, his mark.
136. Wah ah kiny, his mark.
137. Pa nah, his mark.
138. Che su wy, his mark.
139. Mo neth-tath che, his mark.
140. Wah hah da ka, his mark.
141. Ah cut, his mark.
142. Pom mo chi, his mark.
143. Chappey, his mark.
144. Wum ma vicheah, his mark.
145. Che yeck we, his mark.
146. Titchy wy, his mark.
147. Se voy ya, his mark.
148. Per ha de sof py, his mark.
149. Maw wat, his mark.
150. To pau, his mark.
151. Pas sah, his mark.
152. Ho a wy, his mark.
153. Ho ah ke mah, his mark.
154. Oh-ty, his mark.
155. Sat-teo, his mark.
156. Moo da waud, his mark.
157. Ti-nema-wat, his mark.
158. Kah kas Sy, his mark.
159. Ah-cey, his mark.
160. Coas-cho-ek-i-vit, his mark.
161. E-sa-to-ho-vit, his mark.
162. Kas ses seah, his mark.
163. Black Horse, his mark.
164. Henry Wallace, his mark.
165. Woos ah whe, his mark.
166. Cha na po ha cut, his mark.
167. Quer dy, his mark.
168. Nah dof deah, his mark.
169. No yo cy, his mark.
170. Saw pit ty, his mark.

171. Pe he teth ka, his mark.
172. Quas se che ky, his mark.
173. Pat cho ko pado ah, his mark.
174. Pit chu e na, his mark.
175. Tah doo nif pa, his mark.
176. Ko he yah, his mark.
177. Mah tso, his mark.
178. Be-ho, his mark.
179. To nar cy, his mark.
180. Quas se yah, his mark.
181. Taum of tooah, his mark.
182. Mer de ky, his mark.
183. Hau no vich, his mark.
184. We yah po yah, his mark.
185. Weath tipe, his mark.
186. Beaf pe wer dy, his mark.
187. Ek i moo di wau, his mark.
188. Take wa ker, his mark.
189. Chicken, his mark.
190. Peas san itht, his mark.
191. At ta wyef per, his mark.
192. Yacky an ny, his mark.
193. Tath chah chah, his mark.
194. Henry Pratt, his mark.
195. Tarcy a poke a dooah, his mark.
196. Woof suka wa, his mark.
197. Oat te poby, his mark.
198. Croos, his mark.
199. Peah cose, his mark.
200. Wah kah quah, his mark.
201. Pas che pap py, his mark.
202. Mo be tarcy, his mark.
203. Ach havit, his mark.
204. Wah bof py, his mark.
205. Wah hah to nah, his mark.
206. E sa toux sa, his mark.
207. Chah ner bitty, his mark.
208. Chah ta ne yeck wy, his mark.
209. Way sef py, his mark.
210. Black Otter, his mark.
211. Ur yay, his mark.
212. Ick a bitty, his mark.
213. Po tah da, his mark.
214. Eck i vit, his mark.
215. Wah woonard, his mark.
216. Tah su dy, his mark.
217. Tay yef per, his mark.
218. Che ko vi, his mark.
219. To wer, his mark.
220. Nah her, his mark.
221. Tim ma wuth ky, his mark.
222. Yan ny ve too ah, his mark.
223. Pah ka wat, his mark.
224. Nah waux sy, his mark.
225. Tah ka ver, his mark.
226. Ate te wuth ta qua, his mark.
227. On hah ty, his mark.
228. Too nev ah, his mark.
229. Big Kiowa, his mark.
230. Yo ko rarce, his mark.
231. Moth tem my, his mark.
232. Titchy mi chi, his mark.
233. Chah tey, his mark.
234. Maw-wat, his mark.
235. Mo too doo ah, his mark.
236. Tabby kin ny, his mark.
237. Po yhat ty, his mark.
238. Chap poo, his mark.
239. Pah kar cy, his mark.
240. Nerm a doth ko, his mark.
241. Pav vo neithk, his mark.
242. Tah ve yah, his mark.
243. Bo ne ty, his mark.
244. Ki her by, his mark.
245. Ach hav vy, his mark.
246. He vah, his mark.
247. Kar no, his mark.
248. Par riea quit top, his mark.
249. Cho nip, his mark.
250. You nia cut, his mark.
251. Chee mard ney, his mark.
252. Mi he su ah, his mark.
253. Nah dar cy, his mark.
254. Pat chay nah, his mark.
255. Kof ty, his mark.
256. Ti mer, his mark.
257. Nah kee, his mark.
258. Pe voy, his mark.
259. Ti chan ner whe, his mark.
260. Hen ner cy, his mark.
261. Tom Black Star, his mark.
262. Too ney, his mark.
263. Tey ko ah, his mark.
264. Cat, his mark.

265. Tip py con ny, his mark.
266. Wook we ah, his mark.
267. Kordy pony, his mark.
268. Ay to, his mark.
269. Pigh ty, his mark.
270. Ki-youe, his mark.
271. Chi bit ty, his mark.
272. Big Cow, his mark.
273. Su day, his mark.
274. Tah hah waud, his mark.
275. Nin nah ko, his mark.
276. Pah die, his mark.
277. Nam a qua yu, his mark.
278. Chah tarcy, his mark.
279. Tah kah per, his mark.
280. Poey wat, his mark.
281. Mo cho rook ey, his mark.
282. Pah dey, his mark.
283. E-tau vich, his mark.
284. Ten ne quer, his mark.
285. Nah vit se ah, his mark.
286. Tah vo k[o], his mark.
287. Nay he mah, his mark.
288. Quoie an one, his mark.
289. Sim me no, his mark.
290. Ek i yo vey, his mark.
291. Nan-or-de-ney, his mark
292. Ko we nord (No. 1), his mark.
293. Saw woody qua, his mark.
294. Ko we nord (No. 2), his mark.
295. Oat ty qua he, his mark.
296. Me sa [r]a, his mark.
297. Ek-her by, his mark.
298. Tis so yo, his mark.
299. George Maddox, his mark.
300. John Kiben, his mark.
301. Mo be ko chy, his mark.
302. Tah wau ka, his mark.
303. I-see-o, his mark.
304. Lucius Aitsau, his mark.
305. Hon[a]meahtah, his mark.
306. Taba-hortly, his mark.
307. Dow-a-ton, his mark.
308. George Birzzle, his mark.
309. George Ross, his mark.
310. To-es-sit, his mark.
311. We-he, his mark.
312. Kicking Bird, his mark.
313. Tso-da-ha, his mark.
314. Pearly Whitmore, his mark.
315. Pahsita, same as 301.
315. I-za-che, his mark.
316. Nas-cha-na-ni, his mark.
317. E-ah-pah, his mark.
318. Tone-moh, his mark.
319. Ee-ho-tah, his mark.
320. Sok-kome, his mark.
321. Samuel Ahatone, his mark.
322. Uk an ni chappy, his mark.
323. Ko youah, his mark.
324. Peah nah vo nit, his mark.
325. Nah say que, his mark.
326. No-yo-van, his mark.
327. Wau a dam ah, his mark.
328. Pah cod dy, his mark.
329. Watch su ah, his mark.
330. Rudolph Fisher, his mark.
331. Moby-er, his mark.
332. Be ney ro, his mark.
333. Pe vo, his mark.
334. Wook yey, his mark.
335. Hoas cho, his mark.
336. Tay ten ne quer, his mark.
337. Wan ney, his mark.
338. Pos sa po ney, his mark.
339. Pi e dy, his mark.
340. Meah ker, his mark.
341. Ech hoas cho, his mark.
342. High tos cha, his mark.
343. Cap pio, his mark.
344. Tah pau ka, his mark.
345. An-to nio, his mark.
346. Moaf pey, his mark.
347. Wah bo yah, his mark.
348. Tissy ro quoth ty, his mark.
349. Ch a ve, his mark.
350. Nachon ko, his mark.
351. James Gardloupe, his mark.
352. Wah che kah, his mark.
353. Tay hue, his mark.
354. Yellow Fish, his mark.
355. Hah ney, his mark.

356. Wer yeck we, his mark.
357. Tommie, his mark.
358. Ah-ko, his mark.
359. Pas chy ne ko, his mark.
360. Chay-chay-goots, his mark.
361. Apache Jime, his mark.
362. Bah-sah-e, his mark.
363. Tanar-th-la, his mark.
364. Pah-be, his mark.
365. Tseel-tsi-sah, his mark.
366. Klin ko-le, his mark.
367. Teu-ho, his mark.
368. Nah-coos-see, his mark.
369. Arche laco, his mark.
370. Di-ace-hut-ley, his mark.
371. Tso-tad-dle, his mark.
372. Bah-ah-at-lah, his mark.
373. Tah-sah-ah-che, his mark.
374. Sephe[u], his mark.
375. Bo yo, his mark.
376. Lu-tah, his mark.
377. Bit-see-ty, his mark.
378. George Cha-yet-chey, his mark.
379. Kle-rate-chal-ray, his mark.
380. Koo-yase-tsley, his mark.
381. Cha-lit-coos-sah, his mark.
382. Mulke-hay, his mark.
383. Zah-tah, his mark.
384. [K]lose ta[l]e-to-tschy, his mark.
385. Kah-ra-so, his mark.
386. Acy per my, his mark.
387. Pe way noth ky, his mark.
388. Mah ke do, his mark.
389. Ni vey quey yu, his mark.
390. Commanche George, his mark.
391. Tabby-to-hovit, his mark.
392. To wock ney, his mark.
393. Acey nap, his mark.
394. Charles Oit-toit, his mark.
395. Below Cozad.
396. Paul C. Zoto[m].
397. John D. Jackson.
398. E-om-ty, his mark.
399. Klah sit-te, his mark.
400. Kolth-tah-ray, his mark.
401. Eck-a-roo-ah-nip-ah, his mark.
402. John Sanches, his mark.
403. Ta watchy woof pi, his mark.
404. Pah do ko, his mark.
405. Quio-hort-ty, his mark.
406. Sin-ke-ah-goop-ty, his mark.
407. Solomon Chandler.
408. Boone Chandler.
409. Andy Conover.
410. George Chandler.
411. Sa-ve-oah, his mark.
412. A-chil-tah, his mark.
413. Di-ace-ley, his mark.
414. Mi-ziz-zoon-dy, his mark.
415. Mo-chah, his mark.
416. Ann-ko-ty, his mark.
417. Tsing-ton-keah, his mark.
418. Albert Cat, his mark.
419. Watchy mam suk awa, his mark.
420. Jimmie Quor-tone, his mark.
421. Andres Martinez.
422. Hank Nelson.
423. Jay.
424. Kah [r]ah tis ziz, his mark.
425. Kaun dy, his mark.
426. Wah sah thlan-e, his mark.
427. Big Whip, his mark.
428. Host Chil ty, his mark.
429. Chaun ty, his mark.
430. Tay vav nah, his mark.
431. Pers chy, his mark.
432. High-we-ni, his mark.
433. Aum a cof pop, his mark.
434. William Tivis.
435. Woodah hah by, his mark.
436. Nan nap dey, his mark.
437. Woof to vah, his mark.
438. Tof po ny, his mark.
439. Shau shau ny, his mark.
440. Frank Given, his mark.
441. Mah-se-ta, his mark.
442. To-ah-pe-na, his mark.
443. Tom-mo-ra-re, his mark.
444. Hern-na-hasy, his mark.
445. Ant oine Martinez, his mark.
446. Eld[mo] Melano, his mark.
447. Mi he co by, his mark.

448. James Ahatone, his mark.
449. Yellow Hair, his mark.
450. Charle Zoto[m], his mark.
451. Ah-chil-ty, his mark.
452. Fele-ha, his mark.

453. Pa-poose, his mark.
454. Ba-e-ce-a, his mark.
455. Tone-gai-goudle-ty, his mark.
456. Eck-a-wah-da, his mark.

LONE WOLF V. HITCHCOCK.

187 U.S. 553

Appeal from the Court of Appeals of the District of Columbia.
No. 275. Argued October 23, 1902.—Decided January 5, 1903.

The provisions in article 12 of the Medicine Lodge treaty of 1867 with the Kiowa and Comanche Indians to the effect that no treaty for the cession of any part of the reservation therein described, which may be held in common, shall be of any force or validity as against the Indians unless executed and signed by at least three fourths of all the adult male Indians occupying the same, cannot be adjudged to materially limit and qualify the controlling authority of Congress in respect to the care and protection of the Indians and to deprive Congress, in a possible emergency, when the necessity might be urgent for a partition and disposal of the tribal lands, of all power to act if the assent of three fourths of all the male Indians could not be obtained. Congress has always exercised plenary authority over the tribal relations of the Indians and the power has always been deemed a political one not subject to be controlled by the courts.

In view of the legislative power possessed by Congress over treaties with the Indians, and Indian tribal property, even if a subsequent agreement or treaty purporting to be signed by three fourths of all the male Indians was not signed and amendments to such subsequent treaty were not submitted to the Indians, as all these matters were solely within the domain of the legislative authority, the action of Congress is conclusive upon the courts.

As the act of June 6, 1900, as to the disposition of these lands was enacted at a time when the tribal relations between the confederated tribes of the Kiowas, Comanches and Apaches still existed, and that statute and the statutes supplementary thereto, dealt with the disposition of tribal property and purported to give an adequate consideration for the surplus lands not allotted among the Indians or reserved for their benefit, such legislation was constitutional and this court will presume that Congress acted in perfect good faith and exercised its best judgment in the premises, and as Congress possessed full power in the matter, the judiciary cannot question or inquire into the motives which prompted the enactment of such legislation.

IN 1867 a treaty was concluded with the Kiowa and Comanche tribes of Indians, and such other friendly tribes as might be united with them, setting apart a reservation for the use of such Indians. By a separate treaty the Apache tribe of Indians was incorporated with the two former-named, and became entitled to share in the benefits of the reservation. 15 Stat. 581, 589.

The first named treaty is usually called the Medicine Lodge treaty. By the sixth article thereof it was provided that heads of families might select a tract of land within the reservation, not exceeding 320 acres in extent, which should thereafter cease to be held in common, and should be for the exclusive possession of the Indian making the selection, so long as he or his family might continue to cultivate the land. The twelfth article of the treaty was as follows:

"Article 12. No treaty for the cession of any portion or part of the reservation herein described, which may be held in common, shall be of any validity or force as against the said Indians, unless executed and signed by at least three fourths of all the adult male Indians occupying the same, and no cession by the tribe shall be understood or construed in such manner as to deprive, without his consent, any individual member of the tribe of his rights to any tract of land selected by him as provided in article III (VI) of this treaty."

The three tribes settled under the treaties upon the described land. On October 6, 1892, 456 male adult members of the confederated tribes signed, with three commissioners representing the United States, an agreement concerning the reservation. The Indian agent, in a certificate appended to the agreement, represented that there were then 562 male adults in the three tribes. Senate Ex. Doc. No. 27, 52d Congress, second session, page 17. Four hundred and fifty-six male adults therefore constituted more than three fourths of the certified number of total male adults in the three tribes. In form the agreement was a proposed treaty, the terms of which, in substance, provided for a surrender to the United States of the rights of the tribes in the reservation, for allotments out of such lands to the Indians in severalty, the fee simple title to be conveyed to the allottees or their heirs after the expiration of twenty-five years; and the payment or setting apart for the benefit of the tribes of two million dollars as the consideration for the surplus of land over and above the allotments which might be made to the Indians. It was provided that sundry named friends of the Indians (among such persons being the Indian agent and an army officer) "should each be entitled to all the benefits, in land only, conferred under this agreement, the same as if members of said tribes." Eliminating 350,000 acres of mountainous land, the quantity of surplus lands, suitable for farming and grazing purposes was estimated at 2,150,000 acres. Concerning the payment to be made for these surplus lands, the commission, in their report to the President announcing the termination of the negotiations, said (Senate Ex. Doc. No. 17, second session, 52d Congress):

"In this connection it is proper to add that the commission agreed with the Indians to incorporate the following in their report, which is now done:

"The Indians upon this reservation seem to believe (but whether from an exercise of their own judgment or from the advice of others the commission cannot determine) that their surplus land is worth two and one half million dollars, and Congress may be induced to give them that much for it. Therefore, in compliance with their request, we report that they desire to be heard through an attorney and a delegation to Washington upon that question, the agreement signed, however, to be effective upon ratification, no matter what Congress may do with their appeal for the extra half million dollars."

In transmitting the agreement to the Secretary of the Interior, the Commissioner of Indian Affairs said:

"The price paid, while considerably in excess of that paid to the Cheyennes and Arapahoes, seems to be fair and reasonable, both to the government and the Indians, the land being doubtless of better quality than that in the Cheyenne and Arapahoe reservation."

Attention was directed to the provision in the agreement in favor of the Indian agent and an army officer, and it was suggested that to permit them to avail thereof would establish a bad precedent.

Soon after the signing of the foregoing agreement it was claimed by the Indians that their assent had been obtained by fraudulent misrepresentations of its terms by the interpreters, and it was asserted that the agreement should not be held binding upon the tribes because three fourths of the adult male members had not assented thereto, as was required by the twelfth article of the Medicine Lodge treaty.

Obviously, in consequence of the policy embodied in section 2079 of the Revised Statutes, departing from the former custom of dealing with Indian affairs by treaty and providing for legislative action on such subjects, various bills were introduced in both Houses of Congress designed to give legal effect to the agreement made by the Indians in 1892. These bills were referred to the proper committees, and before such committees the Indians presented their objections to the propriety of giving effect to the agreement. (H. R. Doc. No. 431, 55th Congress, second session.) In 1898 the Committee on Indian Affairs of the House of Representatives unanimously reported a bill for the execution of the agreement made with the Indians. The report of the committee recited that a favorable conclusion had been reached by the committee "after the fullest hearings from delegations of the Indian tribes and all parties at interest." (H. R. Doc. No. 419, first session, 56th Congress, p. 5.)

The bill thus reported did not exactly conform to the agreement as signed by the Indians. It modified the agreement by changing the time for making the allotments, and it also provided that the proceeds of the surplus lands remaining after allotments to the Indians should be held to await the judicial decision of a claim asserted by the Choctaw and Chickasaw tribes of Indians to the surplus lands. This claim was based upon a treaty made in 1866, by which the two tribes ceded the reservation in question, it being contended that the lands were impressed with a trust in favor of the ceding tribes, and that whenever the reservation was abandoned, so much of it as was not allotted to the confederated Indians of the Comanche, Kiowa and Apache tribes reverted to the Choctaws and Chickasaws.

The bill just referred to passed the House of Representatives on May 16, 1898. (31st Cong. Rec. p. 4947.) When the bill reached the Senate that body, on January 25, 1899, adopted a resolution calling upon the Secretary of the Interior for information as to whether the signatures attached to the agreement comprised three fourths of the male adults of the tribes. In response the Secretary of the Interior informed the Senate, under date of January 28, 1899, that the records of the department "failed to show a census of these Indians for the year 1892," but that "from a roll used in making a payment to them in January and February, 1893, it appeared that there were 725 males over eighteen years of age, of which 639 were twenty-one years and over." The Secretary further called attention to the fact that by the agreement of 1892 a right of selection was conferred upon each member of the tribes over eighteen years of age, and observed:

"If 18 years and over be held to be the legal age of those who were authorized to sign the agreement, the number of persons who actually signed was 87 less than three fourths of the adult male membership of the tribes; and if 21 years be held to be the minimum age, then 23 less than three fourths signed the agreement. In either event, less than three fourths of the male adults appear to have so signed."

With this information before it the bill was favorably reported by the Committee on Indian Affairs of the Senate, but did not pass that body.

At the first session of the following Congress (the Fifty-sixth) bills were introduced in both the Senate and House of Representatives substantially like that which has just been noticed. (Senate, 1352; H. R. 905.)

In the meanwhile, about October, 1899, the Indians had, at a general council at which 571 male adults of the tribes purported to be present, protested against the execution of the provisions of the agreement of 1892, and adopted a memorial to Congress, praying that that body should not give effect to the agreement. This memorial was forwarded to the Secretary of the Interior by the Commissioner of Indian Affairs with lengthy comments, pointing out the fact that the Indians claimed that their signatures to the agreement had been procured by fraud and that the legal number of Indians had not signed the agreement, and that the previous bills and bills then pending contemplated modification of the agreement in important particulars without the consent of the Indians. This communication from the Commissioner of Indian Affairs, together with the memorial of the Indians, were transmitted by the Secretary of the Interior to Congress. (Senate Doc. No. 76; H. R. Doc. No. 333; first session, Fifty-sixth Congress.) Attention was called to the fact that although by the agreement of October 6, 1892, one half of each allotment was contemplated to be agricultural land, there was only sufficient agricultural land in the entire reservation to average thirty acres per Indian. After setting out the charges of fraud and complaints respecting the proposed amendments designed to be made to the agreement, as above stated, particular complaint was made of the provision in the agreement of 1892 as to allotments in severalty among the Indians of lands for agricultural purposes. After reciting that the tribal lands were not adapted to such purposes, but were suitable for grazing, the memorial proceeded as follows:

"We submit that the provision for lands to be allotted to us under this treaty are insufficient, because it is evident we cannot, on account of the climate of our section, which renders the maturity of crops uncertain, become a successful farming community; that we, or whoever else occupies these lands, will have to depend upon the cattle industry for revenue and support. And we therefore pray, if we cannot be granted the privilege of keeping our reservation under the treaty made with us in 1868, and known as the Medicine Lodge treaty, that authority be granted for the consideration of a new treaty that will make the allowance of land to be allotted to us sufficient for us to graze upon it enough stock cattle, the increase from which we can market for support of ourselves and families."

With the papers just referred to before it, the House Committee on Indian Affairs, in February, 1900, favorably reported a bill to give effect to the agreement of 1892.

On January 19, 1900, an act was passed by the Senate, entitled "An act to ratify an agreement made with the Indians of the Fort Hall Indian reservation in Idaho, and making an appropriation to carry the same into effect." In February, 1900, the House Committee on Indian Affairs, having before it the memorial of the Indians transmitted by the Secretary of the Interior, and also having for consideration the Senate bill just alluded to, reported that bill back to the House favorably, with certain amendments. (H. R. Doc. No. 419, 56th Congress, first session.) One of such amendments consisted in adding to the bill in question, as section 6, a provision to execute the agreement made with the Kiowa, Comanche and Apache Indians in 1892. Although the bill thus reported embodied the execution of the agreement last referred to, the title of the bill was not changed, and consequently referred only to the execution of the agreement made with the Indians of the Fort Hall reservation in Idaho. The provisions thus embodied in section 6 of the bill in question substantially conformed to those contained in the bill which had previously passed the House, except that the previous enactment on this subject was changed so as to do away with the necessity for making to each Indian one half of his allotment in agricultural land and the other held in grazing land. In addition a clause was inserted in the bill providing for the setting apart of a large amount of grazing land to be used in common by the Indians. The provision in question was as follows:

"That in addition to the allotment of lands to said Indians as provided for in this agreement, the Secretary of the Interior shall set aside for the use in common for said Indian tribes four hundred and eighty thousand acres of grazing lands, to be selected by the Secretary of the Interior, either in one or more tracts as will best subserve the interest of said Indians."

The provision of the agreement in favor of the Indian agent and army officer was also eliminated.

The bill, moreover, exempted the money considerations for the surplus lands from all claims for Indian depredations, and expressly provided that in the event the claim of the Choctaws and Chickasaws was ultimately sustained, the consideration referred to should be subject to the further action of Congress. In this bill as in previous ones provision was made for allotments to the Indians, the opening of the surplus land for settlement, etc. The bill became a law by concurrence of the Senate in the amendments adopted by the House as just stated.

Thereafter, by acts approved on January 4, 1901, 31 Stat. 727, c. 8; March 3, 1901, 31 Stat. 1078, c. 832, and March 3, 1901, 31 Stat. 1093, c. 846, authority was given to extend the time for making allotments and opening of the surplus land for settlement for a period not exceeding eight months from December 6, 1900; appropriations were made for surveys in connection with allotments and setting apart of grazing lands; and authority was conferred to establish counties and county seats, townsites, etc., and proclaim the surplus lands open for settlement by white people.

On June 6, 1901, a bill was filed on the equity side of the Supreme Court of the District of Columbia, wherein Lone Wolf (one of the appellants herein) was named as complainant, suing for himself as well as for all other members of the confederated tribes of the Kiowa, Comanche and Apache Indians, residing in the Territory of Oklahoma. The present appellees (the Secretary of the Interior, the Commissioner of Indian Affairs and the Commissioner of the General Land Office) were made respondents to the bill. Subsequently, by an amendment to the bill, members of the Kiowa, Comanche and Apache tribes were joined with Lone Wolf as parties complainant.

The bill recited the establishing and occupancy of the reservation in Oklahoma by the confederated tribes of Kiowas, Comanches and Apaches, the signing of the agreement of October 6, 1892, and the subsequent proceedings which have been detailed, culminating in the passage of the act of June 6, 1900, and the acts of Congress supplementary to said act. In substance it was further charged in the bill that the agreements had not been signed as required by the Medicine Lodge treaty, that is, by three fourths of the male adult members of the tribe, and that the signatures thereto had been obtained by fraudulent misrepresentations and concealment, similar to those recited in the memorial signed at the 1899 council. In addition to the grievance previously stated in the memorial, the charge was made that the interpreters falsely represented, when the said treaty was being considered by the Indians, that the treaty provided "for the sale of their surplus lands at some time in the future at the price of $2.50 per acre;" whereas, in truth and in fact, "by the terms of said treaty, only $1.00 an acre is allowed for said surplus lands," which sum, it was charged, was an amount far below the real value of said lands. It was also averred that portions of the signed agreement had been changed by Congress without submitting such changes to the Indians for their consideration. Based upon the foregoing allegations, it was alleged that so much of said act of Congress of June 6, 1900, and so much of said acts supplementary thereto and amendatory thereof as provided for the taking effect of said agreement, the allotment of certain lands mentioned therein to members of said Indian tribes, the surveying, laying out, and platting townsites and locating county seats on said lands, and the ceding to the United States and the opening to settlement by white men of two million acres of said lands, were enacted in violation of the property rights of the said Kiowa, Comanche and Apache Indians, and if carried into effect would deprive said Indians of their lands without due process of law, and that said parts of said acts were contrary to the Constitution of the United States, and were void, and conferred no right, power or duty upon the respondents to do or perform any of the acts or things enjoined or required by the acts of Congress in question. Alleging the intention of the respondents to carry into effect the aforesaid claimed unconstitutional and void acts, and asking discovery by answers to interrogatories propounded to the respondents, the allowance of a temporary restraining order, and a final decree awarding a perpetual injunction was prayed, to restrain the commission by the respondents of the alleged unlawful acts by them threatened to be done. General relief was also prayed.

On January 6, 1901, a rule to show cause why a temporary injunction should not be granted was issued. In response to this rule an affidavit of the Secretary of the Interior was filed, in which in substance it was averred that the complainant (Lone Wolf) and his wife and daughter had selected allotments under the act of June 6, 1900, and the same had been approved by the Secretary of the Interior and that all other members of the tribes, excepting twelve, had also accepted and retained allotments in severalty, and that the greater part thereof had been approved before the bringing of this suit. It was also averred that the 480,000 acres of grazing land provided to be set apart, in the act of June 6, 1900, for the use by the Indians in common, had been so set apart prior to the institution of the suit, "with the approval of a council composed of chiefs and headmen of said Indians." Thereupon an affidavit verified by Lone Wolf was filed, in which in effect he denied that he had accepted an allotment of lands under the act of June 6, 1900, and the acts supplementary to and amendatory thereof. Thereafter, on June 17, 1901, leave was given to amend the bill and the same was amended, as heretofore stated, by adding additional parties complainants and by providing a substituted first paragraph of the bill, in which was set forth, among other things, that the three tribes, at a general council held on June 7, 1901, had voted to institute all legal and other proceedings necessary to be taken, to prevent the carrying into effect of the legislation complained of.

The Supreme Court of the District on June 21, 1901, denied the application for a temporary injunction. The cause was thereafter submitted to the court on a demurrer to the bill as amended. The demurrer was sustained, and the complainants electing not to plead further, on June 26, 1901, a decree was entered in favor of the respondents. An appeal was thereupon taken to the Court of Appeals of the District. While this appeal was pending, the President issued a proclamation, dated July 4, 1901, (32 Stat. Appx. Proclamations, 11,) in which it was ordered that the surplus lands ceded by the Comanche, Kiowa and Apache and other tribes of Indians should be opened to entry and settlement on August 6, 1901. Among other things, it was recited in the proclamation that all the conditions required by law to be performed prior to the opening of the lands to settlement and entry had been performed. It was also therein recited that, in pursuance of the act of Congress ratifying the agreement, allotments of land in severalty had been regularly made to each member of the Comanche, Kiowa and Apache tribes of Indians; the lands occupied by religious societies or other organizations for religious or educational work among the Indians had been regularly allotted and confirmed to such societies and organizations, respectively; and the Secretary of the Interior, out of the lands ceded by the agreement, had regularly selected and set aside for the use in common for said Comanche, Kiowa and Apache tribes of Indians, four hundred and eighty thousand acres of grazing lands.

The Court of Appeals (without passing on a motion which had been made to dismiss the appeal) affirmed the decree of the court below, and overruled a motion for reargument. 19 App. D. C. 315. An appeal was allowed, and the decree of affirmance is now here for review.

Mr. William M. Springer and Mr. Hampton L. Carson, for appellants.

Mr. Assistant Attorney General Van Devanter, for appellee.

MR. JUSTICE WHITE, after making the foregoing statement, delivered the opinion of the court.

By the sixth article of the first of the two treaties referred to in the preceding statement, proclaimed on August 25, 1868, 15 Stat. 581, it was provided that heads of families of the tribes affected by the treaty might select, within the reservation, a tract of land of not exceeding 320 acres in extent, which should thereafter cease to be held in common, and should be for the exclusive possession of the Indian making the selection, so long as he or his family might continue to cultivate the land. The twelfth article reads as follows:

"Article 12. No treaty for the cession of any portion or part of the reservation herein described, which may be held in common, shall be of any validity or force as against the said Indians, unless executed and signed by at least three fourths of all the adult male Indians occupying the same, and no cession by the tribe shall be understood or construed in such manner as to deprive, without his consent, any individual member of the tribe of his rights to any tract of land selected by him as provided in article III (VI) of this treaty."

The appellants base their right to relief on the proposition that by the effect of the article just quoted the confederated tribes of Kiowas, Comanches and Apaches were vested with an interest in the lands held in common within the reservation, which interest could not be divested by Congress in any other mode than that specified in the said twelfth article, and that as a result of the said stipulation the interest of the Indians in the common lands fell within the protection of the Fifth Amendment to the Constitution of the United States, and such interest—indirectly at least—came under the control of the judicial branch of the government. We are unable to yield our assent to this view.

The contention in effect ignores the status of the contracting Indians and the relation of dependency they bore and continue to bear towards the government of the United States. To uphold the claim would be adjudge that the indirect operation of the treaty was to materially limit and qualify the controlling authority of Congress in respect to the care and protection of the Indians, and to deprive Congress, in a possible emergency, when the necessity might be urgent for a partition and disposal of the tribal lands, of all power to act, if the assent of the Indians could not be obtained.

Now, it is true that in decisions of this court, the Indian right of occupancy of tribal lands, whether declared in a treaty or otherwise created, has been stated to be sacred, or, as sometimes expressed, as sacred as the fee of the United States in the same lands. *Johnson* v. *McIntosh,* (1823) 8 Wheat. 543, 574; *Cherokee Nation* v. *Georgia,* (1831) 5 Pet. 1, 48; *Worcester* v. *Georgia,* (1832) 6 Pet. 515, 581; *United States* v. *Cook,* (1873)

19 Wall. 591, 592; *Leavenworth &c. R. R. Co.* v. *United States,* (1875) 92 U. S. 733, 755; *Beecher* v. *Wetherby,* (1877) 95 U. S. 517, 525. But in none of these cases was there involved a controversy between Indians and the government respecting the power of Congress to administer the property of the Indians. The questions considered in the cases referred to, which either directly or indirectly had relation to the nature of the property rights of the Indians, concerned the character and extent of such rights as respected States or individuals. In one of the cited cases it was clearly pointed out that Congress possessed a paramount power over the property of the Indians, by reason of its exercise of guardianship over their interests, and that such authority might be implied, even though opposed to the strict letter of a treaty with the Indians. Thus, in *Beecher* v. *Wetherby,* 95 U. S. 517, discussing the claim that there had been a prior reservation of land by treaty to the use of a certain tribe of Indians, the court said (p. 525):

"But the right which the Indians held was only that of occupancy. The fee was in the United States, subject to that right, and could be transferred by them whenever they chose. The grantee, it is true, would take only the naked fee, and could not disturb the occupancy of the Indians; that occupancy could only be interfered with or determined by the United States. It is to be presumed that in this matter the United States would be governed by such considerations of justice as would control a Christian people in their treatment of an ignorant and dependent race. Be that as it may, the propriety or justice of their action towards the Indians with respect to their lands is a question of governmental policy, and is not a matter open to discussion in a controversy between third parties, neither of whom derives title from the Indians."

Plenary authority over the tribal relations of the Indians has been exercised by Congress from the beginning, and the power has always been deemed a political one, not subject to be controlled by the judicial department of the government. Until the year 1871 the policy was pursued of dealing with the Indian tribes by means of treaties, and, of course, a moral obligation rested upon Congress to act in good faith in performing the stipulations entered into on its behalf. But, as with treaties made with foreign nations, *Chinese Exclusion Case,* 130 U. S. 581, 600, the legislative power might pass laws in conflict with treaties made with the Indians. *Thomas* v. *Gay,* 169 U. S. 264, 270; *Ward* v. *Race Horse,* 163 U. S. 504, 511; *Spalding* v. *Chandler,* 160 U. S. 394, 405; *Missouri, Kansas & Texas Ry. Co.* v. *Roberts,* 152 U. S. 114, 117; *The Cherokee Tobacco,* 11 Wall. 616.

The power exists to abrogate the provisions of an Indian treaty, though presumably such power will be exercised only when circumstances arise which will not only justify the government in disregarding the stipulations of the treaty, but may demand, in the interest of the country and the Indians themselves, that it should do so. When, therefore, treaties were entered into between the United States and a tribe of Indians it was never doubted that the *power* to abrogate existed in Congress, and that in a contingency such power might be availed of from considerations of governmental policy, particularly if consistent with perfect good faith towards the Indians. In *United States* v. *Kagama,* (1855) 118 U. S. 375, speaking of the Indians, the court said (p. 382):

"After an experience of a hundred years of the treaty-making system of government, Congress has determined upon a new departure—to govern them by acts of Congress. This is seen in the act of March 3, 1871, embodied in § 2079 of the Revised Statutes: 'No Indian nation or tribe, within the territory of the United States shall be acknowledged or recognized as an independent nation, tribe, or power, with whom the United states may contract by treaty; but no obligation of any treaty lawfully made and ratified with any such Indian nation or tribe prior to March third, eighteen hundred and seventy-one, shall be hereby invalidated or impaired.'"

In upholding the validity of an act of Congress which conferred jurisdiction upon the courts of the United States for certain crimes committed on an Indian reservation within a State, the court said (p. 383):

"It seems to us that this is within the competency of Congress. These Indian tribes *are* the wards of the nation. They are communities *dependent* on the United States. Dependent largely for their daily food. Dependent for their political rights. They owe no allegiance to the States, and receive from them no protection. Because of the local ill feeling, the people of the States where they are found are often their deadliest enemies. From their very weakness and helplessness, so largely due to the course of dealing of the Federal government with them and the treaties in which it has been promised, there arises the duty of protection, and with it the power. This has always been recognized by the Executive and by Congress, and by this court, whenever the question has arisen.

* * *

"The power of the general government over these remnants of a race once powerful, now weak and diminished in numbers, is necessary to their protection, as well as to the safety of those among whom they dwell. It must exist in that government, because it has never existed anywhere else, because the theatre of its exercise is within the geographical limits of the United States, because it has never been denied, and because it alone can enforce its laws on all the tribes."

That Indians who had not been fully emancipated from the control and protection of the United States are subject, at least so far as the tribal lands were concerned, to be controlled by direct legislation of Congress, is also declared in *Choctaw Nation* v. *United States*, 119 U. S. 1, 27, and *Stephens* v. *Cherokee Nation*, 174 U. S. 445, 483.

In view of the legislative power possessed by Congress over treaties with the Indians and Indian tribal property, we may not specially consider the contentions pressed upon our notice that the signing by the Indians of the agreement of October 6, 1892, was obtained by fraudulent misrepresentations and concealment, that the requisite three fourths of adult male Indians had not signed, as required by the twelfth article of the treaty of 1867, and that the treaty as signed had been amended by Congress without submitting such amendments to the action of the Indians, since all these matters, in any event, were solely within the domain of the legislative authority and its action is conclusive upon the courts.

The act of June 6, 1900, which is complained of in the bill, was enacted at a time when the tribal relations between the confederated tribes of Kiowas, Comanches and

Apaches still existed, and that statute and the statutes supplementary thereto dealt with the disposition of tribal property and purported to give an adequate consideration for the surplus lands not allotted among the Indians or reserved for their benefit. Indeed, the controversy which this case presents is concluded by the decision in *Cherokee Nation* v. *Hitchcock*, 187 U. S. 294, decided at this term, where it was held that full administrative power was possessed by Congress over Indian tribal property. In effect, the action of Congress now complained of was but an exercise of such power, a mere change in the form of investment of Indian tribal property, the property of those who, as we have held, were in substantial effect the wards of the government. We must presume that Congress acted in perfect good faith in the dealings with the Indians of which complaint is made, and that the legislative branch of the government exercised its best judgment in the premises. In any event, as Congress possessed full power in the matter, the judiciary cannot question or inquire into the motives which prompted the enactment of this legislation. If injury was occasioned, which we do not wish to be understood as implying, by the use made by Congress of its power, relief must be sought by an appeal to that body for redress and not to the courts. The legislation in question was constitutional, and the demurrer to the bill was therefore rightly sustained.

The motion to dismiss does not challenge jurisdiction over the subject matter. Without expressly referring to the propositions of fact upon which it proceeds, suffice it to say that we think it need not be further adverted to, since, for the reasons previously given and the nature of the controversy, we think the decree below should be

Affirmed.

MR. JUSTICE HARLAN concurs in the result.

NOTES

CHAPTER 1, INTRODUCTION

1. Paraphrased from Dawes, "Indian Territory," Fifteenth Annual Meeting of Lake Mohonk Conference, in Commissioner of Indian Affairs, *Annual Report*, 1897, p. 991, and Dawes, "Have We Failed With the Indian?" 281. The General Allotment Act of 8 February 1887 is found at 24 Stat. 388. After 1883 the various individuals who made up the Friends of the Indian held an annual conference in upstate New York at Lake Mohonk Lodge.

2. Roosevelt's First Annual Message to Congress, 3 December 1901, in *Works*, 15:129.

3. Prucha, *American Indian Policy in Crisis*, v.

4. Vine Deloria, Jr., in response to the increasing demand at the start of the decade of the 1970s for Indian-related printed materials, produced a document collection that mentioned the case but failed to include an excerpt from it (*Of Utmost Good Faith*, 63).

5. Walter L. Williams, "From Independence to Wardship"; Prucha, *Great Father*, 2:775–76; Hoxie, *Final Promise;* and Hagan, *Indian Rights Association*, 212–15, 247–48.

6. Including Wilkinson and Volkman, "Judicial Review of Indian Treaty Abrogation"; Barsh and Henderson, *The Road*, which devotes a short chapter to the case; Estin, *"Lone Wolf v. Hitchcock"*; Newton, "Federal Power over Indians." A casebook example is Getches, Rosenfelt, and Wilkinson, *Federal Indian Law*, 185–88. The leading legal guide is *Felix S. Cohen's Handbook*, 43–44, 63–64, 214, 222, 468, and 516.

CHAPTER 2, THE SUPREME COURT

1. Art. III, Sec. 2. The Judiciary Act of 24 September 1789, 1 Stat. 72, set up circuit courts to accompany district courts. I found useful Arthur S. Miller, *The Supreme Court in American Life* (New York: Free Press, 1968); Sklar, *Corporate Reconstruction;* and Ziegler, *Supreme Court*.

2. Argued in *San Mateo County v. Southern Pacific Railroad*, 116 U.S. 138 (1885); accepted in *Santa Clara County v. Southern Pacific Railroad*, 118 U.S. 394 (1886).

3. Spencer, *Social Statics; or, The Conditions Essential to Human Happiness Specified* (London: Chapman, 1851), 322, quoted in Alpheus T. Mason, "The Conservative World of Mr. Justice Sutherland, 1883–1910," *American Political Science Review* 32 (1938): 453.

4. *Wilson v. New*, 243 U.S. 332 (1917) at 347, cited in Highsaw, *Edward Douglas White*, 106.

5. Dissent in *Lochner v. New York*, 198 U.S. 45 (1905) at 75, dealing with a ten-hour work law for bankers, cited in Highsaw, *Edward Douglas White*, 65.

6. *Wabash, St. Louis and Pacific Railway Co. v. Illinois*, 118 U.S. 557 (1886) at 577 for quotations that follow.

7. *Slaughter-House Cases*, 16 Wall. 36 (1873) at 78. Another interventionist opinion was *Munn v. Illinois* (1877), in which Chief Justice M. R. Waite's opinion for the majority stated pointedly that "the State may exercise all the powers of government over them [warehouses], even though in so doing it may indirectly operate upon commerce outside its immediate jurisdiction" 94 U.S. 113 at 135.

8. *U.S. v. E. C. Knight*, 156 U.S. 1 (1895).

9. 156 U.S. 1 at 9.

10. 156 U.S. 1 at 12 and 17.

11. Highsaw, *Edward Douglas White*, 100.

12. *Civil Rights Cases*, 109 U.S. 3 (1883) at 24 for quotation from Justice Joseph P. Bradley's opinion later on.

13. *U.S. v. Reese*, 92 U.S. 214 (1875).

14. *Plessy v. Ferguson*, 163 U.S. 537 (1896) at 548 and 550.

15. 163 U.S. 551.

16. For Asians see *Yick Wo v. Crowley*, 26 F. 207, and *Yick Wo v. Hopkins*, 118 U.S. 356 (1886), from the District Court in California, and the later case of *U.S. v. Ju Toy*, 198 U.S. 253 (1904). Smith, "Federal Courts and the Black Man"; Hall, "Children of Cabins."

17. John Smith in Commissioner of Indian Affairs, *Annual Report*, 1876, p. x.

18. Garland, "Red Man's Present Needs," 485.

19. Paraphrasing William G. Sumner, "Indians in 1887," *Forum* 3 (1887): 256.

20. Prucha, *Great Father*, devotes two volumes to the reform impulse in Indian-white relations.

21. Commissioner of Indian Affairs, *Annual Report*, 1876, p. 384.

22. IRA founder Herbert Welsh in 1884 and his father's formal invitation in 1882 for the establishment of the IRA are quoted in Introduction to *The IRA Papers: A Guide to the Microfilm Edition, 1884–1973* (Glen Rock, N.J.: Microfilming Corp. of America, 1975), p. 1.

23. *Fletcher v. Peck*, 10 U.S. 87 (1810).

24. *Johnson and Graham's Lessee v. McIntosh*, 21 U.S. 542 (1823).

25. *Gibbons v. Ogden*, 19 U.S. (6 Wheat) 1 (1824).

26. *Cherokee Nation v. Georgia*, 30 U.S. (5 Pet.) 1 (1831), 16–17.

27. *Worcester v. Georgia*, 31 U.S. (6 Pet.) 515 (1832) concurring opinion of Justice John McLean at 593.

28. *U.S. v. Rogers*, 45 U.S. 567 (1846) at 573. Newton, "Federal Power over Indians," 209–11, and Williams, "From Independence to Wardship," 18.

29. *The Cherokee Tobacco*, 78 U.S. 616 (1870) at 621.

30. Sen. Rept. 268, *Effect of the Fourteenth Amendment*, 1, 11.

31. *Ex Parte Crow Dog*, 109 U.S. 556 (1883) at 569. The invitation at 572 dealt with past *non*interference on the part of the United States, but stated: "To justify such a departure, in such a case, requires a clear expression of the intention of Congress."

32. Major Crimes Act, sec. 9 of Indian Appropriation Act of 1885, 23 Stat. 385. Crow Dog was accused in federal court of murdering another Indian on the reservation after federal authorities determined that the tribe's customary law punishment of Crow Dog was insufficient for them.

33. *U.S. v. McBratney*, 104 U.S. 621 (1882) at 624.

34. *Elk v. Wilkins*, 112 U.S. 94 (1884). The Indian, Elk, voluntarily left his reservation and resided in the city of Omaha. When he sought to vote in a municipal election, he was denied that right. See Bodayla, " 'Can an Indian Vote?' "

35. *U.S. v. Kagama*, 118 U.S. 379 (1886). See Rotenberg, "American Indian Tribal Death."

36. *Choctaw Nation v. U.S.*, 119 U.S. 1 (1886) at 27.

37. Cannon speaking on HR 10049, *Cong. Rec.*, v. 31, pt. 5, 55th Cong., 2d sess., House, 16 May 1898, p. 4954.

38. *Cherokee Nation v. Southern Kansas Railway*, 135 U.S. 641 (1890), in which the Court agreed that Congress was empowered to grant right-of-way through the territory under the authority of an 1884 law to regulate commerce; see also *Stephens v. Cherokee Nation*, 174 U.S. 483 (1899) at 488; *Cherokee Nation v. Hitchcock*, 187 U.S. 294 (1902) at 306.

39. *Talton v. Mayes*, 163 U.S. 196 (1896) at 197; *U.S. v. Winans*, 73 F. 72 (1896) at 75.

40. *Stephens v. Cherokee Nation*, 1899, at 483.

41. *Jones v. Meehan*, 175 U.S. 1 (1899) at 10.

42. *Lone Wolf v. Hitchcock*, 187 U.S. 553 (1903).

43. Art. VI.

44. *The Cherokee Tobacco*, 78 U.S. 616 (1870). See Wilkinson and Volkman, "Judicial Review of Indian Treaty Abrogation."

45. *U.S. v. McBratney*, 104 U.S. 621 (1882) at 623.

46. *Whitney v. Robinson*, 124 U.S. 190 (1888).

47. Chinese Exclusion case, 130 U.S. 581 (1889).

48. *Cong. Rec.*, v. 44, pt. 3, 41st Cong., 3d sess., House, 1 March 1871, p. 1812.

49. 16 Stat. 566, 3 March 1871. See John Wunder, "No More Treaties: The Resolution of 1871 and the Alteration of Indian Rights to Their Homelands," in idem, ed., *Working the Range*, 39–56.

50. *Cherokee Nation v. Southern Kansas Railway*, 135 U.S. 641 (1890).

51. Morgan, "The Indian Territory," in Report of the 13th Annual Mohonk Conference of Friends of the Indians in Commissioner of Indian Affairs, *Annual Report*, 1895, p. 1056, unknowingly using the international law doctrine of *rebus sic stantibus*, under which one party may end a treaty as a result of basic changes in circumstances.

52. Platt, "Problems in the Indian Territory," 201.

53. *U.S. v. Winans,* 73 F. 72 (1896) at 75, so remarked, leaving those rights to the discretion of Congress, although the Indians did have the right to fish along the Columbia River at "the usual and accustomed places," a phrase that would be revived in the famous Boldt decision of 1974.

54. *Ward v. Race Horse,* 163 U.S. 504 (1896) at 516.

55. *Stephens v. Cherokee Nation,* 174 U.S. 445 (1899) at 488.

56. *Jones v. Meehan,* 175 U.S. 1 (1899). Quotation from *U.S. v. Rickert,* 188 U.S. 432 (1903). A dispute over former Chippewa Indian land in Minnesota led the Court to declare an 1894 Joint Resolution of Congress unconstitutional because the judiciary reserved to itself the review of treaty rights unless an overpowering political question was involved.

CHAPTER 3, KIOWAS AND AMERICANS

1. The classic ethnographic account is Mooney, "Calendar History of the Kiowa Indians"; and the anthropological account of Mildred Mayhall, *The Kiowas,* as well as the tribal history, *Kiowa Voices,* edited by Maurice Boyd, provide information. Useful for the Comanches are Fehrenbach, *Comanches,* and Wallace and Hoebel, *Comanches.* Homeland and alliances in Mayhall, *Kiowas,* 9–12; Boyd, *Kiowa Voices,* 2:1. Momaday, *Way to Rainy Mountain,* chronicles the journey. A Kiowa version of making "relatives of Comanche" is in Parsons, *Kiowa Tales,* 85–88.

2. DeMallie, "Early Kiowa and Comanche Treaties"; Richardson, *Comanche Barrier to Southern Plains Settlement.* Discussions of plains treaty-making are Lindquist and Seymour, "Indian Treaty Making"; DeMallie, "American Indian Treaty Making"; idem, "Touching the Pen"; and Fixico, "As Long as the Grass Grows." Discussion of kinship terms in diplomacy is in DeMallie, "Touching the Pen," 50, and in Fixico, "As Long as the Grass Grows," 142.

3. In Commissioner of Indian Affairs, *Annual Report,* 1837, pp. 558–59, as well as DeMallie, "Early Kiowa and Comanche Treaties," 22, and 7 Stat. 533.

4. 10 Stat. 10–13, 27 July 1853.

5. The Comanche Confederate Treaty, August 12, 1861, is in *War of the Rebellion,* 4th ser., vol. 1, 542–54. Kiowa leaders and the remainder of the Comanche chiefs on October 24 signed the treaty of October 18 that "a portion of the Comanche chiefs" had already signed. The Treaty of the Little Arkansas is at 10 Stat. 1013, and in Commissioner of Indian Affairs, *Annual Report,* 1865, p. 394. See Hagan, *United States–Comanche Relations;* Monahan, "Kiowa-Federal Relations"; and Unrau, "Indian Agent vs. the Army."

6. *Cong. Globe,* 40th Cong., 1st sess., Senate, 20 July 1867, p. 753, for passage of S. 136; signature of president on p. 755. 15 Stat. 17.

7. *Cong. Globe,* vol. 39, pt. 1, 40th Cong., 1 sess., Senate, 12 July 1867, pp. 623–24.

8. Parrish, "Indian Peace Commission," 36.

9. Official records are "Transcript of the Minutes and Proceedings of the Indian

Peace Commission Appointed by an Act of Congress, 20 July 1867," Records of the Office of the Secretary of the Interior, RG 48, National Archives.

10. Mooney, "Calendar History," 321.

11. Jones, *Treaty of Medicine Lodge;* idem, "Medicine Lodge Revisited"; and Prucha, *Great Father,* 1:488–92, who places Commission efforts into national perspective.

12. Mardock, *Reformers and the American Indian,* 60.

13. The Kiowa–Comanche Treaty of 21 October is at 15 Stat. 581. The Kiowa–Comanche–Apache Treaty is at 15 Stat. 589.

14. Reprinted in Rister, "Satanta," 83, and for Ten Bears see Parrish, "Indian Peace Commission," 43–44; Hagan, *United States–Comanche Relations,* 29–31.

15. An-pay-kau-te in Nye, *Bad Medicine and Good,* 138. See also Mooney, "Calendar History," 321.

16. Poor Buffalo in Minutes of the Council, 3 October 1892, in Sen. Doc. 77, 55th Cong., 3d sess., 26 January 1899, Serial No. 3731, vol. 7, p. 28; Sherman in his annual report for 1866 quoted in the Report of Indian Peace Commission, 7 January 1868, in Commissioner of Indian Affairs, *Annual Report,* 1868, p. 40.

CHAPTER 4, TEARS IN THEIR EYES

1. Mooney, "Calendar History," 219.

2. Hunt in Commissioner of Indian Affairs, *Annual Report,* 1879, p. 66, and in *Annual Report,* 1880, p. 73. Annuities and beef rations were still issued through headmen for a time. Contemporary accounts of 1870–73 issues through headmen are in Butler, "Pioneer School Teaching," 502, 519, 527.

3. Mooney, "Calendar History," 344.

4. White, *Experiences of a Special Indian Agent,* 310. Flour and bacon on ration day from Susie Peters, in Boyd, *Kiowa Voices,* 2:264.

5. Scott, *Some Memories of a Soldier,* 206; Mayhall, *Kiowas,* 181; Letter, James Randlett to Mr. Bacchus, 4 January 1900, Kiowa Agency, vol. 74, Letterpress Book, microfilm roll KA53, p. 382, Oklahoma Historical Society.

6. William D. Pennington, "Government Policy and Farming."

7. Laura Pedrick interview in Boyd, *Kiowa Voices,* 2:233–36. Lone Wolf's genealogy is traced in Momaday, *Names.*

8. Report of Special Agent E. E. White in Commissioner of Indian Affairs, *Annual Report,* 1888, p. 96.

9. Entry for 16th Day of 5th Month, 1871, in Butler, "Pioneer School Teaching," 503.

10. Commissioner of Indian Affairs, *Annual Report,* 1874, p. 72. The Kiowa-Comanche School contained only Caddo pupils during Josiah Butler's 1870–1873 teaching tenure.

11. Letter, James Mooney to unknown, 21 June 1893, BAE Records, Letters Received, box 14, 1893 folder, National Anthropological Archives.

12. Sources on missionary activity include Hume, "Pioneer Missionary Enterprises"; Corwin, "Protestant Missionary Work"; and Forbes, "John Jasper Methvin."

13. Methvin, *In the Limelight*, 84; and W. W. Bray interview in Indian–Pioneer Papers, Oklahoma Historical Society, vol. 16, p. 231.

14. Butler, "Pioneer School Teaching," 494. Battey's account is *Life and Adventures.*

15. Crawford, *Kiowa*, 55.

16. Ibid., 24.

17. Journal entry for 3rd Day of 6th Month, 1872, in Butler, "Pioneer School Teaching," 517.

18. Commissioner of Indian Affairs, *Annual Report*, 1898, p. 238. The count includes the Kiowas, Comanches, and Apaches, as well as the Wichitas and affiliated tribes.

19. Commissioner of Indian Affairs, *Annual Report*, 1887, 83.

20. Minutes of the council in Sen. Doc. 77, 55th Cong., 3d sess., 26 January 1899, Serial No. 3731, vol. 7, p. 23.

21. Conover, *Sixty Years in Southwest Oklahoma*, records the view of one intermarried white rancher.

22. Hagan, *United States–Comanche Relations*, 175–76, 219, for amounts yielded by leasing. Interview with Forest Lee for a description of the types of grasses and their nutritional richness in Indian–Pioneer Papers, vol. 109, p. 115, Oklahoma Historical Society.

23. Minutes of Jerome Commission, Fort Sill, 27 September 1892, in Sen. Doc. 77, 55th Cong., 3d sess., 26 January 1899, Serial No. 3731, vol. 7, p. 14.

24. Frank Armstrong, 27 November 1889, Report of Inspection of Field Jurisdictions of the Office of Indian Affairs, RG 75, Microcopy 1070, reel 21 (microcopy, Newberry Library).

25. Frizzle Head quoted first and Chad-Dle-Kaung-Ky quoted second, 1890 Council, in W. W. Junkin, Report of Inspection of Field Jurisdictions, 28 June 1890, ibid. Agent W. D. Myers recorded Kiowa sentiment regarding allotment in Commissioner of Indian Affairs, *Annual Report*, 1889, p. 192, as did Indian Inspector James McLaughlin in 1898 in Sen. Doc. 77, pp. 57–58.

26. Mooney, "Calendar History," 378.

27. Sec. 14 of Act of 2 March 1889, 25 Stat. 1005.

28. Address at Crawford Opera House, Wichita, Kansas, in *Kansas City Gazette*, 21 November 1888, cited in Hoig, *Oklahoma Land Rush*, 12.

29. Hagan, *United States–Comanche Relations*, 204.

30. Chapman, "Final Report of the Cherokee Commission"; idem, "Secret 'Instructions and Suggestions' "; and Jerome's remarks at Fort Sill, 28 September 1892, in Sen. Doc. 77, p. 21.

CHAPTER 5, THE JEROME NEGOTIATIONS

1. *Annual Report* of the Department of the Interior for Fiscal Year Ending 30 June 1903, *Indian Affairs* (1904), Serial No. 4644, vol. 18, pp. 2–3. Attitudes of commissioners and views on Indian title are presented in Chapman, "How the Cherokees Acquired," and House Rept. 3768, *Cherokee Outlet,* as well as in Sen. Ex. Doc. 63, *Report on Cherokee Outlet.* The 1903 quotation of the Commissioner of Indian Affairs closely mirrors the sentiment in opening remarks to the Kiowa meeting by Jerome Commissioner Warren Sayre at Ft. Sill, 6 October 1892, in Sen. Doc. 77, *Jerome Commission Journal,* p. 38.

2. Tohauson in Sen. Doc. 77, p. 38.

3. Frizzle Head quoted, then Quanah quoted, in 1890 Council in W. W. Junkin, Report of Inspection of Field Jurisdictions, 28 June 1890 (microcopy, Newberry Library).

4. Minutes of Fort Sill meeting, 28–29 September 1892, in Sen. Doc. 77, pp. 9–10, 21. Another compilation is DeMallie, *Jerome Agreement.*

5. Sen. Doc. 77, 14.

6. Ibid., 19–20.

7. Ibid., 11.

8. Ibid., 18.

9. Ibid., 25.

10. Ibid., 21.

11. Ibid., Iseeo on p. 23; Komalty, p. 33.

12. Ibid., 29–30.

13. Ibid., 38, and Letter, Randlett to Merrill Gates, 15 December 1899, Kiowa Agency, vol. 74, Letterpress Book, Microfilm roll KA53, p. 294, Oklahoma Historical Society. Per capita figure in Commissioner of Indian Affairs, *Annual Report,* 1892, p. 387.

14. Hagan, *United States–Comanche Relations,* 204.

15. Sen. Doc. 77, p. 21.

16. Hagan, *United States–Comanche Relations,* 208–9. Testimony in Sen. Doc. 77, p. 30. Tabananca confessed that he and the other head chiefs knew nothing about any such lawyer; ibid., 31.

17. Ibid., 37.

18. Ibid., 38.

19. Letter, Givens to Methvin, 11 October 1892, Kiowa Agency, vol. 74, Letterpress Book, Microfilm roll KA53, p. 405, Oklahoma Historical Society.

20. Hagan, *United States–Comanche Relations,* 210–11. John Hill eventually received his allotment under an amendment to the Indian Appropriation Act of 27 May 1902, 32 Stat. 245.

21. Letter, Jerome to Secretary of the Interior Noble, 7 October 1892, in *Kiowa-Comanche Indians* 2:9–10.

22. Minutes of 11 October, Sen. Doc. 77, p. 41.

23. Ibid., Jerome on p. 40; Iseeo, p. 43.

24. Testimony of Yellow Boy Tonemah and Jimmie Quetone, 10–11 May 1949, in *Kiowa-Comanche Indians*, 2:42; 1:195, 200, 203; Ahatone, p. 218.

25. Biographical information on Givens is from Commissioner of Indian Affairs, *Annual Report*, 1890, pp. 188–89; Toyebo testimony, 10 May 1949, in *Kiowa-Comanche Indians*, 1:181, 185; and Boyd, *Kiowa Voices*, 2:48–49.

26. Sen. Doc. 77, p. 44.

27. Ibid., 47.

28. Ibid., 51–52. Versions of the Big Tree–Givens exchange in testimony of Odle-pah-quoit (Rev. Pauahty, White Fox) in *Kiowa-Comanche Indians*, 2:30–32; Jimmie Quetone, 1:197–99. Givens's comment to Big Tree from testimony of Guy Quetone in House, Committee on Indian Affairs, *KCA Jurisdictional Act*, Hearings on J. Res. 290, 67th Cong., 1st sess., 18 and 21 July 1939, p. 37.

29. Ibid., 54. The Minutes do not include the demand for removal of the Indian signatures; that incident is in Sen. Misc. Doc. 102, 53rd Cong., 2d sess., 1894, Serial No. 3167, vol. 1, p. 2.

30. Affidavits in Sen. Misc. Doc. 102, pp. 15ff.; testimony in *KCA Jurisdictional Act*, pp. 21ff.; Hoy-koy-bitty comments in Comanche Council Minutes, 27 February 1920, in Hugh Scott Papers, Kiowa Agency folder, No. 4525, National Anthropological Archives, and correspondence in Sen. Ex. Doc. 17, 52d Cong., 2d sess., 1893, Serial No. 3055, vol. 1.

31. Newspaper clipping accompanying Letter, George Day to Commissioner, 9 January 1893, Kiowa file no. 1910-j, National Anthropological Archives, and Methvin, "Reminiscences," 174.

32. Scott, *Some Memories of a Soldier*, 157–58; Boyd, *Kiowa Voices*, 2:209. Eventually Lone Wolf sponsored the Feather Dance.

33. Sen. Doc. 84, 55th Cong., 3d sess., 28 January 1899, Serial No. 3731, vol. 7; and Office of Indian Affairs, Letters Received, RG 75, No. 8094-1892, National Archives.

CHAPTER 6, THE KIOWAS LOBBY

1. *Report* of the Board of Indian Commissioners, 1894, p. 36.

2. Mooney in Hagan, *Indian Rights Association*, 167; Scott in Letter, Scott to Daniel S. Lamont, 11 May 1893, in Sen. Doc. 77, p. 5.

3. Lone Wolf affidavit, 6 October 1893, in Sen. Misc. Doc. 102, p. 14, and Petition, 10 April 1897, Hugh Scott Papers, Kiowa Agency file no. 4525, National Anthropological Archives, and Memorials of 9 October 1899 and 13 January 1900, in Sen. Doc. 76, and Petition of 1892 by Methvin in Kiowa Agency, Vol. 74, Letterpress Book, Microfilm roll KA58, p. 403, Oklahoma Historical Society, as examples.

4. Quoted in Crawford, *Kiowa*, 64–65.

5. IRA Papers, reel 102.

6. Letter, Commissioner of Indian Affairs W. A. Jones to Interior Secretary Hitchcock, 23 December 1899, in Sen. Doc. 75, 56th Cong., 1st sess., 15 January 1900, Serial No. 3850, vol. 8, p. 6; Letter, Hitchcock to President of the Senate, 13 January 1900, in Sen. Doc. 76, p. 2. Baldwin in Commissioner of Indian Affairs, *Annual Report*, 1896, p. 256. Randlett in Letter, Randlett to Merrill E. Gates, 15 December 1899, Kiowa Agency, vol. 74, LetterPress Book, Microfilm roll KA58, p. 294, Oklahoma Historical Society, and Letter, Randlett to Samuel Brosius, 12 December 1899, ibid., p. 277.

7. *An Appeal on Behalf of the Apache, Kiowa and Comanche*, 1899, IRA Papers, reel 102; Sen. Doc. 75, 56th Cong., 1st sess., 1900; Sen. Doc. 170, Pt. 1, 14 February 1900; Pt. 2, 3 March; Pt. 3, 6 March, Serial No. 3852, vol. 10; *El Reno Globe*, 4 July 1901.

8. The quotation is from Scott, *Some Memories of a Soldier*, 201. Other sources are Letter by Scott, 11 May 1893, in Scott Papers, No. 1909, National Anthropological Archives, and testimony of Kiowa-Apache Tennyson Berry, who accompanied one of the delegations, in Indian Claims Commission, *Kiowa, Comanche, and Apache v. United States*, 11 May 1949, *Kiowa-Comanche Indians*, 2:82.

9. *Cong. Rec.*, vol. 31, pt. 5, 55th Cong., 2d sess., House, 22 April 1898, p. 4201; vol. 32, pt. 2, 55th Cong., 3d sess., Senate, 9 February 1899, p. 1639. See Sen. Doc. 75, 56th Cong., 1st sess., 15 January 1900, Serial No. 3850, vol. 8.

10. Ibid., vol. 33, pt. 1, 56th Cong., 1st sess., Senate, 11 January 1900, p. 762; pt. 2, House, 15 February 1900, p. 1857; pt. 3, Senate, 6 March 1900, p. 2581; House Rept. 419 to acc. S. 255, 22 February 1900, p. 5.

11. Letters, Brosius to Matthew Sniffen, 10 and 12 March 1900, and Letter, Brosius to Welsh, 13 June 1900, IRA Papers, reel 15; For background see Hagan, *Indian Rights Association*, 15–22, 197.

12. Act of 6 June 1900, 31 Stat. 672, as Sec. 6 of the Fort Hall Agreement. Enactment at *Cong. Rec.*, vol. 33, pt. 8, Senate, 56th Cong., 1st sess., 6 June 1900, p. 6799.

13. Letter, Brosius to Editor, *Washington Post*, 20 October 1902.

14. Letter, Philip Garrett and Welsh to President, 6 June 1900, IRA Papers, reel 75.

15. Letter, District Superintendent J. A. Buntin to Tatro of the Senate Committee on Indian Affairs, 8 April 1929, in Senate, Committee on Indian Affairs, *Survey of Conditions of Indians in the U.S.*, Hearings, 71st Cong., 3d sess., 17–22 November 1930, Pt. 15, p. 7271.

16. Letter, Brosius to Welsh, 13 June 1900, IRA Papers, reel 15.

17. Commissioner of Indian Affairs, *Annual Report*, 1900, pp. 538–40.

18. *Washington Post*, 20 October 1902.

19. Testimony of Thomas P. Gore in House, Committee on Indian Affairs, *KCA Jurisdictional Act*, Hearings on J. Res. 290, 67th Cong., 1st sess., 18 and 21 July 1939, p. 8; Findings of Fact in *Kiowa-Comanche Indians*, 2:184–85.

20. Report of Francis Leupp, 30 November 1903, in Interior Department, *Annual*

Report, 1903, Indian Affairs, Pt. 2, *Commission to Five Civilized Tribes*, 1904, p. 494; *El Reno Weekly Globe*, 28 June and 4 July 1901.

CHAPTER 7, THE LONE WOLF MOVEMENT

1. Springer Collection, Chicago Historical Society; *Chicago Daily Tribune*, 5 December 1903, p. 5; *Chicago Record-Herald*, 5 December 1903, p. 2. Quotations are from his 1897 letter printed in Sen. Doc. 164, 54th Cong., 2d sess., 1897, Serial No. 3471, vol. 5, pp. 11–12.

2. *El Reno Weekly Globe*, 28 June 1901.

3. Virtually no record exists of local legal involvement on behalf of Indians, with the exception of probates of deceased Indians' estates. See *Harry Whitebead v. Barker*, September 1899, Canadian County District Court, Appearance Docket No. 7, p. 257, El Reno, Oklahoma, for the return of possessions. Federal Indian agents mentioned the presence of local attorneys during some annuity payments. Randlett's quotation in Commissioner of Indian Affairs, *Annual Report*, 1903, pt. 1, p. 266.

4. Berthrong, "Cattlemen on the Cheyenne-Arapaho Reservation," sees absence of a cattle lobby as the reason for the earlier allotment of the Cheyenne-Arapaho country. The lobby's delaying effort for the KCA Reserve is the subject of Hagan, "Kiowas, Comanches, and Cattlemen," esp. 355.

5. Southward, "History of Comanche County," 72.

6. Hagan, "Kiowas, Comanches, and Cattlemen," 355.

7. Hagan, *United States–Comanche Relations*, 263–64, and Pennington, "Government Policy and Farming," 333, for the controversy. Pedrick's family link in Boyd, *Kiowa Voices*, 2:235. Also known for a time as Laura Doanmoe, she was the first Kiowa woman ever to attend college, in Carlisle, Pennsylvania.

8. Randlett's version of the Lone Wolf suit in Commissioner of Indian Affairs, *Annual Report*, 1903, pt. 1, 260–66.

9. Records are found in the Canadian County District Court, El Reno, Oklahoma.

10. *Rebecca, Bettie, and Floyd Young, et al., v. United States*, Old Court Records microfilm, case no. 804, Canadian County District Court, El Reno, Oklahoma. The files of the case were not closed until 1913 because they were used in other litigation. The Youngs were defeated. Correspondence on the Cox suit in the Springer Collection, Chicago Historical Society. Richards's comment in *Report of W. A. Richards*, Sen. Doc. 341, 57th Cong., 1st sess., 5 May 1902, Serial No. 4241, vol. 22, p. 13.

11. 118 U.S. 375 (1886).

12. 11 Wall. 616 (1871).

13. 2 Pet. 253 (1829) at 314.

14. Citing *Foster v. Neilson*, 2 Pet. 253 (1829) at 307, again; *Fellows v. Blacksmith*, 19 How. 366 (1856) at 372; *Cherokee Nation v. Southern Kansas Railway Co.*, 135 U.S. 641 (1890); *U.S. v. Old Settlers*, 148 U.S. 427 (1892); and *U.S. v. Choctaws et al. Nations*,

179 U.S. 4494 (1900) at 532, 535. Case no. 1109, Supreme Court of the District of Columbia, 20 June 1901, RG 267, file 18454, National Archives.

15. Decree of the Court of Appeals of the District of Columbia, No. 1109, 4 March 1902, RG 267, file 18454, National Archives, as well as Opinion of Court on Motion for Re-Argument, No. 1109, Case No. 22338, Docket 50, 14 March 1902, IRA Papers, reel 16. Springer's deposit in Matthew Sniffen correspondence, IRA Papers, reel 75.

16. Letter, Brosius to Welsh, 25 March 1902, IRA Papers, reel 16; clippings attached to Letter, Sniffen to Springer, 24 June 1901, May–December 1901 Correspondence, Springer Collection, Box 1901–1903.

17. Clipping, no date, Hugh Scott Papers, Box 2, No. 4396, National Anthropological Archives.

18. Letter, Springer to IRA, 25 June 1901, May–December 1901 Correspondence file, Springer Collection, Chicago Historical Society. Another example is Letter, Springer to Welsh, 23 June 1901, IRA Papers, reel 134, which enclosed the Indian correspondence.

19. Letter, Springer to Sniffen, 10 November 1902, IRA Papers, reel 16.

20. Meeting Minutes, 7 May 1902, IRA Papers, reel 99.

21. Springer served as counsel for the Indian side in *Cherokee Nation v. Hitchcock*, 187 U.S. 294 (1902). Carson in Letter to Clerk J. H. McKenney, 24 March 1902, Supreme Court Appellate Cases, RG 267, file 18454, National Archives.

22. Hagan, *Indian Rights Association*, 3, 17, 214.

23. 32 Stat. Appendix 11. Widely reprinted in newspapers; an example, *El Reno Weekly Globe*, 12 July 1901.

24. Speed, "Oklahoma Land Lottery," 668.

25. Chapman, "Land Office Business."

26. *El Reno Globe*, 12–13 July 1901.

27. Letter, Van Devanter to Hitchcock, 28 July 1901, Hitchcock Papers, Letters Received 1899–1906, RG 316, National Archives.

28. House Document No. 5, *Annual Report of Commissioner of the General Land Office, 1901*, 57th Cong., 1st sess., Serial No. 4289, vol. 22, pp. lxxiv–lxxvii and cclviii–cclxxi; Richards's Report, Sen. Doc. 341, 57th Cong., 1st sess., 5 May 1902, Serial No. 4241, vol. 22; Murphy, "History of the Opening," 26–42; Haley, "Opening of the Kiowa and Comanche Country," 53–74; *El Reno Weekly Globe*, 12–19 July 1901; and clippings attached to letter of August 9 in the Springer Collection, Correspondence May–December 1901.

CHAPTER 8, KIOWAS BEFORE THE SUPREME COURT

1. Estin, "*Lone Wolf v. Hitchcock*," 236.

2. Chapman, "Day in Court," 1.

3. *U.S. v. Cook*, 19 Wall. 591 (1873), discussed in Letter, Brosius to Welsh, 7 March

1902, IRA Papers, reel 16, and in Letter, Commissioner of Indian Affairs W. A. Jones to Interior Secretary Ethan A. Hitchcock, 5 January 1900, in Sen. Doc. 76, 56th Cong., 1st sess., p. 7.

4. 12 Stat. 512 (1862).

5. Brosius, "The Government Denying the Indian Title," *Proceedings* of the 20th Annual Meeting of the Lake Mohonk Friends of the Indian and Other Dependent Peoples in 1902 (1903), 23, and correspondence on the importance of the appeal in IRA Papers, reel 16. The Fort Hall Act thought the first instance of action without Indian consent in Brosius article above; not a case on record of treaty lands being taken without native consent in Letter, Springer to Matthew Sniffen, 26 June 1901, IRA Papers, reel 16; Supreme Court will favor KCA contract in Brosius to Herbert Welsh, 27 October 1902, ibid. Words regarding 1862 Minnesota seizure nearly identical to those of Commissioner of Indian Affairs Thomas Jefferson Morgan in 1890 *Annual Report,* p. xxix. The Crow Creek discussed in *City and State* 12 (13 March 1902): 167.

6. Brosius to Welsh, 15 March 1902, IRA Papers, reel 16.

7. *Cherokee Nation v. Hitchcock,* 187 U.S. 294 (1902). Sources for Lone Wolf litigation include: Agent James Randlett's simplistic account in Commissioner of Indian Affairs, *Annual Report,* 1903, pt. 1, 260–66; Springer Collection, Chicago Historical Society; the IRA Papers, reels 16 and 134; Ethan Allen Hitchcock Private Papers, Letters Received 1899–1906, RG 316, National Archives; Records of the Supreme Court, Supreme Court Appellate Cases, Judicial, Fiscal, and Legislative Branch, RG 267, file 18454, National Archives; and Sen. Doc. 217, 57th Cong., 2d sess., 3 March 1903, Serial No. 4430, vol. 15.

8. Letter, Brosius to Sniffen, 17 November 1902, IRA Papers, reel 16.

9. Letter, Springer to Sniffen, 10 November 1902, IRA Papers, reel 16. Binney of the IRA thought Carson was "very able"; IRA Executive Committee Minutes, 5 November 1902, IRA Papers, reel 99.

10. Letter to Welsh, 27 October 1902, IRA Papers, reel 16.

11. Letter, Van Devanter to Hitchcock, 30 July 1901, in Hitchcock Papers, RG 316, Letters Received 1899–1906, Box 3, National Archives, and clippings in Lands, Forestry, and Irrigation, Box 41; also clippings in Hugh Scott Papers, Library of Congress. Individual newspapers have been cited already.

12. Transcript of Record, Supreme Court, October Term 1901, Docket No. 601; *Lone Wolf v. Hitchcock in Equity, Appeal from the Court of Appeals of the District of Columbia, Motion to Advance* (Washington, D.C.: Gibson Brothers, 1902), in IRA Papers, reel 16; Reply Brief of Appellants in Opposition to Motion to Dismiss Appeal, in Letter, Brosius to Welsh, 2 December 1902, ibid. IRA efforts to respond to Van Devanter's claim regarding payment of money in IRA Papers, reel 75.

13. Highsaw, *Edward Douglas White,* 6, 24–25, 59.

14. Justice Philip Nichols, Jr., concurring in *Sioux Nation v. U.S.,* 601 F. 2d 1157 (1979) at 1173.

15. *Kansas Indians,* 5 Wall. 737 (1866) at 755.

16. Justices Marion Bennett and Robert Kunzig dissenting in *Sioux Nation v. U.S.*, 601 F. 2d 1157 (1979) at 1180. Dollar amount from *U.S. v. Kiowa, Comanche, and Apache Tribes*, 143 Ct. Cl. 534 (1958). See *Three Affiliated Tribes of Ft. Berthold Reservation v. U.S.*, 390 F. 2d 686 (1968) for discussion of "good faith effort."

17. Ibid., 566, citing *The Cherokee Tobacco* case, 11 Wall. 616 (1871).

18. Ibid., 566.

19. *Lone Wolf v. Hitchcock*, 187 U.S. 553 (1903) at 565, 568.

20. Ibid., 568.

21. 187 U.S. 553 at 568.

22. Ibid.

23. Ibid.

24. Ibid.

25. 118 U.S. 375 (1885) at 383.

26. 11 Wall. 616 (1871).

27. 163 U.S. 504 (1896) at 511.

28. 95 U.S. 517 (1877) at 525.

29. 174 U.S. 445 (1899) at 483.

30. 187 U.S. 294 (1902) at 306.

31. Letter, McKenney to Acting Commissioner I. C. Tonner, 31 January 1903, Supreme Court Appellate Cases, RG 267, file 18454, National Archives.

32. Twenty-first Annual Report of the IRA, 1903, p. 20, IRA Papers, reel 103. On the heels of the Court of Appeals pronouncement, another IRA writer stated that the case "contains doctrine of a very startling nature"; *City and State* 12 (13 March 1902): 166.

33. Brosius's *A New Indian Policy*, IRA Pamphlet No. 62, 2nd Series, IRA Papers, reel 102. The word "discouraging" is from Brosius, too, in Proceedings of Twenty-first Annual Meeting of IRA, 1903 (1904), 35. Identical language is used in Twentieth Annual Report of IRA, 1902 (1903), 40. Leupp, *Indian and His Problem*, 83, remarked that the decision was met with "dismay" among humanitarians. The historian William T. Hagan noted that the decision "dealt the Indians and their supporters a crushing blow" (*Indian Rights Association*, 214).

34. Brosius, "The Government Denying the Indian Title, "Proceedings of Twentieth Annual Meeting of Lake Mohonk, 1902 (1903), 24.

35. Brosius, "Report of Washington Agency," *Lone Wolf* case file, 4 March 1902, IRA Papers, reel 16.

36. Kennan, "Have Reservation Indians Any Vested Rights?" 765.

37. Idem, "Indian Lands and Fair Play," 501, as well as 498.

38. Humphrey, *Indian Dispossessed*, 274–75.

39. *Another "Century of Dishonor"?* IRA Papers, reel 102; "A Startling Decision," *City and State* 12 (13 March 1902): 166–67, which was Herbert Welsh's municipal reform publication; Kennan, "Have Reservation Indians Any Vested Rights?" 765; idem, "Indian Lands and Fair Play," 498; and Brosius in Twenty-first Annual Report of IRA, 1903, p. 35, IRA Papers, reel 103.

40. Ibid., p. 24.

41. Letter, A. Breuninger of Un-a-quaw Home Defense Bureau, June 1920, Scott Papers, Box 49, Library of Congress.

42. Matthew Sniffen, *Record of Thirty Years,* IRA Tract No. 87, 1912, p. 9, IRA Papers, reel 102.

43. Twenty-fourth Annual Report of Executive Committee of IRA (Philadelphia, 1912), 2.

44. Leupp Report, 30 November 1903, Interior Department, *Annual Reports, 1903, Indian Affairs,* pt. 2, *Commission to Five Civilized Tribes,* 1904, p. 472.

45. Garland, "Red Man's Present Needs," 488; citizenship, p. 486.

46. *Barker v. Harvey,* 181 U.S. 481 (1901), reversed *Byrne v. Alas,* 74 Cal. 628 (1888). Brosius obtained some of the Warner Ranch bond back through congressional re-imbursement of the surety company. The IRA Papers are filled with Mission Indian issues—a pet topic of the very active Helen Hunt Jackson, a longtime friend of many members of the IRA, even though she had died (1885) before Brosius himself took over the Washington, D.C., office of the IRA (1898). Hagan, *Indian Rights Association,* 109–12, discusses the cases. See Sniffen, *Record of Thirty Years,* p. 2, for reconsidering litigation as a viable avenue for redress and protection of rights. The following quotations from the Barker case are at pp. 491 and 488.

47. Henry Pancoast, *Indian Before the Law,* IRA Pamphlet, 1884, p. 20, IRA Papers, reel 102.

48. Sniffen, *Record of Thirty Years,* 1912, p. 2; Thirtieth Annual Report of IRA, 1912, p. 80; and Brosius, Thirty-third Annual Report of IRA, 1915, p. 70.

49. Minutes, 7 January 1903, IRA Papers, reel 99.

50. *Quick Bear v. Leupp,* 210 U.S. 50 (1908). Prucha, *Churches and the Indian Schools,* esp. 149–60; Hagan, *Indian Rights Association,* 247–48; and Viken, *"Quick Bear v. Leupp."* The court brief is in IRA Papers on reel 119. The IRA Papers are filled with pamphlets and speeches on the topic, 1905–1915.

CHAPTER 9, MORE INDIAN LAND LOST

1. George Kennan, *Outlook,* 70 (April 1900): 958.

2. Quoted in *Another "Century of Dishonor?"* 1904, IRA Papers, reel 102.

3. Minutes of meeting, 5 March 1902, p. 8, IRA Papers, reel 99.

4. Brosius, Report of the Washington Agency, 4 March 1902, IRA Papers, reel 16. IRA efforts are presented in *City and State* 12 (19 June 1902): 389.

5. Rev. T. L. Riggs, Report on Standing Rock Leasing, 17 March 1902, IRA Papers, reel 16.

6. *City and State* 12 (19 June 1902): 389.

7. Letter, Brosius to Welsh, 17 April 1902, IRA Papers, reel 16. See also Welsh, *The Action of the Interior Department in Forcing the Standing Rock Indians to Lease Their Lands*

to Cattle Syndicates, IRA Papers, 1902, reel 102, and Rev. Riggs, Report on Standing Rock Leasing, 17 March, 1902, ibid., reel 16.

8. Letters, Brosius to Welsh, 22 February and 12 March 1902, IRA Papers, reel 16.

9. Welsh, *Action of Interior Department in Forcing the Standing Rock Indians to Lease*, IRA Papers, reel 102.

10. His brief report is in IRA Papers, reel 102.

11. Special Agent E. B. Reynolds in Sen. Misc. Doc. 70, 53d Cong., 2d sess., 1 February 1894, Serial No. 3167, vol. 1, p. 3.

12. Letter, Browning to Acting Sec. of Int. William H. Sims, 14 September 1893, Sen. Misc. Doc. No. 70, p. 6.

13. Matthew Sniffen to Leupp, 8 July 1896, IRA Papers, reel 73; Leupp to Welsh, 27 March 1897, reel 13; Hagan, *Indian Rights Association*, 165; 29 Stat. 334.

14. Letter, Commissioner Jones to Sec. Hitchcock, 22 November 1901, in Sen. Rept. 265 to acc. S. 2513, 57th Cong., 1st sess., 30 January 1902, Serial No. 4257, vol. 2, p. 3.

15. Sen. Doc. 31, 57th Cong., 1st sess., 9 December 1901, Serial No. 4220, vol. 2, for the journal proceedings. Price on p. 5; signatures on p. 37. See Hagan, *Indian Rights Association*, 244–49, and Hoxie, *Final Promise*, 156–57.

16. House Rept. 3839 to acc. HR 17467, 57th Cong., 2d sess., 21 February 1903, Serial No. 4415, vol. 3, esp. pp. 1–2.

17. *Cong. Rec.*, vol. 38, pt. 2, House, 58th Cong., 2d sess., 30 January 1904, pp. 1421–23, on HR 10418.

18. Ibid., pt. 3, 4 March 1904, p. 2829.

19. *Cong. Rec.*, vol. 38, pt. 3, House, 58th Cong., 2d sess., 4 March 1904, pp. 2828–32. Burke included excerpts from Kennan's article, "Indian Lands and Fair Play."

20. Letter, Jones to Hitchcock, 9 January 1904, in House Rept. 443, 58th Cong., 2d sess., 21 January 1904, Serial No. 4578, vol. 2, p. 8.

21. Ibid., 4.

22. Ibid., 5. See Prucha, *Great Father*, 2: 867–68.

23. House Rept. 443, pp. 12–19.

24. Brosius, *Need for Protecting Indian Allotments*, 1904, IRA Papers, reel 102.

25. 33 Stat. 254, Ch. 1484, Act of 23 April 1904. See Hagan, *Indian Rights Association*, 244–49.

26. 34 Stat. 1230, Act of 2 March 1907. See Sniffen, *The Record of Thirty Years*, p. 11, IRA Papers, reel 102.

27. *Chickasha Express*, 8 April 1897, cited in Crawford, *Kiowa*, 65.

28. *Daily Oklahoman*, 28 June 1901, p. 2, cited in Hagan, *United States–Comanche Relations*, 268.

29. Letter, Brosius to Welsh, 19 April 1900, IRA Papers, reel 15.

30. Telegram, Randlett to Int. Sec., 25 July 1901, Kiowa Agency, vol. 90, Letterpress Book, Microfilm roll KA61, p. 165, Oklahoma Historical Society.

31. Reports of Randlett in Commissioner of Indian Affairs, *Annual Reports*, 1901–

1905; correspondence in Kiowa Agency, Letterpress Books, Oklahoma Historical Society.

32. Letter, Agent Frank Baldwin to Commissioner of Indian Affairs, 24 March 1895, Kiowa Agency, vol. 44, Letterpress Book, Microfilm roll KA22, p. 253, Oklahoma Historical Society; *Thomas Wilbourne v. Frank Baldwin and Frank Farwell*, 5 Okla. Rep. 266 (Dale ed., 1897); Letter, Baldwin to District Attorney C. R. Brooks, 2 October 1895, vol. 47, roll KA22, p. 235; Letter, Randlett to E. M. Fuller, 20 December 1899, vol. 74, roll KA53, p. 325.

33. Ibid., Letter, Randlett to Emmet Cox, 29 December 1899, p. 367.

34. Monahan, "Kiowa-Comanche Reservation," 452, 454.

35. Letter, Randlett to Huston, 16 February 1900, vol. 83, roll KA58, p. 105; Huston's deposition, p. 231.

36. Randlett in Commissioner of Indian Affairs, *Annual Report*, 1904, p. 293. Discussion of need, *Annual Report*, 1903, pt. 1, p. 262.

37. Ibid., 1905, p. 300.

38. Hagan, *United States–Comanche Relations*, 270. See Hitchcock's 9 April 1903 letter as a separate Interior Department document, and the Senate Report on the subject, Sen. Doc. No. 135, 57th Cong., 1st sess., 21 January 1902, Serial No. 4231, vol. 13.

39. Tah-ko-we-ah and Kome-ta-me-ah were permitted in 1903 to sell one-half of their allotments, subject to the approval of the secretary of the interior, in Sec. 9 of 1903 Indian Appropriation Act, 32 Stat. 1008.

40. This and the earlier quotation from Randlett, Annual Report, 1 September 1902, in Commissioner of Indian Affairs, *Annual Report*, 1902, p. 289.

41. Brosius to Welsh, 20 October 1902, IRA Papers, reel 16.

42. Randlett in Commissioner of Indian Affairs, *Annual Report*, 1903, pt. 1, p. 266.

43. Sen. Doc. No. 217, 57th Cong., 2d sess., 3 March 1903, Serial No. 4430, vol. 15, in 14 pages. Randlett's numbers are in his 23 October 1903 Annual Report in Commissioner of Indian Affairs, *Annual Report*, 1903, pt. 1, p. 264.

44. House Doc. No. 5, 58th Cong., 2d sess., 1903, pt. 2, and Hagan, *United States–Comanche Relations*, 281.

45. Letter, E. F. Baker to Springer, 16 October 1902, IRA Papers, reel 16.

46. Leupp Report, 30 November 1903, Sen. Doc. No. 26, 58th Cong., 2d sess., 15 December 1903, Serial No. 4587, vol. 2. Comment on Randlett's "grind," p. 474. Hagan, *United States–Comanche Relations*, 282–83, discusses it from the Comanche side.

47. Randlett Annual Report in Commissioner of Indian Affairs, *Annual Report*, 1905, 304.

48. *Lawton Constitution*, 27 April 1905.

49. Hagan, *United States–Comanche Relations*, 283.

50. *Cong. Rec.*, vol. 36, pt. 3, 57th Cong., 2d sess., House, 16 February 1903, p. 2291.

51. Randlett Annual Report of 4 November 1904 in Commissioner of Indian Affairs, *Annual Report*, 1904, 294.

52. John J. Fitzgerald (N.Y.) of the Committee of Indian Affairs in *Cong. Rec.*, Senate, p. 2292.

53. See the historical account, *Daily Oklahoman*, 1 August 1988; Haley, "Opening of the Kiowa and Comanche Country," 105.

54. *Cong. Rec.*, vol. 41, pt. 4, 59th Cong., 1st sess., House, 14 March 1906, p. 3825; pt. 5, 29 March, p. 4454.

55. Ibid., House, p. 4739, for payment; passage at p. 4741; signature of HR 17507 at 4 April 1906, p. 4738; 34 Stat. 213.

56. House Doc. 382, 2d sess., 1906, Serial No. 5154, vol. 51. Both Gore and Ferris began their Lawton law practices with the original opening in 1901, also the year of the start of Lone Wolf's litigation. HR 11783 signed at *Cong. Rec.*, vol. 40, pt. 4, 14 March 1906, p. 3825; 34 Stat. 550.

57. *Lawton News Republican*, 12 September 1906.

58. Blackman in Annual Report in Secretary of the Interior, *Annual Report*, 1907, 113.

59. Ibid., 114, Act of 20 March 1906, 34 Stat. 80.

60. Sen. Rept. 924 on HR 27400, 61st Cong., 3d sess., 15 December 1910, Serial No. 5843, vol. A (microfiche).

61. Act of 29 May 1908, 35 Stat. 456; Act of 25 June 1910, 36 Stat. 861; Act of 27 April 1912, 37 Stat. 91.

62. Delos K. Lone Wolf Testimony in Senate, *Survey of Conditions of Indians in the United States*, 71st Cong., 3d sess., 17–22 November 1930, pt. 15, pp. 7410 and 7413. George Hunt expressed anger over the preferential right of purchase being taken from Indians and given to white lessees nearly a quarter century later in Letter, Hunt to Senator Lynn Frazier, 26 November 1930, p. 7471.

CHAPTER 10, THE LEGACY OF *LONE WOLF*

1. Barsh and Henderson, *The Road*, 95.

2. Nebraska Rep. Edgar Howard, *Cong. Rec.*, vol. 78, pt. 11, 73rd Cong., 2d sess., House, 15 June 1934, p. 11726, and U.S., American Indian Policy Review Commission, *Final Report* (Washington, D.C.: Government Printing Office, 1977), 1:524.

3. Howard, *Cong. Rec.*, 15 June 1934, p. 11728.

4. Recommendation No. 7 of the House, *Indians of the United States, Field Investigation*, House Rept. 1133, 66th Cong., 3d sess., Serial No. 7776, vol. 1, 18 December 1920, p. 18.

5. Letter, Warren K. Moorhead to Malcolm McDowell, 22 March 1920, Scott Papers, Kiowa Agency folder, National Anthropological Archives.

6. Leasing scandals discussed in G. E. E. Lindquist Report on Kiowa Agency,

25 April 1932, for Board of Indian Commissioners, Hugh Scott Papers, National Anthropological Archives, No. 4525; "Meeting at Anadarko," 11; and Report of Kiowa Area Field Office in Senate, Committee on Interior and Insular Affairs, *Indian Land Transactions,* 85th Cong., 2d sess., 1 December 1958, p. 242.

7. Lindquist Report, 25 April 1932, Scott Papers, National Anthropological Archives, and Jasper Saunkeah Testimony, Senate *Survey of the Conditions of the Indians of the U.S.,* Pt. 15, pp. 7337–39.

8. *City and State* 12 (13 March 1902): 167. The point is made by Estin, *"Lone Wolf* v. *Hitchcock,"* 240, citing *Tee-Hit-Ton Indians v. U.S.,* 348 U.S. 272 (1955).

9. Quotation from Pound, "Nationals without a Nation," 102.

10. *U.S. v. Celestine,* 215 U.S. 278 (1909) at 290. See also *Cramer v. U.S.,* 261 U.S. 219 (1923).

11. *Gritts v. Fisher,* 224 U.S. 640 (1912); liquor in *Mosier v. U.S.,* 198 U.S. 54 (1912).

12. 197 U.S. 488 (1905) at 498.

13. 197 U.S. 488 at 499. Full control at 498.

14. Ibid., 499.

15. Quotation from Moses Clapp, *Cong. Rec.,* vol. 40, pt. 6, 59th Cong., 1 sess., Senate, 11 April 1906, p. 5052.

16. *Cong. Rec.,* vol. 41, pt. 3, 59th Cong., 3d sess., Senate, 6 February 1907, p. 2342.

17. Ibid., p. 2346, Senator Clapp.

18. McCumber Amendment, Sec. 19 of Five Tribes Act of 26 April 1906, 34 Stat. 137.

19. 221 U.S. 286 (1911).

20. 221 U.S. 286 at 316.

21. 224 U.S. 665 (1912) esp. at 671 and 678.

22. 224 U.S. 665 at 671. See Cohen, "Indian Rights and the Federal Courts," 199; Newton, "Federal Power over Indians," 195.

23. 56 L. Ed. 820 (1912) at 832.

24. *U.S. v. Sandoval,* 231 U.S. 28 (1913) at 46.

25. *Lane v. Pueblo of Santa Rosa,* 249 U.S. 110 (1919) at 113. This opinion limited executive authority, which the courts have held to a tighter fiduciary standard in dealing with Indians than Congress has.

26. *U.S. v. Creek Nation,* 295 U.S. 103 (1935) at 110, using identical language from *Lane,* 294 U.S. 110 (1919) at 113. See also *Seminole Nation v. U.S.,* 316 U.S. 286 (1942); *Menominee Tribe v. U.S.,* 59 F.2d 135 (Ct. Cl., 1944); and *Manchester Band of Pomo Indians v. U.S.,* 363 F.2d 1238 (N. C. Cal., 1973).

27. *Alcea Band of Tillamooks v. U.S.,* 329 U.S. 40 (1946) at 54, citing *Stephens v. Cherokee Nation,* 174 U.S. 445 (1899) at 478.

28. *Choate v. Trapp,* 224 U.S. 941 (1912) at 945.

29. *Shoshone Tribe v. U.S.,* 299 U.S. 476 (1937). Quotation from 5th Amendment at 497. See also *Choate v. Trapp,* 224 U.S. 941 (1912) at 945.

30. Harring, "Crow Dog's Case," book manuscript, pp. 6–7, which I am grateful to

the author for sharing with me. See also idem, "Crazy Snake and the Creek Struggle for Sovereignty"; "Crow Dog's Case."

31. Barsh and Henderson, *The Road*, 93; Clow, "Taxing the Omaha and Winnebago Trust Lands."

32. *U.S. v. Sandoval*, 231 U.S. 28 (1913) at 45.

33. Quotation from Russell, "Indian before the Law," 329.

34. Editorial, *The Nation* 71 (10 May 1900): 350.

35. *Cong. Rec.*, vol. 33, pt. 3, 56th Cong., 1st sess., Senate, 7 March 1900, p. 2618.

36. From Circularized Letter of Herbert Welsh, 16 May 1902, IRA Papers, reel 16. Welsh was outspoken in his opposition to America's overseas dominion, leading to falling support for his various pet projects such as the IRA and his reform journal *City and State*. Perhaps it also contributed to his failed health at the same time.

37. Root, *Military and Colonial Policy*, 39.

38. *Lone Wolf v. Hitchcock*, 187 U.S. 553 at 565, quoting *Beecher v. Wetherby*, 95 U.S. 517 (1877) at 525. The following quotations are from pp. 564, 565, 567. I relied on Williams, "United States Indian Policy," and Hoxie, *A Final Promise*.

39. Root, *Military and Colonial Policy*, 293. Root's use of Indian case law, 320–21.

40. Magoon, *Reports of the Law of Civil Government*, 54, 87, 119, 698–730.

41. 212 U.S. 449 (1909) at 458.

42. 182 U.S. 244 (1901). Chief Justice Melville Fuller dissenting at 372.

43. Highsaw, *Edward Douglas White*, 11.

44. Ibid., 173, 186.

45. "The Philippine Problem," 138. Mark Twain, following, at p. 154.

46. Roosevelt, *Strenuous Life*, 18.

47. Taft, Address of 13 December 1903 in Sen. Doc. 191, *The Duty of Americans in the Philippines*, 58th Cong., 2d sess., 8 March 1904, Serial No. 4591, vol. 6, pp. 7 and 3.

48. Beveridge, *Cong. Rec.*, vol. 33, pt. 1, 56th Cong., 1st sess., 9 January 1900, p. 711, and Proceedings of 19th Annual Meeting of Lake Mohonk Conference in 1901 (1902), p. vi.

49. Leupp, *Indian and His Problem*, 93.

50. IRA President Merrill Gates, "President's Address" to Seventeenth Annual Lake Mohonk Conference in Commissioner of Indian Affairs, *Annual Report*, 1899, p. 296.

51. Randolph, "Constitutional Aspects of Annexation," 309.

52. *Lone Wolf v. Hitchcock*, 187 U.S. 553 at 565, borrowed from *Beecher v. Wetherby*, 95 U.S. 517 (1877) at 525. Identical phrasing in Leupp, *Indian and His Problem*, 83.

53. Cover letter from Welsh, 17 February 1899, IRA Papers, reel 102.

54. *Buffalo* (N.Y.) *Courier*, 21 November 1899, in Hitchcock Papers, Box 41, National Archives. Hagan, *Indian Rights Association*, 191–93, deals with Welsh's views.

55. Editorial, *The Nation* 70 (8 February 1900): 104.

56. Simeon Baldwin, "Constitutional Questions," *Harvard Law Review*. Baldwin in

an earlier version stated that while Indian tribes in the United States were *not* subject to federal jurisdiction, citing the *Elk v. Wilkins* and *Kagama* cases, "the more civilized natives" of the islands surely would be subject to United States jurisdiction under the terms of the treaty with Spain concluding the warfare ("Constitutional Questions," American Historical Association, *Annual Report*, 331).

CHAPTER 11, CONCLUSION

1. *Sioux Nation v. U.S.*, 448 U.S. 371 (1980) at 413–14.
2. Charles F. Wilkinson, *American Indians, Time and the Law*, 79–80.
3. As one example, Newton, "Judicial Role in Fifth Amendment Taking," 248, hypothesizes that as natural resources become more scarce and Indian land becomes more coveted, Congress will "take" more tribal property.
4. Phillipa Strum, "The Supreme Court and the 'Political Question'" (Ph.D. dissertation, New School for Social Research, 1964), and Henkin, "Is There a 'Political Question' Doctrine?"
5. *Delaware Tribal Business Committee v. Weeks*, 430 U.S. 73 (1977) at 84. See Alfred Ziontz, "Indian Litigation," in S. Cadwalader and V. Deloria, eds., *The Aggressions of Civilization*, (Philadelphia: Temple University Press, 1984): 167.
6. *Sioux Nation v. U.S.*, 448 U.S. 371 (1980) at 413.
7. 448 U.S. 371 at 408, citing *Lone Wolf.* See "Federal Plenary Power"; Newton, "Judicial Role in Fifth Amendment Taking"; and Justice Hugo Black's dissent in *Federal Power Commission v. Tuscarora Indian Nation*, 362 U.S. 99 (1960).
8. *Hodel v. Irving*, 481 U.S. 704 (1986) at 734, quotation marks deleted.
9. Ross O. Swimmer Testimony, House, Committee on Interior and Insular Affairs, *To Provide for the Exchange of Certain Lands between the Hopi and Navajo Indian Tribes*, Hearing on HR 4281, 99th Cong., 2d sess., 8 May 1986, Serial No. 99-32, p. 92.
10. *Delaware Tribal Business Committee v. Weeks*, 430 U.S. 73 (1977) at 84.
11. *U.S. v. Nice*, 241 U.S. 591 (1916) at 597.
12. *Delaware* case above, at 83; *Solem v. Bartlett*, 104 S. Ct. 1161 (1984) in a footnote at 1166 reaffirming congressional power under the Lone Wolf decision.
13. *Yankton Sioux v. U.S.*, 623 F.2d 159 (Ct. Cl., 1980) at 181.
14. *U.S. v. Lane*, 258 F. 520 (1919) at 522; *Mickadiet v. Payne*, 269 F. 194 (1920) at 197; *McClanahan v. Arizona Tax Commission*, 411 U.S. 164 (1973) at 172; *Montana v. U.S.*, 450 U.S. 544 (1980) at 564.
15. *Muscogee (Creek) Nation v. Hodel*, 851 F.2d 1439 (D. C. Cir., 1988), discussing abolition of tribal courts.
16. *U.S. v. Wheeler*, 435 U.S. 313 (1978) at 323; *Santa Clara Pueblo v. Martinez*, 436 U.S. 49 (1978) at 56; *National Farmers Union Insurance Companies v. Crow Tribe*, 105 S. Ct. 2447 (1985) at 2451. Many other examples exist.
17. *Santa Clara Pueblo v. Martinez*, 436 U.S. 49 at 56. Also see *Merrion v. Jicarilla*

Apache Tribe, 455 U.S. 130 (1985) at 184, Justice John Paul Stevens's dissent. See Worthen, "Shedding New Light," 99–111.

18. *U.S. v. Wheeler,* 435 U.S. 313 (1978) at 323.

19. *Merrion v. Jicarilla Apache Tribe,* 455 U.S. 130 (1980). Justice Thurgood Marshall at 155, esp. note 21; dissenting Justice John Paul Stevens at 172, esp. note 23. See *Solem v. Bartlett,* 104 S. Ct. 1161 (1984) at 1166 note 11.

20. Newton, "Federal Power over Indians," 197.

21. Grossman, "Indians and the Law," 112. Also see Coulter, "Denial of Legal Remedies"; Ball, "Constitution, Courts, Indian Tribes," 54; Barsh, "Indigenous North America"; and Wyatt, "Supreme Court, *Lyng,*" 649–54, esp. 651.

22. Permits required for killing eagles for religious purposes only reflected Congress's belief "that it was abrogating the rights of Indians to take eagles," *U.S. v. Dion,* 476 U.S. 734 (1986) at 743; "The intent to abrogate inconsistent treaty rights is clear enough from the express terms of Pub. L. 280, "*Washington v. Yakima Indian Nation,* 439 U.S. 463 (1979) at 478 note 22; and, "Congress understood that it was not bound by the three-fourths consent requirement of the 1868 Treaty with the Sioux Nation," *Rosebud Sioux Tribe v. Kneip,* 430 U.S. 584 (1977) at 594; as well as the examination of federal legal requirements to abrogate an Indian treaty in Laurence, "Abrogation of Indian Treaties," 862–86.

23. Wilkinson and Volkman, "Judicial Review of Indian Treaty Abrogation," 645–59, urge adoption of an explicit statement by the legislature tied to specific action; while Mike Townsend calls for supplementing the last-in-time rule with an express statement that offers a justification satisfactory to international law's *rebus sic stantibus;* Townsend, "Congressional Abrogation of Indian Treaties," 810–11. Laurence supports the vague tests established in selected environmental cases involving Indians; Laurence, "Abrogation of Indian Treaties," 866–70, 878–85.

EPILOGUE

1. House, Committee on Indian Affairs, *KCA Jurisdiction Act,* Hearings on J. Res. 290, 67th Cong., 1st sess., 18–21 July 1939, pp. 3–13.

2. Chapman, "Day in Court."

APPENDIX 2

1. Brackets in the list of signatories enclose the author's emendations of names that are given in nonstandard or mistaken form in the published Agreement.

BIBLIOGRAPHY

MANUSCRIPTS

Chicago, Illinois
  Chicago Historical Society
    William McKendree Springer Papers
El Reno, Oklahoma, Canadian County Courthouse
  County and District Court Civil Cases, Old Court Records, Microcopy
Forth Worth, Texas
  Federal Records Center
    RG 75, Records of Bureau of Indian Affairs
    Kiowa Agency Files Microcopy
Oklahoma City, Oklahoma
  Oklahoma Historical Society
    Berlin B. Chapman Papers
    Indian-Pioneer Papers
    Kiowa Agency Files Microcopy
  State Capitol, Court Clerk's Office
    Oklahoma State Bar Records
Philadelphia, Pennsylvania
  Historical Society of Pennsylvania
    Indian Rights Association Papers Microcopy
Washington, D.C.
  Library of Congress
    Charles J. Bonaparte Papers
    Hugh L. Scott Papers
  National Archives and Records Service
    RG 46, Records of the Senate
    RG 48, Records of the Office of the Secretary of the Interior
      Letters Sent, 1849–1907
      Letters Sent, 1849–1903, Microcopy M606
    RG 75, Records of the Bureau of Indian Affairs
      Inspection Reports of Field Jurisdictions, Kiowa Agency, 1875–1898,
        Microcopy
      Letter press copy volumes for 1871–1901
      Letters Received, 1824–1907, Microcopy M234
      Letters Sent, 1824–1907, Microcopy M21
      Report books, 1838–1885, Microcopy M348

Superintendents' Annual Narrative and Statistical Reports from Field Juris-
dictions, 1907–1938, Microcopy M1070
RG 267, Supreme Court Appellate Cases
RG 316, Ethan Allen Hitchcock Private Papers
Smithsonian Institution, National Anthropological Archives
Bureau of American Ethnology Records
Hugh Scott Papers

FEDERAL GOVERNMENT DOCUMENTS

American Indian Policy Review Commission, *Final Report*, vol. 1. Washington, D.C.:
Government Printing Office, 1977.
Board of Indian Commissioners Annual Reports, reprinted as part of the Annual
Report of the Commissioner of Indian Affairs, 1880–1933.
Congressional Globe, 1867–1869.
Congressional Record, 1880–1990.
House, Committee on Indian Affairs, *Investigation of the Administration of Indian Affairs
in the State of Oklahoma*, Hearings, 11 November–12 December 1924, 68th Cong.,
1st Sess.
House, Committee on Indian Affairs, *Kiowa, Comanche, and Apache Indians Jurisdic-
tional Act*, Hearings on J. Res. 290, 67th Cong., 1st Sess., 18–21 July 1939.
House Document No. 5, *Annual Report of the Commissioner of the General Land Office,
1901*, 57th Cong., 1st sess., Serial No. 4289, vol. 22.
House Executive Document No. 47, *Report of the Public Land Commission*, Parts 1–2,
46th Cong., 3d Sess., 18 January 1881, Serial No. 1975–1976, vols. 25–26.
House, Joint Commission to Investigate Indian Affairs, Hearings, Part 9: Kiowa and
Comanche Reservation, 21 January–25 March 1914, Serial No. 1.
House Report No. 1095, *Reserving Lands in Oklahoma*, 52th Cong., 1st Sess., 15 April
1892, Serial No. 3045, vol. 4.
House Report No. 1133, *Indians of the United States, Field Investigation*, 66th Cong., 3d
Sess., 18 December 1920, Serial No. 7776, vol. 1.
House Report No. 3768, *Cherokee Outlet*, 51st Cong., 2d Sess., 11 February 1891,
Serial No. 2888, vol. 4.
Indian Affairs: Laws and Treaties. Kappler, Charles J., ed. 3 vols. Washington, D.C.:
Government Printing Office, 1904.
Interior Department, *Annual Reports*, 1890–1907.
Interior Department, Indian Inspector for Indian Territory, *Annual Reports*, 1899–
1907.
Interior Department, Office of Indian Affairs, *Report of the Commissioner of Indian
Affairs*, 1869–1940.
Morgan, Thomas Jefferson. "The Political Status of Indians." In Interior Depart-
ment, Commissioner of Indian Affairs, *Annual Report, 1891*, Vol. 1, pp. 9–37.

National Resources Board, Land Planning Committee, *Report.* Washington, D.C.: Government Printing Office, 1934.

Proceedings of the Annual Meeting of the Lake Mohonk Conference of Friends of the Indian and Other Dependent Peoples, 1897–1903, printed as part of the annual report of the Board of Indian Commissioners in the Commissioner of Indian Affairs Annual Reports.

"Report of the Joint Committee on Securing for the Indians the Protection of the Civil Law," General Convention of the Protestant Episcopal Church of the United States. In Interior Department, Commissioner of Indian Affairs, *Annual Report, 1888,* pp. 185–88.

"Report to the President by the Indian Peace Commission, 7 January 1868." In Interior Department, Commissioner of Indian Affairs, *Annual Report, 1868,* House Executive Document No. 97, 40th Cong., 2d Sess., 14 January 1868, Serial No. 1337, vol. 11.

Richards, W. A. "Report of W. A. Richards: The Opening of the Kiowa, Comanche, and Apache and Wichita Lands in Oklahoma." In Senate Document No. 341, 57th Cong., 1st Sess., 5 May 1902, Serial No. 4241, vol. 22.

Senate, Committee on Indian Affairs, *Investigation of Affairs at the KCA Indian Reservation,* Senate Document No. 34, 55th Cong., 1st Sess., 13 April 1897, Serial No. 3559, vol. 2.

Senate, Committee on Indian Affairs, *Report on Conditions of the Indians in Indian Territory,* Senate Report No. 1278, 49th Cong., 1st Sess., 4 June 1886, Part I, Serial No. 2362, vol. 8, esp. Senator Dawes, pp. i–xxvi.

Senate, Committee on Indian Affairs, *Survey of Conditions of the Indians of the United States,* Hearings, 1928–35.

Senate, Committee on Interior and Insular Affairs, *Indian Land Transactions,* Committee print, 85th Cong., 2d Sess., 1 December 1958.

Senate Document No. 26, *Kiowa Indian Agency, Results of Investigation,* 58th Cong., 2d Sess., 15 December 1903, Serial No. 4587, vol. 2 (Leupp Report).

Senate Document No. 191, *The Duty of Americans in the Philippines,* 58th Cong., 2d Sess., 8 March 1904, Serial No. 4591, vol. 6.

Senate Executive Document No. 32, *Survey of Land in Indian Territory,* 45th Cong., 2d Sess., 21 February 1878, Serial No. 1780, vol. 1.

Senate Executive Document No. 63, *Report on the Cherokee Outlet,* 52d Cong., 1st Sess., 21 March 1892, Serial No. 2900, vol. 5.

Senate Executive Document No. 109, *Lands in Indian Territory,* 48th Cong., 1st Sess., 18 February 1884, Serial No. 2167, vol. 6.

Senate Executive Document No. 78, *Legal Status of Indians in the Indian Territory,* 51st Cong., 1st Sess., 12 March 1890, Serial No. 2686-78, vol. 9.

Senate Report No. 268, *Effect of the Fourteenth Amendment to the Constitution upon Indian Tribes,* 41st Cong., 3d Sess., 1870, Serial No. 1443, vol. 1.

Senate Report No. 744, *Affairs in Indian Territory,* 45th Cong., 3d Sess., 11 February 1879, Serial No. 1839, vol. 3.

Statutes at Large, 1900–1920.
Supreme Court Reports, 1829–1978.

JEROME AGREEMENT WITH KIOWA, COMANCHE, APACHE INDIANS

Senate, Committee on Indian Affairs, *Indian Memorial,* Senate Document No. 76, 56th Cong., 1st Sess., 15 January 1900, Serial No. 3850, vol. 8.

Senate, Committee on Indian Affairs, *Petition,* Senate Miscellaneous Document No. 102, 53d Cong., 2d Sess., 1 March 1894, Serial No. 3167, vol. 1.

Senate, Committee on Indian Affairs, *Quality, Nature, and Character of Lands of the KCA Reservation,* Senate Document No. 75, 56th Cong., 1st Sess., 15 January 1900, Serial No. 3850, vol. 8.

Senate Document No. 77, *Jerome Commission Journal,* 55th Cong., 3d Sess., 26 January 1899, Serial No. 3731, vol. 7.

Senate Document No. 84, *Number of Adult Males among Kiowa, Comanche, and Apache Indians, October, 1892,* 55th Cong., 3d Sess., 28 January 1899, Serial No. 3731, vol. 7.

Senate Document No. 170, Part 2, *Memoranda Respecting KCA Treaty,* 56th Cong., 1st Sess., 3 March 1900, Serial No. 3852, vol. 10.

Senate Document No. 217, *Memorial,* 57th Cong., 2d Sess., 3 March 1903, Serial No. 4430, vol. 15.

Senate Executive Document No. 17, *Jerome Agreement,* 52d Cong., 2d Sess., 4 January 1893, Serial No. 3055, vol. 1.

AGREEMENTS WITH SIOUX INDIANS

Senate Doc. No. 31, *Agreement with Indians of Rosebud Reservation, South Dakota,* 57th Cong., 1st Sess., 9 December 1901, Serial No. 4220, vol. 2.

Senate Miscel. Doc. No. 70, *Communication from Commissioner of Indian Affairs on Ratification of Agreement between Indians of Rosebud Agency and Certain Indians of Lower Brule Agency,* 53d Cong., 2d Sess., 1 February 1894, Serial No. 3167, vol. 1.

Senate Report No. 265 to acc. S.2513, *To Ratify Agreement with Indians of Lower Brule Agency, South Dakota,* 57th Cong., 1st Sess., 30 January 1902, Serial No. 4257, vol. 2.

House Report No. 443, *To Ratify and Amend Agreement with Indians of Rosebud Reservation in South Dakota,* 58th Cong., 2d Sess., 21 January 1904, Serial No. 4578, vol. 2.

CONGRESSIONAL BILLS

Senate Report No. 924 on HR 27400, *To Repeal Act Issuing Land Patent to James F. Rowell,* 61st Cong., 3d Sess., 15 December 1910, Serial No. 5843, vol. A (microfiche).

House, Committee on Interior and Insular Affairs, *To Provide for the Exchange of Certain Lands between the Hopi and Navajo Indian Tribes,* Hearing on HR 4281, 99th Cong., 2d Sess., 8 May 1986, Serial No. 99-32.

House Doc. No. 382, *Draft of Bill for Allotments to Certain Children of Kiowa, Comanche, and Apache Indians,* 59th Cong., 2d Sess., 1906, Serial No. 5154, vol. 51.

House Report No. 3839 to acc. HR 17467, *To Ratify and Amend Agreement with Indians of Rosebud Reservation, South Dakota,* 57th Cong., 2d Sess., 21 February 1903, Serial No. 4415, vol. 3.

BOOKS, ARTICLES, AND UNPUBLISHED MATERIALS

Baldwin, Simeon E. "Constitutional Questions Incident to the Acquisition and Government by the U.S. of Island Territory." American Historical Association *Annual Report,* 1898, pp. 313–43. Washington, D.C.: Government Printing Office, 1899.

———. "The Constitutional Questions Incident to the Acquisition and Government by the U.S. of Island Territory." *Harvard Law Review* 12 (25 January 1899): 393–416.

Ball, Milner. "Constitution, Courts, Indian Tribes." American Bar Foundation *Research Journal* 1 (1987): 3–140.

Barsh, Russel. "Indigenous North America and Contemporary International Law." *Oregon Law Review* 62 (1983): 73–125.

Barsh, Russel, and James Y. Henderson. *The Road: Indian Tribes and Political Liberty.* Berkeley and Los Angeles: University of California Press, 1980.

Battey, Thomas C. *Life and Adventures of a Quaker among the Indians.* Boston: Lee and Shepard, 1875.

Berthrong, Donald. "Cattlemen on the Cheyenne-Arapaho Reservation, 1883–1885." *Arizona and the West* 13 (Spring 1971): 5–32.

Bodayla, Stephen D. "'Can an Indian Vote?': *Elk v. Wilkins,* A Setback for Indian Citizenship." *Nebraska History* 67 (Winter 1986): 372–80.

Boyd, Maurice, ed. *Kiowa Voices.* 2 vols. Fort Worth: Texas Christian University Press, 1981–83.

Butler, Josiah. "Pioneer School Teaching at the Comanche-Kiowa Agency School, 1870–1873." *Chronicles of Oklahoma* 6 (September 1928): 483–528.

Chapman, Berlin B. "The Day in Court for the Kiowa, Comanche and Apache Tribes." *Great Plains Journal* 2 (Fall 1962): 1–21.

———. "Final Report of the Cherokee Commission." *Chronicles of Oklahoma* 19 (December 1941): 356–58.

———. "How the Cherokees Acquired and Disposed of the Outlet." *Chronicles of Oklahoma* 16 (March 1938): 36–51.

———. "Land Office Business at Lawton and El Reno." *Great Plains Journal* 7 (Fall 1967): 1–25.

———. "Secret 'Instructions and Suggestions' to the Cherokee Commission." *Chronicles of Oklahoma* 26 (Winter 1948–49): 449–58.

Clow, Richmond L. "Cattlemen and Tribal Rights: The Standing Rock Leasing Conflict of 1902." *North Dakota History* 54 (Spring 1987): 23–30.

———. "Taxing the Omaha and Winnebago Trust Lands, 1910–1917." *American Indian Culture and Research Journal* 9, no. 4 (1985): 1–22.

Cohen, Felix S. *Felix S. Cohen's Handbook of Federal–Indian Law,* ed. Rennard Strickland. Charlottesville, Va.: Michie Bobbs-Merrill, 1982.

———. "Indian Rights and the Federal Courts." *Minnesota Law Review* 24 (January 1940): 145–200.

Conover, George. *Sixty Years in Southwest Oklahoma.* Anadarko, Okla.: Plummer, 1927.

Corwin, Hugh D. "Protestant Missionary Work among the Comanches and Kiowas." *Chronicles of Oklahoma* 46 (Spring 1968): 41–57.

Coulter, Robert T. "The Denial of Legal Remedies to Indian Nations under U.S. Law." *American Indian Journal* 3 (September 1977): 5–11.

Crawford, Isabel. *Kiowa: The History of a Blanket Indian Mission.* New York: Fleming H. Revell, 1915.

Dawes, Henry L. "Have We Failed with the Indian?" *Atlantic Monthly* 84 (August 1899): 280–85.

Deloria, Vine, Jr., ed. *Of Utmost Good Faith.* San Francisco: Straight Arrow Press, 1971.

Deloria, Vine, Jr., and Clifford M. Lytle. *American Indians, American Justice.* Austin: University of Texas Press, 1983.

DeMallie, Raymond J. "American Indian Treaty Making: Meanings and Motives." *American Indian Journal* 3 (1977): 2–10.

———. "Early Kiowa and Comanche Treaties: The Treaties of 1835 and 1837." *American Indian Journal* 9 (1986): 16–20.

———. *The Jerome Agreement between the Kiowa, Comanche & Apache Tribes and the United States Government.* Washington, D.C.: Institute for the Development of Indian Law, 1977.

———. "Touching the Pen: Plains Indian Treaty Councils in Ethnohistorical Perspective." In *Ethnicity on the Great Plains,* ed. Frederick E. Luebke, pp. 38–53. Lincoln: University of Nebraska Press, 1980.

Estin, Ann Laquer. "*Lone Wolf v. Hitchcock:* The Long Shadow." In *The Aggressions of Civilization,* ed. Sandra Cadwalader and Vine Deloria, Jr., pp. 215–45. Philadelphia: Temple University Press, 1984.

"Federal Plenary Power in Indian Affairs after *Weeks* and *Sioux Nation.*" *University of Pennsylvania Law Review* 131 (November 1982): 235–70.

Fehrenbach, T. R. *Comanches: Destruction of a People.* New York: Knopf, 1974.

Fixico, Donald L. "As Long as the Grass Grows . . . The Cultural Conflicts and Political Strategies of U.S.–Indian Treaties." In *Ethnicity and War*, ed. Winston A. Van Horne and Thomas V. Tonnesen, pp. 128–49. Milwaukee: University of Wisconsin System, American Ethnic Studies Coordinating Committee/Urban Corridor Consortium, 1984.

Forbes, Bruce David. "John Jasper Methvin, Methodist 'Missionary to the Western Tribes' (Oklahoma)." In *Churchmen and the Western Indians, 1820–1920*, ed. Floyd A. O'Neil and Clyde A. Milner, II, pp. 41–73. Norman: University of Oklahoma Press,1985.

Garland, Hamlin. "The Red Man's Present Needs." *North American Review* 174 (April 1902): 476–88.

Getches, David H., Daniel M. Rosenfelt, and Charles F. Wilkinson, eds. *Federal–Indian Law: Cases and Materials*. St. Paul: West Publishing Co., 1979.

Grossman, George. "Indians and the Law." In *New Directions in American Indian History*, ed. Colin G. Calloway, pp. 97–127. Norman: University of Oklahoma Press, 1988.

Hagan, William T. *The Indian Rights Association: The Herbert Welsh Years, 1882–1904*. Tucson: University of Arizona Press, 1985.

———. "Kiowas, Comanches, and Cattlemen, 1867–1906: A Case Study of the Failure of U.S. Reservation Policy." *Pacific Historical Review* 40 (August 1971): 333–55.

———. *United States–Comanche Relations: The Reservation Years*. New Haven: Yale University Press, 1976.

Haley, John Curry. "The Opening of the Kiowa and Comanche Country." M.A. thesis, University of Oklahoma, 1940.

Hall, Kermit. "The Children of Cabins: The Lower Federal Judiciary, Modernization, and the Political Culture, 1789–1899." *Northwestern University Law Review* 75 (October 1982): 423–65.

Harring, Sidney L. "Crazy Snake and the Creek Struggle for Sovereignty: The Native American Legal Culture and American Law." *American Journal of Legal History* 34 (October 1990): 365–80.

———. "Crow Dog's Case: A Chapter in the History of Tribal Sovereignty." *American Indian Law Review* 14, no. 2 (1989): 191–239.

Henkin, Louis. "Is There a 'Political Question' Doctrine?" *Yale Law Review* 85 (April 1976): 597–625.

Highsaw, Robert B. *Edward Douglas White: Defender of the Conservative Faith*. Baton Rouge: Louisiana State University Press, 1981.

Hoig, Stan. *The Oklahoma Land Rush of 1889*. Oklahoma City: Oklahoma Historical Society, 1984.

Hoxie, Frederick E. *A Final Promise: The Campaign to Assimilate the Indians, 1880–1920*. Lincoln: University of Nebraska Press, 1984.

Hume, C. Ross. "Pioneer Missionary Enterprises of Kiowa, Comanche, and Wichita Indian Reservations." *Chronicles of Oklahoma* 29 (Spring 1951): 113–16.

Humphrey, Seth K. *The Indian Dispossessed*. Boston: Little, Brown, 1905.

Jones, Douglas C. "Indian Lands and Fair Play." *Outlook* 76 (27 February 1904): 498–501.

———. "Medicine Lodge Revisited." *Kansas Historical Quarterly* 35 (Summer 1969): 130–42.

———. *The Treaty of Medicine Lodge.* Norman: University of Oklahoma Press, 1966.

Kennan, George. "Have Reservation Indians Any Vested Rights?" *Outlook* 70 (29 March 1902): 759–65.

Kiowa-Comanche Indians. 2 vols. New York: Garland Publishers, 1974.

Kvasnicka, Robert M., and Herman J. Viola, eds. *The Commissioner of Indian Affairs, 1824–1977.* Lincoln: University of Nebraska Press, 1979.

Laurence, Robert. "The Abrogation of Indian Treaties by Federal Statutes Protective of the Environment." *Natural Resources Journal* 31 (Fall 1991): 859–86.

Leupp, Francis E. *The Indian and His Problem.* New York: Scribner's, 1910.

Lindquist, G. E. E., with Flora Warren Seymour. "Indian Treaty Making." *Chronicles of Oklahoma* 26 (Winter 1948–49): 416–48.

Magoon, Charles E. Reports of the Law of Civil Government in Territory Subject to Military Occupation by the Military Forces of the United States. Washington, D.C.: Government Printing Office, 1902.

Mardock, Robert. *Reformers and the American Indian.* Columbia: University of Missouri Press, 1971.

Mayhall, Mildred. *The Kiowas.* Norman: University of Oklahoma Press, 1962.

"Meeting at Anadarko." *Indians at Work* 1 (15 April 1934): 11.

Methvin, John Jasper. *In the Limelight; or, A History of Anadarko and Vicinity.* Anadarko, Okla.: author, 1925; repr. Anadarko: Plummer, 1928.

———. "Reminiscences of Life among the Indians." *Chronicles of Oklahoma* 5 (June 1927): 166–79.

Miller, Arthur S. *The Supreme Court in American Life.* New York: Free Press, 1968.

Momaday, N. Scott. *The Names: A Memoir.* New York: Harper and Row, 1976.

———. *The Way to Rainy Mountain.* Albuquerque: University of New Mexico Press, 1969.

Monahan, Forrest D., Jr. "The Kiowa-Comanche Reservation in the 1890s." *Chronicles of Oklahoma* 45 (Winter 1967–68): 451–63.

———. "Kiowa–Federal Relations in Kansas, 1865–68." *Chronicles of Oklahoma* 49 (Winter 1971–72): 477–91.

Mooney, James. "Calendar History of the Kiowa Indians." In Bureau of American Ethnology, *Seventeenth Annual Report,* for the Years 1895–96, vol. 1, pt. 1, pp. 141–447. Washington, D.C.: Government Printing Office, 1898.

Murphy, William Hymen. "A History of the Opening of the Wichita-Caddo-Kiowa-Comanche-Apache Reservation." M.A. thesis, Oklahoma State University, 1932.

Newton, Nell Jessup. "Federal Power over Indians: Its Source, Scope and Limitations." *University of Pennsylvania Law Review* 132 (January 1984): 195–288.

———. "The Judicial Role in Fifth Amendment Taking of Indian Land: An Analysis of the *Sioux Nation* Rule." *Oregon Law Review* 61 (1982): 245–65.

Nye, Wilbur S. *Bad Medicine and Good: Tales of the Kiowas.* Norman: University of Oklahoma Press, 1962.

Parrish, Cora Hoffman. "The Indian Peace Commission of 1867 and the Western Indians." M.A. thesis, University of Oklahoma, 1948.

Parsons, Elsie Clews. *Kiowa Tales* (Memoirs of the American Folklore Society, 22). New York: Stechert, 1929.

Pennington, William D. "Government Policy and Farming on the Kiowa Reservation, 1869–1901." Ph.D. dissertation, University of Oklahoma, 1972.

"The Philippine Problem" (editorial). *Harper's Weekly* 45 (9 February 1901): 138.

Platt, Orville H. "Problems in the Indian Territory." *North American Review* 160 (February 1895): 195–202.

Pound, C. W. "Nationals without a Nation." *Columbia Law Review* 22 (February 1922): 97–102.

Prucha, Francis Paul. *American Indian Policy in Crisis: Christian Reformers and the Indian, 1865–1900.* Norman: University of Oklahoma Press, 1976.

———. *The Churches and the Indian Schools.* Lincoln: University of Nebraska Press, 1979.

———. *The Great Father.* 2 vols. Lincoln: University of Nebraska Press, 1984.

Prucha, Francis Paul, ed. *Americanizing the American Indian: Writings of the "Friends of the Indians," 1880–1900.* Cambridge: Harvard University Press, 1973.

Randolph, Carman F. "Constitutional Aspects of Annexation." *Harvard Law Review* 12 (25 December 1898): 291–315.

Richardson, Rupert N. *The Comanche Barrier to Southern Plains Settlement.* Glendale, Calif.: Arthur H. Clark, 1933.

Rister, Carl C. "Satanta: Orator of the Plains." *Southwest Review* 17 (Autumn 1931): 77–99.

Roosevelt, Theodore. *The Strenuous Life: Essays and Addresses.* New York: Century Co., 1918.

———. *The Works of Theodore Roosevelt,* vol. 15: *State Papers as Governor and President, 1899–1909.* New York: Scribner's Sons, 1926.

Root, Elihu. *Military and Colonial Policy of the United States: Address and Reports.* Cambridge: Harvard University Press, 1916.

Rotenberg, Daniel L. "American Indian Tribal Death–A Centennial Remembrance." *University of Miami Law Review* 41 (1986): 409–23.

Russell, Isaac F. "The Indian before the Law." *Yale Law Journal* 18 (March 1909): 328–37.

Sanger, George P., ed. *The Statutes at Large, Treaties, and Proclamations of the United States of America,* vol. 15. Boston: Little, Brown, 1869.

Scott, Hugh L. *Some Memories of a Soldier.* New York: Century, 1928.

Sklar, Martin J. *The Corporate Reconstruction of American Capitalism, 1890–1916.* New York: Cambridge University Press, 1988.

Smith, Jordan Marshall. "The Federal Courts and the Black Man in America, 1800–

1883: A Study of Judicial Policy Making." Ph.D. dissertation, University of North Carolina, Chapel Hill, 1977.

Southward, Claude. "A History of Comanche County." M.A. thesis, University of Oklahoma, 1929.

Speed, John Gilmer. "The Oklahoma Land Lottery." *Outlook* 68 (20 July 1901): 667–68.

Townsend, Mike. "Congressional Abrogation of Indian Treaties." *Yale Law Journal* 98 (February 1989): 793–812.

Twain, Mark. "Is the Philippine Policy of the Administration Just? No." *Harper's Weekly* 45 (9 February 1901): 154.

Unrau, William E. "Indian Agent vs. the Army: Some Background Notes on the Kiowa-Comanche Treaty of 1865." *Kansas Historical Quarterly* 30 (Summer 1964): 129–52.

Viken, Jeffrey. "*Quick Bear* v. *Leupp:* Amalgamation of Church and State on the Rosebud." *South Dakota Historical Collections* 38 (1977): 1–72.

Wallace, Ernest, and E. Adamson Hoebel. *The Comanches: Lords of the South Plains.* Norman: University of Oklahoma Press, 1952.

The War of the Rebellion: A Compilation of the Official Records of the Union and Confederate Armies. 128 vols. Washington, D.C.: Government Printing Office, 1880–91.

White, E. E. *Experiences of a Special Indian Agent.* Norman: University of Oklahoma Press, 1965.

Wilkinson, Charles F. *American Indians, Time and the Law: Native Societies in a Modern Constitutional Democracy.* New Haven: Yale University Press, 1987.

Wilkinson, Charles F., and John M. Volkman. "Judicial Review of Indian Treaty Abrogation: 'As Long as Water Flows, or Grass Grows upon the Earth–How Long a Time Is That?" *California Law Review* 63 (January 1975): 601–61.

Williams, Walter L. "From Independence to Wardship: The Legal Process of Erosion of American Indian Sovereignty, 1810–1903." *American Indian Culture and Research Journal* 7, no. 4 (1984): 5–32.

———. "United States Indian Policy and the Debate over Philippine Annexation: Implications for the Origins of American Imperialism." *Journal of American History* 66 (March 1980): 810–31.

Worthen, Kevin J. "Shedding New Light on an Old Debate: A Federal Indian Law Perspective on Congressional Authority to Limit Federal Question Jurisdiction." *Minnesota Law Review* 75 (October 1990): 65–121.

Wunder, John R., ed. *Working the Range: Essays on the History of Western Land and the Environment.* Westport, Conn.: Greenwood, 1985.

Wyatt, Kathryn C. "The Supreme Court, *Lyng,* and the *Lone Wolf* Principle." *Chicago-Kent Law Review* 65 (Spring 1989): 623–55.

Ziegler, Benjamin. *The Supreme Court and American Economic Life.* Evanston, Ill.: Row, Peterson, 1962.

INDEX

Other titles in the Law in the American West series include:

Volume 1
Christian G. Fritz
Federal Justice in California: The Court of Ogden Hoggman, 1851–1891

Volume 2
Gordon Morris Bakken
Practicing Law in Frontier California

Volume 3
Shelley Bookspan
A Germ of Goodness: The California State Prison System, 1851–1944

Volume 4
M. Catherine Miller
Flooding the Courtrooms: Law and Water in the Far West

Volume 5
Blue Clark
*Lone Wolf v. Hitchcock: Treaty Rights and Indian Law at the End of the
Nineteenth Century*

Volume 6
Mark R. Scherer
Imperfect Victories: The Legal Tenacity of the Omaha Tribe, 1945–1995